DATE DUE

The
Reference
Shelf

Russia & Eastern Europe

Edited by Clifford Thompson

The Reference Shelf
Volume 70 • Number 2

The H. W. Wilson Company
New York • Dublin
1998

eference Shelf

nts of articles, excerpts from books, addresses on
nds in the United States and other countries. There
ach volume, all of which are usually published in
the same calendar year. Numbers one through five are each devoted to a single subject,
providing background information and discussion from various points of view and con-
cluding with a subject index and comprehensive bibliography that lists books, pamphlets,
and abstracts of additional articles on the subject. The final number of each volume is a
collection of recent speeches, and it contains a cumulative speaker index. Books in the
series may be purchased individually or on subscription.

Visit H.W. Wilson's web site: www.hwwilson.com

Library of Congress Cataloging-in-Publication Data

Russia & Eastern Europe / edited by Clifford Thompson
    p. cm.—(The reference shelf; v. 70, no. 2)
   Includes bibliographical references and index.
   ISBN 0-8242-0942-7
1. Former Soviet republics—Politics and government. 2. Former Soviet republics—
Economic conditions. 3. Europe, Eastern—Politics and government—1989- 4. Europe,
Eastern—Economic conditions—1989- 5. Foreign aid—Former Soviet republics. 6.
Foreign aid—Europe, Eastern. 7. North Atlantic Treaty Organization. I. Series.
DK293.R868 1998   98–14348
947.086—dc21   CIP

Cover: Demonstrators carry a bust of Joseph Stalin adorned with a sign, translated from
   Czech as "Nothing lasts forever."
Photo: AP/Wide World Photos

Printed in the United States of America

Contents

IV. Aid to Russia and Eastern Europe

Bibliography

Index

Preface

Little more than a decade ago, the current states of affairs in Russia, the other former constituent republics of the Soviet Union, and Eastern Europe might have been unimaginable. In 1986 the United States failed to reach arms-control agreements with the Soviet Union, which U.S. president Ronald Reagan had characterized three years earlier as an "evil empire" and as "the focus of evil in the modern world." In the wake of that failure, the existence of two superpowers, the antagonism between them (the Cold War), and Russia's role as the leader of the world's Communist nations seemed to many observers to be permanent arrangements. Even as *glasnost* ("openness") and *perestroika* (economic "restructuring") became the watchwords of the day in Moscow, many regarded these policies as innovations of uncertain staying power within a system as fixed and predictable as time itself.

Similarly, for most of the 1980s, the reunification of Communist East Germany and democratic West Germany—divided since the end of World War II—seemed a far-off goal. In Poland, where communism had reigned since 1947 and Lech Wałesa's Solidarity movement had been illegal since 1981, radical change did not appear imminent. Hungary and Czechoslovakia likewise seemed to be firmly in the grip of communism.

As the 1980s drew to a close, however, undeniable signs of change emerged. In 1989 mass demonstrations by those seeking reform and democracy in East Germany preceded the formation of the New Forum, a citizens' action group that was soon given legal sanction and became a major political force in the country. The Berlin Wall, which was built in 1961 and eventually stretched along the entire border between East and West Germany, was dismantled in 1990—a year before the official reunification of the two countries. Legalized in 1989, Poland's Solidarity party went on to win a majority in both houses of parliament in free elections later in the same year. In Czechoslovakia, the scene of the brutal 1968 Soviet-led invasion to halt democratization, the Communist party leadership stepped down amidst popular opposition in 1989, and the Czech Republic was born. Meanwhile, an almost identical process was unfolding in Hungary.

Most dramatically of all, Soviet president Mikhail Gorbachev had proven as good as his word in bringing about changes in the Soviet Union. While the troubled Soviet economy failed to respond as hoped to the increased trade and communication with other nations, surprising strides toward political freedom and international peace were made: the Soviet Union struck a major arms-reduction pact with the United States in 1987, many Soviet dissidents were freed and allowed to speak openly, and the USSR had withdrawn troops from Afghanistan by February 1989. Two and a half years later, as Gorbachev prepared to grant greater autonomy to the constituent republics of the USSR, he was detained in an attempted coup by reactionary hard-line government officials. The coup failed after three days, in the face of opposition from military leaders and the heads of the republics, in particular the Russian president, Boris Yeltsin. Even after Gorbachev was reinstated as the head of the Soviet Union, true power remained with the leaders of the republics; in late 1991 Gorbachev resigned, and the Soviet Union was dissolved.

While the entire free world celebrated the demise of communism in Russia and Eastern Europe and the end of the Cold War, few seemed able to predict what would take their place. The aim of this volume is to shed light on the conditions that exist today in Russia, Eastern Europe, and the former Soviet Union as a result of the events of a few years ago. (For the purposes of this book, the term *Eastern Europe* is used loosely, to reflect past ideological as well as present geographical designation.) While most of the nations under discussion have made at least nominal efforts to establish democracy and free-market economies, such tasks are easier said than done, and levels of success vary widely.

The first section of this book, "Contemporary Russia," comprises six articles that focus on the internal state of Russia—from an economical and political standpoint—and the relationship of the United States, as the lone remaining superpower, to the "new" Russia. The five pieces in the second section, "NATO Expansion," discuss the ramifications of the possible extension of the North Atlantic Treaty Organization to include Hungary, Poland, and the Czech Republic—a decision being made as this volume goes into production. The third section, "How Viable Are the 'New' States?", is composed of seven articles. This section's focus is on how well the nations under discussion, either newly formed or newly democratized, are functioning as self-sustaining, free societies. It is my hope that this section will begin to create a picture of the current state of Central and Eastern Europe, a task that perhaps no single volume could accomplish completely. Finally, four articles make up the fourth section, "Aid to Russia and Eastern Europe."

For their invaluable guidance and input during the preparation of this book, I would like to thank Michael Schulze, the H.W. Wilson Company's director of general reference; Joseph Sora, managing editor; Frank McGuckin, associate editor; Hilary D. Claggett, senior editor; and Rhonda Bell, editorial assistant.

Clifford Thompson
March 1998

I. Contemporary Russia

Editor's Introduction

For many years, the word *Russia* was often used synonymously with the Union of Soviet Socialist Republics (USSR), which emerged in the wake of the Russian revolution of 1917 and eventually grew to include 15 constituent republics: Armenia; Azerbaijan; Belarus; Estonia; Georgia; Kazakhstan; Kyrgyzstan; Latvia; Lithuania; Moldova; Tajikistan; Turkmenistan; Ukraine; and Uzbekistan; as well as Russia itself.

When the USSR dissolved, in 1991, Russia found itself—for the first time in seven decades—regulating the activities of no nation other than itself. It has since, under the leadership of President Boris Yeltsin, struggled to adapt to a free-market economy, to reap the benefits and shoulder the burdens of democracy, and to find its new place in a world that it once occupied as a superpower. This section examines the state of that struggle in its various aspects: how Russia is faring economically, how successfully it has adjusted to democracy, and how well the United States—Russia's former rival as a superpower—has responded to the changes in Russia. This section contains six articles. The views they present of the challenges facing Russia range from hopeful to grim.

Two articles discuss at length the general state of Russia. In a piece from the *Washington Quarterly*, Anatol Lieven, in scathing language, dismisses as evidence of "Western arrogance and ideological blindness" the notion that Russia has made the transition to democratic capitalism. The Russia portrayed in Lieven's essay is a weak one morally, economically, and militarily, one whose "private sector" is aimed "not at competition and the maximization of profits" but at the "creation of monopolies with the help of state support, and at the extraction of state favors and subsidies," a Russia in which organized crime, "if...as important as most analyses say...has reached a stage at which many state policies and economic reforms are simply irrelevant." The optimism Lieven offers is of the most vague and general sort.

Hope of a more substantial nature is offered by the democracy-minded Russian politician Sergei Kovalev, in his article "Russia After Chechnya," from the *New York Review of Books*. His piece concerns Russia's 1994–96 war with the breakaway republic of Chechnya and focuses on the causes of the conflict and the future of both sides. While Kovalev echoes many of the points made by Lieven, he sees cause for guarded optimism in the Russian people themselves, who let politicians running for office in 1996 know that they wanted the fighting stopped. "This, in fact, is democracy at work," Kovalev writes.

Two other articles focus on the policies of the West (particularly the United States) concerning Russia. In "Is Russia Still an Enemy?", from *Foreign Affairs*, Richard Pipes declares that a "battle for Russia's soul is in progress," being waged between a young, educated, mostly urban crowd that seeks to build a "new" Russia on the Western model and an older, more conservative set, "suspicious of...Western ways and nostalgic for the more secure Soviet past." Pipes fears that certain factions in Russia may try to compensate for internal weaknesses by "posturing on the global stage," and he feels that the West can deal with Russia most effectively with a policy containing both "toughness" and "understanding of Russian sensitivities." In an article originally published in the *New York Times Magazine*, the Russian Grigory Yavlinsky echoes Anatol Lieven, lamenting the United States' recent tendency to declare Russia a democracy and so belittle its grinding internal problems. Yavlinsky calls on the United States to return to its tradition of speaking truthfully about the situation in Russia, rather than heaping praise on a supposedly democratic government, "which the people no longer trust." He urges the U.S. to "not give up" on Russia, where "reform is possible and...necessary."

A brief article from Reuters offers details of the alarming birth-to-death ratio in contemporary Russia.

Finally, on a more hopeful note, there is the address given at Stanford University in the fall of 1997 by Unitesd States deputy secretary of state Strobe Talbott and printed in the State Department publication *Dispatch*. It is Talbott's view not only that the United States has much to gain from the emergence of a forward-looking, freedom-embracing Russia—but that there are signs that this process is taking place. Talbott points to Yeltsin's election victory over communism in 1996, the relatively stable Russian gross national product of 1997, and the pact that ended the war with Chechnya.

The Future of Russia: Will It Be Freedom or Anarchy?[1]

Every Russian with a sense of history ought to go down on his or her knees every morning and thank his or her God for the existence of nuclear weapons. They might also—however hard this might be for them—offer up a subsidiary prayer of thanks that they live during a period of an unusually stable and peaceful international order under the generally beneficent, quasi-hegemony of the United States.

They should give thanks because, in previous and more warlike eras, when conventional armies were the final arbiters of international decision, the Russia of today would have been in the gravest danger. Inspired by the Chechen war and its evidence of unprecedented Russian military decline, several other powers would already have sent their forces into the former Soviet Union to take bites out of the enormous, decaying Russian whale, to recover former territory, and to expand their spheres of influence. China would likely have been among those powers to invade, as Russia is rapidly falling further and further behind its biggest neighbor—at present economically, but in future without doubt militarily as well—and without any real prospect of closing the gap. As for the United States, the idea that Russia might be a serious direct threat to vital U.S. interests over the next 10 to 15 years is quite simply ludicrous—whatever some Russians themselves might wish. Indirectly, of course, the very weakness of the Russian state poses many threats, above all in the area of crime and smuggling.

When assessing the future of Russia in the light of President Boris Yeltsin's latest political victory and simultaneous physical collapse, it is necessary always to keep in mind the underlying weakness of the Russian state and economy. It is true that many of the Russian central government's immediate difficulties and divisions derive from the particular problems of Yeltsin's presidency: his heart disease, alcohol habit, desire to evade responsibility for potentially unpopular decisions, and chronic tendency to govern by playing one subordinate against another rather than by taking the lead himself.

Over the past two years, this has frequently led to a virtual paralysis of major decision-making and the suspension of all serious reforms. For the near future, the new ascendancy of Anatolii Chubais as Yeltsin's chief of staff gives some hope of a renewal of the reform process, but this may well be hindered or brought to nothing by the increasing struggle over the succession

---

[1]Article by Anatol Lieven, a senior fellow at the United States Institute of Peace, from "Freedom and Anarchy: Russia Stumbles Toward the Twenty-First Century," *The Washington Quarterly*, 20/1:41-58 Win 1997. Copyright © 1996 by the Center for Strategic and International Studies (CSIS) and the Massachusetts Institute of Technology. Reprinted with permission.

within the regime itself; Chubais's apparent attempts in August and September 1996 to sabotage General Aleksandr Lebed's peace process in Chechnya give little reason to hope that, in their battles with each other, most members of the Yeltsin administration will be constrained by considerations of national or public interest, let alone morality.

In any case, the weaknesses of the contemporary Russian state, society, and economy go much deeper than the problems of Yeltsin's government; they are structural and systemic. Some may sort themselves out over time, but it seems most unlikely that the Yeltsin administration will be able to do much about them. For that matter, Russia's problems may be so deep-rooted by now as to be beyond the cure of any government.

"...the weaknesses of the contemporary Russian state... go much deeper than the problems of Yeltsin's government..."

The phrase so incessantly repeated by Western advisers, journalists, and governments—a "transition from totalitarianism to democracy and the free-market"—is profoundly misleading and betrays Western arrogance and ideological blindness. For, after all, most of the world lives neither under totalitarianism nor under a prosperous, Western-style, capitalist democracy. Most people live under systems more akin to the anarchic quasi-feudalism incisively described by Vladimir Shlapentokh. ...Rather than use as a model medieval feudalism—which was at its height a formal, recognized system enshrined in law, religion, and culture—a closer historical analogy might be the *cacique* (chieftain) system prevalent in liberal Spain a century ago, when Spain's mildly authoritarian, incompetent, corrupt, self-serving, and often brutal governments never ceased to trumpet their allegiance to constitutionalism, law, and enlightened progress. Another key difference between the two traditions, very applicable to Russia today, was incisively remarked on by Gerald Brenan, the classic historian of pre–Civil War Spain:

> The defects of the Spanish upper classes are sometimes put down to their having a feudal mentality. I do not think this word has been well chosen: Feudalism implies a sense of mutual obligations that has long been entirely lacking in Spain...

Weak quasi-liberal states like those of Spain in the past and Russia and much of Latin America today can prove remarkably stable and long-lasting and can even generate considerable economic growth as well as real, though limited, elements of a "civil society." To their better-off inhabitants, and to those with some form of "protection," they offer major personal freedoms and opportunities. They also, however, tend to be characterized by unstable elite politics, extreme levels of organized crime, personal insecurity, poor public health, bad public education, rampant bureaucracy, corruption, and vicious exploitation of the poor and the environment. Such states are generally far too weak and corrupt to enforce the law, raise taxes efficiently and fairly, and protect the weaker sections of society. In extreme cases, like

Columbia and to an increasing extent Mexico, the state itself may be largely taken over by criminal forces. Such states are also of course highly incompetent in projecting power and influence beyond their borders.

By contrast, in the days of apparent Soviet greatness, Western political scientists often used the Soviet Union as the very paradigm of a "strong state," dominating all aspects of internal political, social, and economic life; capable of uniting and mobilizing its resources; and projecting its power successfully beyond its borders. They contrasted this with "weak states" like India and Brazil, where the state's ability to influence social and economic developments, or to mobilize national resources, was extremely limited.

Of course, this was becoming an increasingly false picture of the Soviet Union long before Mikhail Gorbachev came to power. Nonetheless, this picture had the appearance of reality, sufficient to intimidate the Soviet Union's vassals and command the wary respect of its rivals. Today, by contrast, the Russian Federation is quite evidently a weak state incapable of mobilizing resources, raising adequate revenues, stimulating economic development, curbing organized crime, or even maintaining its territorial integrity in the face of a determined secessionist movement.

The West has not fully recognized this fact in part because most of Russia's immediate former-Soviet neighbors are even weaker and suffer from the same problems but in an exaggerated form. Some of these countries—notably the conservative secular dictatorships of Central Asia—have their own good reasons for maintaining close ties with Moscow; others remain linked to Russia by history and ethnicity. These factors have allowed Russia to go on exerting a regional influence considerably greater than its real strength. But, as the defeat in Chechnya shows, this influence is largely hollow; if Russian pressure ever has to be backed up by serious military force, it is liable to collapse.

The Russian establishment's awareness of this is reflected in a recent draft document prepared by the Council on Foreign and Defense Policy under Sergei Karaganov, entitled "Will the Union Revive by 2005?" In many ways this is an over-optimistic document from a Russian point of view, particularly in its vague hopes for drawing Ukraine into a new union. On one point, however, it is clear: "The contemporary situation practically excludes the use of coercive methods of the restoration of a union."

Failing military coercion or the threat of it, however, neither this document nor any other I have read has suggested what the Russian state would be able to do to counter determined opposition, such as could be expected from Ukraine. The case of the Balts is instructive in this regard. Faced with these tiny but strong, cohesive, and determined states—which are supported by the West—the Russians have been forced to back off; all their blustering and bullying against the Balts over the past few years has brought them exactly nothing.

Another reason for the lack of Western recognition that Russia is now a classic weak state is that it would mean admitting that Russia has lost its position of central importance both on the world stage and for Western interests; such recognition does not come easily to Western experts on Russia. (This recognition doesn't come easily to me either—after all, I have devoted a large chunk of my life to studying Russia, and my present livelihood depends on Americans' continuing interest in the place.) For this reason, few Western experts will admit fully to Russia's collapsed role, and of course neither will the Russians.

In the United States, the Russophobes—and anyone with a domestic political or economic interest in Russophobia—are still trying to terrify U.S. taxpayers with tattered Halloween masks portraying a monstrous Russian threat to its neighbors and the world. But many Russian sympathizers also pursue a version of this, only they project it into the future, warning of all the terribly horrible and dangerous things that will happen if we Westerners do not pay to defend the virtue of "Russian democracy" against her would-be violators—when in fact the poor creature has not just been living in a brothel for years; she was actually born there.

"...both a Russian 'democracy' and a 'dictatorship' would desire to restore Russian hegemony over the other states..."

Both groups conduct their respective public dances against a political background overwhelmingly focused on the shortest-term considerations of U.S. electoral politics, and against a rigid and simplistic ideological background that employs brightly colored poster concepts: brave, benign, Western-style "democrats" and "reformists" versus wicked "Communists," "nationalists," and "authoritarians." This frankly childish frame of analysis seems to be believed implicitly by most senior members of President Bill Clinton's foreign policy establishment, and it guides their policies toward Russia and the Yeltsin administration.

Often underlying this analysis is the naive belief that true Russian democrats must always and of their very nature be defenders of U.S. foreign policy and U.S. national interests. This last belief, however, is actually a force for international understanding—as one point at least on which U.S. conservatives and Russian Communists can both agree.

This also leads to the incessant repetition of a black-and-white and completely mistaken set of alternatives for Russia's future: either the development of a pro-Western, free-market democracy, or reversion to "dictatorship and aggressive external policies." In fact, both a Russian "democracy" and a "dictatorship" would desire to restore Russian hegemony over the other states of the former Soviet Union. However, both would also be headed by pragmatists; this is clear from the present line-up of potential future leaders—General Lebed, Prime Minister Viktor Chernomyrdin and Moscow Mayor Yuri Luzhkov may be personally disagreeable, but they are all in their different ways rational and sensible men and certainly not fanatics. Moreover, these pragmatists will realize that they have to operate under the most severe economic, military, social, and international constraints on Russia's behavior.

A Longing for Order, Peace, Stability

The lesson of the Russian presidential elections, in my view, is that, although Russia is unlikely to develop into a successful democracy and economy, it is also unlikely to develop in ways that will directly threaten really important Western interests. Indirectly, of course, there will be threats—from organized crime and above all from the horrible prospect of nuclear smuggling—but such threats will be symptomatic of Russian state weakness rather than of a determined anti-Western strategy. This is not because many in Russia would hesitate to adopt such a strategy, but because they simply do not have the means. Deliberate challenges to the U.S.-dominated international order are therefore likely to be limited and containable, akin to, though worse than, examples of French international behavior over the past generation or so—arms sales to rogue regimes and so on. The Russian election results showed that, although most Russians are pretty unhappy with many of the developments of the past few years, a majority have no desire whatsoever for political upheavals and the risk of civil strife. The great mass of ordinary Russians has a deep yearning for stability and order, which in one way or another was reflected in the votes for all three leading candidates. As the event showed, this feeling at present outweighs even the desire for social justice, let alone wounded nationalism and hopes for the restoration of the Soviet Union. Russians are a tired, depressed, apathetic, people, not one yearning for great deeds of revolution or conquest. In other words—though this may not last forever—they are a Soviet people, a population that Soviet rule has deprived of most instincts and impulses for spontaneous political or social action from below.

The Communist vote—40 percent of the total, but overwhelmingly from the older part of the population—certainly reflected nostalgia for the Soviet Union, but it was nostalgia for the peace, order, stability, and above all economic security of Soviet days. These are very understandable sentiments given the way that older people in particular have suffered in recent years, and such sentiments are at heart hardly revolutionary. Western commentators were not wrong to take worried note of Gennadii Zyuganov, Yeltsin's opponent, and his increasing ideological borrowings from nineteenth-century Russian messianic nationalism—but they would be very wrong to think that they were why 65-year-old Maria Ivanovna of Ufa would vote for him. Moreover, Communism in Russia is fading fast—if only because, for biological reasons, its electorate is fading too.

Some of Yeltsin's supporters, especially in Moscow and St. Petersburg, undoubtedly favored change and economic reform, as reflected in the fact that his voters were on average some 15 years younger than Zyuganov's. The result showed that basic principles of private ownership and free economic activity have now been accepted by most of the population. But, to a great extent, Yeltsin was also elected by Russians who fear disorder, instability, and civil strife. Thanks to the compliance of the Russian media, Yeltsin had been able to convince most Russians of two things: first, that Communist victory would mean a new revolution and massive upheaval; and second, that even if he lost, Yeltsin would not surrender power, which might mean civil war.

As for Lebed, his program was explicitly devoted to calling for peace, order, and a crackdown on organized crime. His campaign—with or without covert help from Yeltsin's team-was a clever one, simultaneously using his image as a tough, patriotic soldier; stressing his opposition to military "adventures" like Chechnya and Tajikistan; and referring to his successful "peacemaking" campaign in Transdniester in 1992: "Others start wars, he ends them," was the slogan. Another was, "Yeltsin: freedom without order. Zyuganov: order without freedom. Lebed: order and freedom."

"Russia is a weak state, not a failed one."

Now it is quite true, of course, that a Moldovan might have some harsh words to say about Lebed's role in 1992 as commander of the 14th Army, but the point is that in his appeal to the Russian public, he portrayed himself as a tough peacemaker, not an aggressive conqueror. And it must be said that, in his peacemaking role in Chechnya in August 1996, he justified the faith of his electorate—albeit only in the wake of the smashing Chechen victory in August. On expansion of the North Atlantic Treaty Organization (NATO) and relations with the Commonwealth of Independent States (CIS), Lebed has recently taken a studiedly moderate and pragmatic line. He remains a worryingly unpredictable figure, though—as Sergei Markov of the Carnegie Foundation told me, "He could end up anywhere on a spectrum between [Charles] de Gaulle and [Benito] Mussolini; we just don't know." Nonetheless, his role has been a positive one, so far—and it also seems very unlikely that a mass party like the Italian Fascists could be created in contemporary Russian conditions. It could also be said that, by trying to end the war in Chechnya, Lebed has already taken a step toward imitating de Gaulle.

And if Russia is unlikely to explode from determined assaults on its neighbors to the West, it is a so unlikely to implode from complete internal collapse, ethnic rebellions, and civil war. Russia is a weak state, not a failed one. For, another lesson of the elections is that, although Russia's chaotic federal system is contributing mightily to the weakness of the central state and the erosion of its revenue base, it has proved very effective in defusing moves for secession by most of Russia's ethnic minorities. The Chechen example of revolt has failed to spread for reasons that stem largely from demography, geography, and economics: In most of Russia's autonomous republics, the titular nationality is actually a minority; many regions remain dependent on financial subsidies from Moscow; and those that are economically strong, like Tatarstan, are surrounded entirely by Russian territory.

The rulers of these republics hail for the most part from the old elite, long accustomed to carrying out an elaborate political dance with the central authorities to extract subsidies and concessions from Moscow, and more than happy that the new weakness of the central state allows them to extract such concessions on a previously undreamed-of scale. The sheer anarchy of the Russian constitutional order and tax code also means that these republics are able to avoid paying many of the taxes they owe to the central state, and Yeltsin's bribes this year as part of his election campaign have strengthened their position still further.

But it is also true, as I have found on visits to Tatarstan and other republics, that the federal system does now give the larger nationalities at least room to develop their national identities and cultures freely. Constraints on this stem from lack of money and the legacy of past russification, not present restrictions by the central Russian state. Another reason for the general lack of radical nationalist movements is that these groups are not exposed to any significant degree of ethnic Russian chauvinism. The exception are the Caucasians, detested by the Russians for their allegedly dominant role in organized crime; but as for the others, one would be hard pressed to get most Russians to utter really harsh words about Tatars or Yakuts, for example. And far from trying to stir up such sentiments, all the main parties in the last two Russian elections (with the partial exception of Vladimir Zhirinovsky's) were assiduously wooing the autonomies for their support. That was true even of a "nationalist" party like Lebed's Congress of Russian Communities.

On the whole, unless they have some particular focus for their dislike—such as beliefs of economic superiority or political unreliability, as with the Jews and Poles in the past and the Chechens today—Russians do not tend to suffer from strong personal ethnic passions; indeed, British officers visiting Russian Central Asia in the later nineteenth century were frequently appalled at the easy intercourse between local Russians and "natives," compared to the rigid racial barriers that operated in British India.

This flexibility derives above all from Russians' historically weak ethnic identity: Throughout history, Russians have mingled with other races along their huge, vague land frontiers, and ethnic loyalty has generally been diffused into other, wider loyalties—to the Orthodox religion, the czar, Communism, the Soviet Union. Of course, all these institutions had a heavily Russian cast, but they were not purely Russian. This weakness of Russian ethnic feeling is of the most critical importance not just for the internal peace of Russia, but also for the stability or even survival of neighboring states with large Russian minorities, most notably Ukraine.

Yet, a more immediate reason exists for the failure of the Russian state or political movements today to try to stimulate ethnic Russian nationalism: Such a move would threaten to destroy any hope of restoring a union of former Soviet states under Russian hegemony. Every serious Russian politician today knows that reunification could not be done by military coercion, or even purely by economic pressure; a large measure of consent, based on Soviet nostalgia widespread throughout the former Union, would be needed. In other words, one cannot have an openly ethnically based Russia and a Russian-dominated union of other states at the same time.

Four Faces of Russian Weakness

"...although Russia remains the world's largest state in terms of land area, its population is no longer so great..."

What are the chances that a future Russian government will in the short-to-medium term be able to strengthen the Russian state, either in the benign sense of suppressing crime, raising revenue, and carrying out orderly reform, or in the potentially dangerous one of strengthening Russia's capacity for external aggression? Let us briefly examine the different aspects of contemporary Russian weakness.

Military

It makes sense to begin with the military, the historical basis of Russia's strength and the state's power. Unlike the past or present Chinese, British, French, U.S., Japanese, and German empires or spheres of influence, the Russian and Soviet empires were only very rarely in a position to dominate their neighbors through the strength of their industrial and commercial economy and the prestige of their material culture (though they might have developed this ability if the Russian economic development of 1894–1917 had not been interrupted).

Today, however, the Russian army is a wreck, and in the estimate of both Russian experts and Western military attachés based in Moscow, it would take 10 years at least, even in optimal circumstances, to restore it as an effective force capable of fighting a major war. In the meantime, with the help of local allies, it can probably maintain existing positions in Transdniester, Abkhazia, and Tajikistan against weak and divided local states and opposition forces; but the threat of military coercion against Ukraine or Uzbekistan, for example, has vanished-perhaps only temporarily, but perhaps also permanently, given general changes in Russian attitudes and cultural patterns. Russian forces in the Caucasus and the Black Sea are for the first time in more than two centuries clearly inferior to Turkish ones, which terrifies Russian strategists into recurrent fits of alarm.

Demography

When making comparisons with the Russian and Soviet empires of the past, it is also worth remembering that although Russia remains the world's largest state in terms of land area, its population is no longer so great by contemporary world standards, and it is dropping as declining birth rates and steeply rising death rates take their toll. This is of critical importance: for four centuries of czarist rule, Russia's demographic growth and surplus population provided much of the engine for imperial expansion; to see the difference today, one has only to visit Kazakhstan, where the Kazakhs, a minority a decade ago, are steadily outnumbering the Russians thanks to their far higher birthrate; or the Far East, where 2.7 million people in the Vladivostok region live next to 74 million people in the two adjacent Chinese provinces. Moreover, the absence of demographic pressure on jobs and services—in other words, the fact that, unlike in most areas of Asia, millions of young people are *not* coming onto the market each year—is a key reason for Russia's relative political stability today, and for the absence of mass unrest or street protests.

From 150 million at the last Soviet census in 1989, the population of the Russian Federation is only 147.8 million today, continues to drop, and would be even lower were it not for the influx into Russia in recent years of migrants and refugees from other republics. This figure is just over half the population of the United States, less than those of Brazil or Indonesia, and not much bigger than those of Japan or Pakistan. Of course, population size alone does not matter so much in terms of international weight when compared to a powerful economy—but the Russian economy today can hardly be called powerful, except in energy and arms exports.

Economy

It is true that official statistics do not fully reflect the true state of the economy or of living standards, which are in reality a good deal higher. Neither Russian business people nor most Russian workers doing three or four part-time jobs declare more than a fraction of their income to the state if they can help it. But this is the whole point; as in India, for example, but to an even greater extent, a very large proportion of economic activity is not being reported—which means that it is not being taxed. And if it is neither being taxed nor being invested in real economic growth, although it is obviously still beneficial to the state in that it helps keep the population happier, it is useless from the point of view both of developing the economic base and of mobilizing national resources for external or internal state tasks.

As is typical of many such countries with a history of state ownership and socialist or communist planning, it appears on the surface that the Russian government still has very great powers over private business, not just because of the role of the tax and regulatory structure in stifling legal entrepreneurship and initiative, but also because so much of Russian business is directly or indirectly dependent on the state. As the leading economist Anders Aslund has written, the contemporary Russian private sector is largely a "rent-seeking" affair, aiming not at competition and the maximization of profits, but at the creation of monopolies with the help of state support, and at the extraction of state favors and subsidies.

Security Forces and Organized Crime

But once again, this is the whole point. These subsidies are not generally being handed out as part of a strategy for national economic development; nor even, most of the time, to buy votes for the government. Rather, the weakness of the state; the corruption or physical intimidation of the bureaucracy, police, and especially tax authorities; and the intimate nomenklatura links with the world of business mean that state coffers are riddled with holes through which an immense variety of rats travel to and fro. To a very real extent, the state itself has been hollowed out, turned into a vessel to be captured and plundered by the piratical forces of a frequently criminalized Russian private enterprise.

"...changes in state policy and the law were necessary to begin the process of change, but what followed was far less a 'reform'..."

As for the security forces, an amusing anecdote from 1994 illustrates their penetration by the better-paying worlds of private and criminal business: In a deliberate blaze of publicity, the elite Alpha special force was sent to arrest Sergei Mavrodi, the notorious pyramid scheme boss. When the Alpha men knocked on his door, the answer was a string of curses in voices they knew. It turned out that Mavrodi's security was made up of other Alpha men. They work only a three-day week; the rest of the time they earn far more as private security guards. And this, God help us, is Russia's supposedly elite anti-terrorist and anti-mafia force.

The lack of real control over the state services severely limits the central government's ability actually to carry out real economic and legal reforms—instead it merely passes decrees to their effect. The motto of many Russian bureaucrats today is no different from that of their past Spanish counterparts: "I obey, but I do not comply."

In fact, the whole Western image of the Russian "reform process" over the past eight years has been to a great extent a mirage. Of course, changes in state policy and the law were necessary to begin the process of change, but what followed was far less a "reform" than a spontaneous process of transformation from below. One aspect of this has certainly been the liberation of enormous amounts of previously suppressed entrepreneurial energy, as any visit to Russia's main urban centers will make clear; another has been the wholesale seizure of public property by the existing Communist nomenklatura—especially factory managers—and the forces of organized crime. From the point of view of morality or historical justice, the privatization process has therefore been a sick joke; insofar as it has mainly led to the continued control of the old Soviet management structures over Russian industry and agriculture, it has also been of questionable utility in promoting real entrepreneurship and efficiency in these fields. Typically, privatization and reform have been attended not by a reduction of the Russian central bureaucracy, but by its mushroom growth—and six years ago, I would not have believed that the Soviet bureaucracy could have become any more bloated without exploding like a balloon. It seems, however, that there is always room somewhere for another mouthful.

The importance of organized crime is of course regularly touched on in Western analyses. But it is often treated in curious isolation—mentioned, and then promptly dropped, as the commentators return to a discussion of what is needed for "economic reform." The truth is, however, that if organized crime is really as important as most analyses say, then it has reached a stage at which many state policies and economic reforms are simply irrelevant. As in Colombia, Mexico, Pakistan, and elsewhere, the state forces are hopelessly out-spent and out-gunned by the criminals, and in any case are largely controlled by them. There can be no serious talk in these circumstances of a successful state crackdown on organized crime; all one can hope for is that the successful criminals will eventually change of their own accord, recognizing the commercial and personal advantages to themselves of a stable legal order. I would not bet on it, however.

The Failure to Invest and Develop

Crime, together with the anarchy, unpredictability, corruption, and petty tyranny of the Russian tax authorities, is a key reason for Russia's failure to attract the foreign investment it so desperately needs, and to draw back the tens of billions of dollars in Russian capital that has flown abroad. Foreign investment is especially important, as it was for Russia before 1917, not just because Russian capital is in relatively short supply, but because Western investment and Western management are necessary to set a standard both for civilized business behavior and for serious and consistent treatment of private companies by the state.

The present Russian state, however, reflecting the interests of the new Russian dominant classes, remains extremely ambivalent about Western investment. Russian executives and managers see such investment far more as a competitor and a threat to themselves and to their way of doing things than as a potential asset—and in many cases they are entirely correct. For this reason it is not clear that the ascendancy of Anatolii Chubais and the reformists in Yeltsin's administration will have a major effect in stimulating Western investment.

The proposed oil-production sharing agreement with U.S. companies in summer 1996 was an encouraging sign that Prime Minister Chernomyrdin and the energy establishment at least understand the urgent need to renew Russia's production capacity with outside help—but the agreement was voted down by the Duma (parliament) amidst a flurry of nationalist rhetoric about "American economic colonization." Depressingly, a key figure in this refusal, and a bitter opponent of incentives for Western investment, is Lebed's close ally, former trade minister Sergei Glaziyev.

In many ways, a rational economic strategy for Russia might be to return to some form of the policies pursued by both Russia and the United States during earlier periods of capitalist economic growth: selective protectionism to defend fragile domestic production—especially in agriculture and consumer goods—coupled with aggressive encouragement of foreign investment through tax incentives, guarantees of profit repatriation, and renewal of infrastructure.

This would, however, affect the new Russian elites in several ways: They are, as already stated, afraid of Western investment and competition, addicted to imported Western luxuries, and heavily dependent on profitable trade deals involving imports of food and consumer goods and exports of raw materials. They would certainly oppose such policies as would hurt them.

Equally important, once again, is the weakness of the Russian state and its officials. A protectionist policy on food would hardly work because corrupt customs officials would not implement it; they would simply raise the level of the bribes necessary to let the imports through: Witness the farcical "blockade" of Chechnya in autumn 1994.

The nature of the new Russian elite in its purest form was revealed to me during a visit to Vladivostok last winter. Unlike Western Russia, which borders on a flagging Europe, this city lies on the edge of the fastest growing economic region in the world, one with immense amounts of available capital. Yet, I found the interest in foreign investment among the regional governments and elites to be practically zero; this was confirmed by the handful of Western business people in the region. The Russian political elite of Vladivostok is obsessed with only three things: personal political survival; fighting each other over the privatization of Soviet state property; and making personal fortunes through the export of timber, fish, minerals, oil, and tiger skins.

It is a comprador class of the crudest kind and, thanks to the elite, Vladivostok is also a comprador town of the crudest kind. Its streets are full of Japanese cars; its casinos and nightclubs contain ample evidence of the wealth of its new elite. But it is also entirely obvious that not a kopek of this wealth has been invested either in public infrastructure or in new private production; the entire prosperity of the region's elites and their employees is being generated by the export of commodities and is being spent on the import of consumer goods. Meanwhile, transport links, energy supplies, and the education system decay, and local miners and electricity workers have been on a hunger strike because their pay is months in arrears.

If, despite all this, Russia has been able to go on supporting most of its population at an acceptable level and even creating real prosperity for large numbers of them in Moscow, the reason is not mainly "economic reform"; it is above all that Russia remains the largest exporter of oil, natural gas, minerals, and timber in the world, and, as long as stocks last, the profits from

"...Russia has been able to go on supporting most of its population at an acceptable level..."

this suffice to maintain social and economic stability, to keep the budget deficit under reasonable control, and therefore to rein in inflation. Unless these revenues are reinvested, however, they will do nothing to stimulate economic growth. The West may contrast Ukraine's failure to implement economic reforms with Russia's alleged success and thus explain Ukraine's greater misery; but if Russia, like Ukraine, lacked massive oil and gas reserves and had to pay for their import, would it really be in a better position than Ukraine today?

The Moral Illegitimacy of the New Order

The decay of Yeltsin's presidency and the lack of any agreed successor mean that the next few years will undoubtedly be disturbed ones in Russian politics. In my opinion, however, the apathy of the population and the ability of the state to guarantee certain basic living standards mean that that these troubles will not spill over into mass civic violence or new mass revolutionary movements. This is above all true because of the prosperity and contentment of the population of Moscow, which voted overwhelmingly for Boris Yeltsin at the last elections. Violence may occur, but if so it will probably be limited to clashes between various praetorian guards and politicians' immediate followers—much as in October 1993, when a handful of troops loyal to President Yeltsin (or bribed or pressured into helping him) bombarded into submission an even smaller number of armed supporters of the parliamentary opposition. It is quite possible that the result may be the establishment of some more-or-less authoritarian regime in Moscow; but given the genuine federal or even confederal nature of the Russian state today, and the underlying weaknesses I have sketched, it is highly unlikely that such a government would be able to impose effective authoritarian rule across the whole country, let alone mobilize the country to project strong Russian influence in the-outside world, or in the last resort to go to war.

Unfortunately, it also seems unlikely that Russia will be able to establish a stable and prosperous democracy, even in the longer term. Public apathy and demoralization, as well as private violence, are so extensive that it will be difficult for a true civil society to emerge. In some areas, after all, a serious threat or even insult to any major local figure is now likely to earn a bullet in the head, no longer from the secret police but from a private gunman.

Contributing to the long-term weakness of the Russian state and democracy is also likely to be a deep underlying popular feeling of their illegitimacy, because of the nature of the changes that have taken place in recent years. This feeling relates to social injustice: the immiseration of pensioners, the most vulnerable part of the population; the increasing destruction of real Soviet achievements, especially in the areas of health and education; the power of organized crime; and above all, the way in which state property, viewed by most Russians as the patrimony of the whole people, was "privatized."

This does not mean that there will be a mass revolt, or even a mass political movement of protest, in anything like the near future. Communism in Russia is dying fast, but there is no new ideology to replace it. Moreover, the mass of the population has accepted the essential elements of the new order—private property, free economic activity, and a political system based ostensibly at least on elections. In the sense of Antonio Gramsci's analysis—or Francis Fukuyama's—liberal capitalist thought has indeed achieved a "hegemony of consciousness" in Russia, one that is likely to persist for decades to come.

It would be hopelessly optimistic and unhistorical, however, to think that this will last forever. A distant analogy might perhaps be drawn with the situation in Spain and Italy following the liberal seizures of power and subsequent reforms in the mid-nineteenth century. Whatever their other justifications, these reforms were a violent affront to the "moral economies" of a large segment of the peasant populations of these countries. Particularly offensive was the privatization and redistribution of ancient communal and church lands, and their purchase not by local peasants, or even the nobility, but by new and alien bourgeois agricultural entrepreneurs from the towns.

"Communism in Russia is dying fast but there is no new ideology to replace it."

Following the suppression of the Carlist and "bandit" revolts, however, these feelings of moral outrage did not generally express themselves in terms of mass movements in support of the old royal, clerical, and peasant order. The peasants were too inarticulate, impoverished, and disorganized for that; the new bourgeois rulers too militarily and intellectually dominant; and the Catholic Church either co-opted or too cautious and conservative to lead a popular revolt. What happened instead was that these feelings of resentment and alienation went underground to surface decades later in a variety of unpredictable forms, often with little apparent relation to the local historical origins of their support: extreme reactionary Catholicism and modern social Catholicism, but also communism, anarchism, and fascism, united only in their common hatred of the liberal bourgeois order. These movements were, moreover, never entirely locally generated—the world was already too interlinked for that. Rather, these societies proved especially receptive to infection by various extreme ideologies that were floating around Europe, which they then developed in local and especially virulent forms.

A new Russian revolutionary ideology, if it appears over the next few decades, is also unlikely to be home-grown. For the past three centuries, all the various "Russian ideas"—from the new imperial thinking of the seventeenth century through Peter the Great's reforms to slavophilism, populism, and communism—have had their intellectual origins outside Russia, although it has often been in Russia that they have taken their most extreme forms.

What new revolutionary ideologies the middle or later twenty-first century has in store for us are—perhaps thankfully—impossible to predict. Venturing into the realms of science fiction, one might speculate about national-socialist reactions against the global economy and migration, or against increasing physical differences between rich and poor produced by medical developments and genetic engineering, along the lines of a quasi-religious or racist revolt to defend the "true image" of humanity.

Two things, however, do seem predictable: first, that if such revolutionary ideologies do emerge, they will as in the past find an especially fertile soil in Russia; and second, that they will not make a serious appearance for many years to come. History has not ended, as Fukuyama suggested, but it does indeed seem to have reached a kind of plateau, doubtless insignificant in terms of the whole span of human history, but reassuring to us, the temporary dwellers on its relatively peaceful and fruitful plains. It may be, therefore, that with all the new Russian order's many problems and weaknesses, it will for a long time be able to stumble on, until we all fall down together.

Russia After Chechnya[2]

And so, it has finally come to pass. In Moscow this May, Boris Yeltsin and Aslan Maskhadov, the recently elected President of Chechnya, signed an agreement "On Peace and the Principles of Relations between the Russian Federation and the Chechen Republic of Ichkeria."

The High Contracting Parties—this is how they refer to themselves—announced their desire to "cease centuries of *confrontation*," "to establish *equal* relations" built on "commonly recognized principles and norms of *international* law." The italics are mine and I think they are indispensable. The terms used in the agreement are entirely unambiguous and can only mean that Russia has recognized that 1) Chechnya was never willingly part of Russia; 2) the Chechens have always resisted Russian dominion; and 3) today Moscow officially views Ichkeria as an independent state.

"...today Moscow officially views Ichkeria as an independent state."

The word "independence," however, is missing from the agreement. This is probably as it should be: last year, in the Dagestan town of Khasavyurt, Alexander Lebed and Maskhadov signed a document ending the war but postponing a final decision on the status of Chechnya until the year 2001. There's no reason to rock the boat right away. But it is clear that such a decision (if, of course, nothing extraordinary occurs) will only strengthen de jure what is Moscow's de facto recognition of the independence of its former province.

It is time to do a preliminary summing up of the Chechen crisis, the most significant event to have occurred so far in the history of the new Russia.

The most important thing, of course, is that the first article of the agreement renounces the use of force or even the threat of force in the resolution of disputes. If we set aside the unpredictability of Russian politics and imagine for a moment that the Kremlin (and the Chechen government in Grozny, for that matter) will keep to the principle that "treaties should be observed," then we can assume that there is little danger of war breaking out again.

And since the war is over, the time is right to attempt to answer some of the questions that inevitably arise at the end of any war.

Why was the war begun, and how was the need to continue it justified?

What were the goals of the warring sides, and what did they actually achieve?

Who was the victor in this war, and who the vanquished?

What does the future hold for both sides?

---

[2] Article by Sergei Kovalev from *New York Review of Books* 44:27-31 Jl 17 '97. Copyright © 1997 NYREV, Inc. Reprinted with permission.

I will try here to answer some of these questions.

The Kremlin officially maintained on many occasions that it resorted to the use of force in order to liquidate the illegitimate and undemocratic regime set up by the Chechen leader General Dzhokhar Dudayev; to prevent Chechnya from separating from Russia; to reestablish law and order and put an end to criminal activity in the republic; to protect human rights (in particular, the rights of Chechnya's Russian-speaking population); and to prevent the creation of a dangerous center of Islamic fundamentalism in the North Caucasus.

In fact, of all these goals, Russia has achieved only one, and even that only in part. The Dudayev regime was not destroyed, but the rebel general himself was killed in a Russian rocket attack in April 1996. In order to accomplish this nearly a hundred thousand other people had to be killed—but who remembers these details today?

It's true, Dudayev's legitimacy was far from indisputable—after all, he disbanded the first Supreme Soviet of the Checheno-Ingush Republic by force in 1991, and then the Chechen parliament in early 1993. Coming from Yeltsin such an accusation may sound grotesque, to put it mildly, but that doesn't change the facts. (And by the end of 1994 Dudayev's dissolution of the Supreme Soviet was no longer much of an issue.)

Elections were supposed to be held in Chechnya in 1995. By then, as it happened, Dudayev's popularity in the republic had been severely shaken. A number of factors conspired to substantially reduce his political prospects: economic problems that he did not know how to resolve, conflicts among the ruling elite, the dissatisfaction of a number of Chechen clans with his appointments to his staff, the traditional Chechen distrust of any kind of "state" power (especially if that power is nearby, in Grozny). If Moscow had waited just a bit, it probably would have found a legitimate negotiating partner in Grozny, and that partner probably would not have been the obstinate Dudayev. The only thing that could have prevented his ouster was what in fact happened: direct intervention by Russia. Dudayev immediately became a symbol of national resistance. Since his death he has become a popular hero.

It cannot be said that Moscow ignored the problem of legitimacy during its military campaign. The Chechen people were constantly offered new governors, each one said to be fairer and more legitimate than the previous. The last of them was Doku Zavgayev—the former Communist Party leader of the Soviet Checheno-Ingush Republic. In December 1995, under the protection of the Central Election Committee and the Supreme Court of Russia (and, alas, with the deliberate silence of the Vienna-based Conference on Security and Cooperation in Europe), Zavgayev shamelessly scheduled "elections" in the republic. As anyone could have predicted, 95 percent of the population turned out to be Zavgayev supporters. No one expressed the least surprise.

Then, in August of 1996, when Maskhadov's militia stormed Grozny, recapturing the city from the Russian forces, Zavgayev publicly stated that "nothing extraordinary is happening—just occasional shooting." All of a sudden everyone was shocked— what do you know, the man's a liar!

Rule by Zavgayev was the kind of legitimacy Moscow offered Chechnya. For some reason the Chechens didn't like it. They preferred instead to consider as legitimate the January 1997 elections in which Maskhadov, leader of the Chechen resistance, won hands down. I served as an official observer of those elections. In my opinion they failed in many ways to live up to democratic principles—above all because the tens if not hundreds of thousands of refugees who were outside the republic were excluded from voting. But where in the world has impeccably correct electoral procedure been observed when a country has been quite literally reduced to ashes by war? In Bosnia, perhaps? In any event, what I saw convinced me that the inhabitants of Chechnya who did take part in the elections believed they were honest, and that the authorities, in turn, tried to do their best. Both sides understood that they were insuring themselves against a new war. And it appears they were right.

The second goal that Kremlin strategists set was keeping Chechnya within the Russian Federation. Well, two and a half years ago that was entirely possible. Even after military conflict had begun, not only simple Chechens but members of the Dudayev cabinet explained to me their view of the republic's "independence": they would accept a common currency with Russia, common security forces (including the army and common defense of external borders), common citizenship, joint foreign policy, an integrated economy, etc. The Chechens wanted certain attributes of independence, however, such as the depiction of a wolf in their state emblem....

More seriously, before the war the Chechen leaders in Grozny probably would have agreed to a degree of sovereignty not greatly exceeding that enjoyed by Tatarstan. By the end of the war, Moscow was ready to accept a far greater degree of Chechen autonomy, much more than the Chechen leaders had in mind up until 1995, just as long as Chechnya remained "within the Russian Federation"—i.e., as long as Russia didn't lose face. It was too late. The unique historical opportunity to legalize democratically the inclusion within Russia of the most intransigent mountain people of the Caucasus disappeared under the thunder of bombs and rockets. And now, I'm afraid, it's gone for good.

The third reason put forth by official Russian propaganda as a *casus belli* was the need to destroy the "Chechen mafia" that was purportedly based in Grozny. I can't assess the accuracy of this assertion; nor can I judge the effectiveness of Russian aircraft, long distance artillery, and blanket rocket attacks in fighting crime. I only hope that Yeltsin won't start using these anticrime methods in Russia itself. In Chechnya the results are all too evident: in addition to the traditional types of crime, we now have terrorism and kidnapping for ransom.

As for the rights of the Russian-speaking population (the small part of it that wasn't killed by Russian bombs or forced to flee to Russia, abandoning its homes), here one can only hope that Maskhadov will have sufficient strength and sense to stop the criminal anarchy from which a handful of elderly and defenseless people suffer inconceivably more today than before the war. However, when we observe how Russia treats its refugees, it is hard to imagine that anyone might be able to surpass the Russian government and its immigration services when it comes to crude and widespread violations of the rights of the Russian-speaking natives of Chechnya. And not only of Chechnya.

Finally, there is the threat of Islamic fundamentalism. General Dudayev did talk about introducing the Shariat—Islamic law— even before the war broke out. But Dudayev said a lot of things in his speeches. I would not like to have been in his shoes had he actually tried to introduce Shariat law to Chechnya before the war. Even now, I have serious doubts about whether such innovations will succeed in Chechnya. Even Shamil—the legendary Muslim leader of the Caucasus revolt against Russia in the nineteenth century—was unsuccessful in his time. The Vainakh, or mountain people of the Caucasus, are followers of the form of belief called *adat*, which is based on tradition. Their version of Islam cannot be called fanatic in any sense, especially if you take into account the many distinctions in religious traditions among the Vainakh themselves, traditions that go back to various religious teachers of the nineteenth or even the eighteenth century.

During the war, however, the leaders of the Chechen resistance took to underscoring their adherence to Islam as a symbol of resistance to Russia. In the beginning this elicited a smile. For instance, I remember the demonstrative reverence the former prosecutor general and minister of justice of Ichkeria, Usman Imaev, displayed regarding his "favorite book"—a collection of speeches and sermons of the Ayatollah Khomeini. The works of the Shi'ite ideological leader were now said to be the favorite reading of a faithful Sunni. How seriously, then, was one to take the Islam of rank and file Chechens?

"Public flogging and stoning became part of the republic's criminal code last fall."

Today, however, there's nothing to smile about. Public flogging and stoning became part of the republic's criminal code last fall. Maskhadov has also recently expressed a desire to introduce "Islamic banks" into the country. The former Komsomol functionary and present field commander Salman Raduyev has issued calls for a jihad. He is tormented by unconcealed jealousy of Shamil Basayev, his braver and more successful rival on the field of terror; and he dreams of surpassing Basayev, at least in piety. In Chechnya, and now in neighboring Dagestan, members of the pious sect of the Wahhabites have appeared; they were previously unknown in the region. These are the fruits of war. I have no doubt that Maskhadov wants to build a secular state functioning on democratic principles. He has told me so himself—face to face. But now even he avoids saying this out loud.

So there is a simple relationship between the reasons for the war and its results. Most of the ghosts that haunted the imagination of Kremlin politicians did not in fact exist before the war. The war breathed life into them, and they became a reality. Everything that Moscow was afraid of (or pretended to be afraid of) in 1994 has come to pass: Chechnya's secession from Russia; an upsurge of Islamic fundamentalism; and a wave of criminal violence in the region that has left the remaining Russian-speaking population defenseless. Moscow created this situation all by itself, when it unleashed the war.

In order to answer the question of who won and who lost this war, we will have to dismiss all the demagogic arguments I listed above, arguments that our Russian "hawks" originally put forth to justify their point of view. The longer the military action continued, the less frequently they resorted to these arguments—after all, no one wants to look like a complete idiot. We must examine the true reasons underlying events.

I am by no means an expert on the various theories proposing "economic" reasons for the conflict. Many such hypotheses exist: the desire to cover up the "Moscow connections" of a number of bank scams related to Chechnya; the collision of interests involved in choosing the route by which Caspian oil would be transported to Europe; etc. One version holds that the war was started so that arms illegally sold in Germany by Russian generals when our troops withdrew could be "written off" as military losses in Chechnya. Another version sees the war as an "international Zionist plot." Most Chechens religiously believe in one or another of these theories; they appear here and there in the pages of the Russian press. Or to be more precise, they used to appear—until the military conflict ended and Russian society set about trying to forget Chechnya as if it had all been a bad dream. Some of these stories seem quite believable; others sound like typical "fairy tales and legends of the peoples of the Caucasus." But in any event, such reasons can only apply to secondary causes. The main reason is the condition of Russia on the eve of the war.

In 1994 the government and the President sharply changed the course of the country's development. Economic reform was halted; the clock was turned back on political and legal reforms. Of the two tendencies fighting each other after August 1991—democratic and antidemocratic—the one that represented a sluggish, reactionary state apparatus, what used to be called the *nomenklatura*, won out. Of course, this was no longer quite the old Party *nomenklatura*. Marxist-Leninist rhetoric had been scrapped, which allowed a lot of politicians who had made their career on democratic rhetoric to attach themselves to the ruling elite. However, democratic procedures and democratic methods were just as new and alien to them as they had been to the old *nomenklatura*.

This could be felt almost everywhere, but principally in two ways: in a growing tendency to keep the decision-making process closed and hidden, and in an equally sharp increase in the importance of the "power ministries," e.g., the ministries of interior and defense, the special police forces, the presidential security force, and intelligence. The increase in their power was facilitated enormously by Yeltsin's forcible dissolution of the parliament in September and October 1993, which ironically was undertaken in the name of democracy's defense.

In public opinion, the value of freedom, it seemed, took a back seat to the passionate desire to "establish order in the country." A new, democratic order had not yet taken root, and for that reason many people associated democracy with disorder and instability. It is hardly surprising that the idea of *derzhavnost'*, of a powerful sovereign state, grew more and more popular. Such a state, it was thought, would be capable of reviving Russia's greatness, which had supposedly been undermined by the "democrats." The Russian tradition of "great state values" in fact consists of the sacralization of government power—and of "the sacred heritage, the legacy of our forebears" Ivan the Terrible, Peter the Great, and Joseph Stalin. In this view, the state is the apotheosis of the Russian national spirit; and therefore the interests of society and the individual must be unconditionally subordinated to state interests.' The state itself should, as much as possible, remain beyond social criticism (which by definition is "antipatriotic"), and completely beyond society's control.

It is clear that such an ideology closely corresponds to the interests of a huge, powerful class of state bureaucrats. (Russian bureaucrats shouldn't be confused with Western "managers"— who represent a completely different social type). Bureaucracy and the *nomenklatura* are in fact the primary source of such ideology. The idea of "powerful statehood" also easily finds support among certain *pochvenniki,* or "back-to-the-land" members of the intelligentsia, as well as among a number of financial barons, who today have quasi-criminal relations with the *nomenklatura,* and the captains of industry who prefer to remain Priests of State Expediency rather than become independent entrepreneurs. Alas, this idea of the all-powerful state is also fairly popular among so-called "simple people," who are accustomed to the paternalism of the authorities; it is particularly popular among those who have suffered from economic chaos and disorder.

Initially, the team of reformers put together by Yeltsin in 1991 was able to resist such moods among the apparatchiks and a good part of the population. But by 1994 most of the reformers had been pushed out of the government, under pressure from

"The tradition of 'great state values' in fact consists of the sacralization of government power..."

that very same apparat. Many of those who remained decided
that it was simpler to advance one's career by taking the side of
the bureaucracy. Yeltsin himself appears to have hesitated for
quite some time before breaking with democracy. On the one
hand, he was probably trying to outmaneuver the nationalist-
Communist opposition in the parliament and the country by co-
opting their slogans. This was in vain: the further he drifted
toward this nationalist-Communist opposition, the more radical
its slogans became and the more intransigent its criticism of the
President and the government. On the other hand, it's likely that
many aspects of the "powerful state" ideology are far from alien
to Yeltsin, who has not fully overcome his own Party apparatchik
past.

In any event, the outcome of this hesitation on Yeltsin's part
was the decision to launch a model military action to establish
order in Chechnya, and defend the honor of the Russian state
and its national interests, if not on the world stage, then in a single, separate republic. Pavel Grachev, then minister of defense,
said it would only take "a couple of hours, and one parachute
regiment."

I am sometimes asked: "Well, all right Mr. Kovalev, you turned
out to be correct about the prospects for an armed resolution of
the Chechen crisis. But what if you had been wrong? What if
they actually had been able to solve the Chechen problem in a
short time, with little force and little blood? Would you have
approved?" I usually answer that this could not have happened,
that the problem simply could not have been solved by force,
and that there's no point in discussing impossible hypotheses. I
am usually accused of evading the question. Or worse, it is said
that I was secretly on Dudayev's side and that I still can't admit
it honestly.

In fact, it seems to me that my answer is to the point. Such is
the nature of the clumsy, unintelligent monster called the traditional Russian state. It is inherently incapable of properly evalu-
ating situations because it feeds off myths alone and in some
sense is a myth itself. It cannot live without using force, because
its essence is deified, impersonal power divorced from the power
of society. The Russian state does not know how to resolve problems bloodlessly, for blood is its favorite food. Moreover, it does-
n't really know how to resolve problems at all. It only knows
how to create them. The wars in the Caucasus—the first and the
second—are not simply testimony to the mediocrity of Russian
statehood: they are its inevitable result.

It was this monster that was defeated in Chechnya. It is painful
for me to think of the thousands of Russian soldiers and officers
who died, or were crippled, or were taken prisoner in this war.
It is painful to think of the thousands of young Chechen boys
who perished in battle against my country's army or were
destroyed by the OMON—the special police forces—in the so-

called filtration camps set up by the Russians. It is particularly painful to think of the tens of thousands of civilian victims of the war, of the hundreds of thousands of refugees wandering through Russia without shelter or aid. But I am glad the monster was defeated.

Who was the victor in this war? The forces of the Chechen resistance won the military victory. In effect, they won in the first three weeks of the war, when the gigantic Russian military machine bloodied its fists trying to take over the smoking remnants of Grozny. This unprecedented humiliation of a great power became the Chechens' decisive moral victory. And even if they had been crushed after that and the part of the population that was able to fight had been annihilated, history would still have named them the victors, just as for history Biafra remained the victor in the war with Nigeria—no matter what the historians say.

But the Chechens were not crushed. They claimed victory after victory and ended the war with a triumphant attack on Grozny. The military victory is theirs. But were the Chechen people victorious?

I'm afraid that here things are not so simple.

"This unprecedented humiliation of a great power became the Chechens' decisive moral victory."

There is nothing more dangerous than a military victory. And Chechnya is no exception to this rule.

A few months ago I addressed the Chechen parliament. Speaking about the fact that corporal punishment was recently introduced into the criminal code of the Republic of Ichkeria, I tried to appeal to the Chechen sense of honor and self-respect. "The wolf, the legendary ancestor of the Vainakh people," I said, "is the symbol of your staunchness. But a beaten wolf is no longer a wolf. He is a mongrel." I fully expected to be shot or at least stoned. But nothing of the kind occurred: there were a few embarrassed smiles and complete silence. Most of the people in the hall agreed with me, but they were afraid to say so aloud. A beaten wolf is not a wolf. A frightened Chechen is not a Chechen.

The Chechen leaders are afraid. They are afraid to resist the terror that criminals untested in battle have now unleashed against defenseless Russians—they might be accused of insufficient patriotic spirit and of "pro-Russian attitudes." They are afraid to speak out against the Islamization of the country—they might be accused of being insufficiently devout and of harboring "pro-Western sympathies." They are afraid to take decisive measures against the criminals that have been kidnapping journalists for ransom—they could be accused of lacking solidarity with their fellow Chechens.

The "hero of Budyonnovsk," Shamil Basayev, a truly courageous man, is afraid of the "hero of the Kizlyar Maternity Ward," the degenerate coward Salman Raduyev, even though Basayev could easily crush Raduyev. The government of Ichkeria fusses over Raduyev like a baby, first declaring him mentally ill (which, by the way, seems to be the case), then timidly wagging a finger at him. The leaders of the Chechen resistance are afraid of their own people and, it appears, of one another. The people are beginning to be afraid of their leaders. The night following a battle belongs to looters. By appeasing Raduyev and others like him, by humoring them, Maskhadov risks losing the authority he has earned and smoothing the road to power in Ichkeria for all sorts of riffraff.

Chechnya got its independence. But the Chechens were fighting first and foremost for their freedom. Now they could easily lose that freedom.

This may well be the price of military victory.

I feel sorry for the Chechens. I have great affection for the Chechen people, a people of poets, traders, farmers, and knights—trusting, talented, theatrical, childishly cruel and childishly vain. I fear for their unparalleled sense of self-esteem, for their inborn hunger for freedom. There are few peoples on earth who have so carefully preserved these ancient virtues in their culture, their traditions, and their everyday life. Culture is created over millennia, but it can be destroyed in an instant.

I admire the Chechens and I hope that they will be able to overcome the present social and psychological crisis brought on by the war and by victory. But Russia concerns me even more.

Did Russia lose the Second Caucasus War?

If we are talking about the Russia that was "lost" by Mr. Govorukhin, or Mr. Zyuganov, the leader of the Communist Party, or Mr. Zhirinovsky, the leader of the largest far-right nationalist party—then yes, of course, that Russia was defeated.

But what about the Russia which, beginning with Gorbachev's first timid declarations, our reformers have been trying to nurture from the seeds scattered here and there across our history and especially our culture? The Russia of Pushkin, Herzen, Sakharov? The Russia that is part of a great European civilization, the Russia without which a new, global human civilization will never arise? I don't yet know, but I have the uncertain hope that this Russia was victorious.

Three times in Russian history the loss of a war has brought about liberal political reforms within the country. The Crimean War of the 1850s led to the end of serfdom and to reforms in the legal structure, the army, and local self-government, as well as the weakening of censorship. After the Russo-Japanese war of 1904–1905, considerable limits were placed on the autocracy; civilian freedoms were strengthened and the beginnings of democratic rule were introduced. The Afghan war of the 1980s led to Gorbachev's perestroika.

Each such reform brought the country nearer to the mainstream of social progress. And in each instance, reform struck a blow against the age-old Russian system of an all-powerful state supported by a large, powerful bureaucratic apparat.

The Chechen crisis has demonstrated the utter impracticality of a system of governance based on the all-powerful state. Under the conditions of an open society, a market economy, and political freedom and partnership with the West, such a system could not possibly work. Therefore...? Therefore, there are two options. One can change—but that means new, and this time decisive, systematic reform in all spheres of government, and an end to the absolute power of the old bureaucratic apparat (which is, according to Milovan Djilas, a "new class"). The other option is to sever ties with surrounding reality and as far as possible restore the "Iron Curtain," thereby returning to autarchy and a closed society, i.e., to a form of state schizophrenia.

At present I have the timid hope that the country will somehow choose the first path. The very signing of the agreement with Ichkeria suggests the victory of sobriety over schizophrenia. But there are other signs of change, which may, given certain conditions, become decisive.

The President's administration and cabinet of ministers have been almost completely changed. Almost none of the people directly responsible for the Caucasian slaughter are left (except for the minister of the interior, Anatoly Kulikov, and, of course, the President himself). There are almost no representatives of the old Soviet *nomenklatura* and the so-called "Sverdlovsk mafia"— people like Oleg Lobov, Oleg Soskovets, and Viktor Iliushin, who owed their high positions to a single virtue: personal devotion to the head of state. Perhaps after the behavior of Alexander Korzhakov, his friend and the head of the presidential security forces—who according to rumors tried to stop last year's elections—Yeltsin finally understood that there is nothing more unreliable in politics than personal devotion. Let's hope so.

> "...Yeltsin finally understood that there is nothing more unreliable in politics than personal devotion."

Once again, people with a reputation as reformers are in the government: Anatoly Chubais, Boris Nemtsov, Yakov Urinson. They've started talking about the second stage of reforms. It is encouraging that this time around reforms are being discussed publicly and openly, that Russian society has the opportunity to learn the truth about the country's condition and about proposed solutions to the crisis. True, the reformers are few; moreover, they are divided and weak. Most of the talk centers around economic reform rather than serious legal reform, or, even more important—reform of the system of government.

Still there appears to be less nationalistic and anti-Western blather about "great statehood" in the speeches of the state's top leaders recently. Anti-NATO hysteria seems to be subsiding; Yeltsin signed the agreement with the North Atlantic Alliance at the end of May. (Regarding NATO expansion, I by no means think that the West's behavior is entirely correct or sensible—but this article is about Russia.)

The subject of human rights has also been remembered,

though in the usual Soviet manner: the President declared a "year of human rights" in Russia, in honor of the fiftieth anniversary of the UN Declaration. But even an anniversary "affair" is a good thing coming from these people. Next thing you know, they might even remember judicial reform, which was abandoned some time ago.

Of course, this is all far from being the victory of democracy.

Supporters of the *nomenklatura* and traditional, Soviet-style bureaucratic rule still have a strong presence in the government, and, alas, in the population at large. These social forces dragged the country down in the dirt and blood of the Chechen war, and will never accept their defeat, for defeat means that they must disappear from Russian history. That they still have a fair amount of power in both the opposition and the government itself can be seen, for example, in the recent attempt to bring about unification with Belarus, when we almost woke up in a single country. True, at the last moment the entire agreement was confined to symbols rather than substance. But I'm not talking about the pluses and minuses of integration with Belarus in general, and the antidemocratic and antiliberal character of Lukashenko's regime in particular; what is disturbing is the covert, closed, secretive way in which the decision in favor of unification was taken. That is the way we began the war with Dudayev.

It can't be forgotten that our nationalists and "great state" adherents have powerful allies in the West as well. Some Western statesmen feel that Russia has no business insinuating itself into Europe and that it should "stay in Asia." One can only speculate about the motives of such a geopolitical doctrine. But there is no doubt that the policies of leading Western countries, to the degree that they are determined by this and similar remarks by proponents of the thesis that Russia is an "extra country," contributed to the unfortunate development of events in Russia that led to the Chechen war. Geopolitical racism, whether it comes from Mr. Zhirinovsky or from like-minded Americans, can only bear one fruit—a Russia transformed into an enormous and extremely dangerous source of instability for the entire world.

All the symptoms of awakening democratic tendencies I have mentioned above are still very, very weak. It wouldn't be difficult to crush them—at present they are not much more than declarations. In essence, the peace agreement between Russia and Ichkeria itself is no more than a declaration of intentions. Both sides still have to work out the concrete procedures of the final settlement. I am hardly an optimist and I have no illusions that these procedures will be based on the principles of law and democracy, on the priority of human rights, as they should be. And if a solution depended on the Russian government taking reasonable steps, I would be utterly pessimistic. At present the government is behaving sensibly, but tomorrow it could easily go mad and crave meat. For that matter, what prevented it from devouring more parts of Russia than it did? Did conscience play a role? Or was it just that the bullets ran out? Neither. I allow myself a certain measured optimism based on the fact that the Russian government did not stop the war voluntarily. It was forced to stop fighting.

The people who prevented this war from continuing until the last Chechen and the last Russian soldier were dead are the ones who won the war.

So who did in fact win the war?

In *Izvestia*, Otto Latsis expressed an opinion that was extremely flattering to me: "The party of peace won, and the first to join it were Sergei Kovalev and other democratic politicians." So it seems that Kovalev won the war. This isn't the case, of course. For instance, I cannot consider Chechnya's attaining state independence to be my victory, because it was never my goal. Contrary to widespread opinion, I never argued for or against Chechnya becoming an independent state. Quite frankly, I don't much care whether Chechnya is part of Russia, or Canada, or whether it exists as independent Ichkeria. Just as long as there's no shooting. I would even say that all things being equal, I would like Chechnya to remain part of Russia. But with one obligatory condition: it should be a free, democratic Chechnya as part of a free, democratic Russia. Or—not part of Russia; as long as this condition is met, sovereignty seems of secondary importance to me.

Needless to say, it wasn't Kovalev and "other democratic politicians" who won this war. At least, not alone. The war was won by those few dozen, and only a few dozen, nongovernment organizations all across the country—the Soldiers' Mothers and Memorial, among others—which from the first day raised their voices against the meat grinder. They were seen and heard by only a small percentage of citizens. But among these citizens were several hundred or so—just a few hundred—who demonstrated and picketed day after day, month after month. Their conviction made an impression on our "silent majority."

This is our arithmetic.

The war was won by freedom of speech. By the several dozen honest journalists—just a few dozen—who continued to describe the truth about Chechnya to hundreds of thousands of readers and tens of millions of television viewers, despite pressure from the government. They were forced to broadcast official lies as well as the truth. But we are adults and know how to distinguish lies from the truth.

We turned out to be too exhausted, too broken and disillusioned, to shake Moscow with a 500,000-strong demonstration in the first days of the Chechen adventure—as we did in January 1991 after events in Vilnius. The price of our civilian passivity was 100,000 corpses in the North Caucasus. But we turned out to be sufficiently sober not to let ourselves be deceived by the government.

In 1996, the more perceptive politicians seeking office understood that the country would not support anyone who didn't promise to stop the bloodshed. The "hawks" had no future. It was at this moment that Yeltsin made several highly public moves toward peaceful settlement of the conflict. It was exactly then that Lebed, a man not entirely devoid of political instinct, it seems, beckoned to the voters with the promise of immediate peace. Those voters who didn't believe Yeltsin believed Lebed.

We are still very naive, of course. No one who knows the Russian political elite could guarantee that pre-election promises would be kept even in part. Maskhadov's military victory in August of last year could have been a prelude to a new, unprecedented round of bloodshed rather than to the agreements that ended the fighting. But during the election campaign there turned out to be a fair number of people who, like Lebed, tried to calculate their political career several steps ahead. These were the ones who dotted the *i*'s on the agreements.

This, in fact, is democracy at work: society has mechanisms with which it can force the authorities to do what it demands, and not what the authorities themselves would like to do.

The Chechen crisis was the first serious battle for democracy in Russia. It would be going too far to say that our newborn, weak, sickly, uncertain civil society won this battle. But at least it didn't lose. Peace in the North Caucasus is probably all we are capable of today. And this is of course much less than is needed in order to win the future for Russia.

Is Russia Still an Enemy?[3]

*Treat your friend as if he will one day be your enemy, and your
enemy as if he will one day be your friend.*
Decimus Laberius, First Century B.C.

It is official: Russia no longer considers the Western democracies
antagonists. The military doctrine that the government of the
Russian Federation adopted in 1993 declares that Russia "does
not regard any state to be its adversary." The May 1997 NATO-
Russia agreement reaffirmed the premise. Although not admitted
to NATO, Russia has been given a seat on the alliance's
Permanent Joint Council, which assures it, if not of a veto, then
of a voice, in NATO deliberations. Given that in last year's presidential election Russian voters rejected the communist candidate for one committed to democracy and capitalism, it is not
unreasonable to assume that in time Russia will become a full-
fledged member of the international community.

Yet doubts linger because so much about post-communist
Russia is unfinished and unsettled. Fledgling democracy contends with ancient authoritarian traditions; private enterprise
struggles against a collectivist culture; frustrated nationalist and
imperialist ambitions impede the enormous task of internal
reconstruction. Russians, bewildered by the suddenness and the
scope of the changes they have experienced, do not know in
which direction to proceed. A veritable battle for Russia's soul is
in progress.

Its outcome is of considerable concern to the rest of the world,
if only because Russia's geopolitical situation in the heartland of
Eurasia enables it, weakened as it is, to influence global stability. Whether it indeed joins the world community or once again
withdraws into its shell and assumes an adversarial posture will
be decided by an unpredictable interplay of domestic and external factors.

From Well-wisher to Cold Warrior

Over the past three centuries, Russia has had its share of conflicts with what are now NATO countries—notably Turkey,
Britain, and Germany—but Russian relations with the United
States before the Bolsheviks' seizure of power were exceptional-
ly friendly. In the early decades of the nineteenth century, the
two countries had some differences over the northwestern territories of the North American continent, but these they peaceful-
ly resolved by treaty in 1824. The czarist government permanently eliminated that source of friction in 1867 when, unwilling

[3] Article by Richard Pipes, professor of History, Emeritus, at Harvard University,
from *Foreign Affairs* 76/5:65-78 S/O '97. Copyright © 1997 by the Council on
Foreign Relations, Inc. Reprinted with permission.

to bear the costs of administering and defending Alaska, it persuaded a reluctant U.S. Congress to take the territory off Russia's hands for a nominal payment. During the American Civil War, Russia boosted the morale of the Northern states by dispatching naval units to New York and San Francisco. Secretary of State William Henry Seward declared at the time that Americans preferred Russia over any other European country because "she always wishes us well."

Relations deteriorated to some extent toward the end of the nineteenth century because of the wave of pogroms against Jews that broke out after the assassination of Czar Alexander II and persistent discrimination against American Jews visiting Russia. Another irritant was Russia's expansion in the Far East: in the 1904–05 Russo-Japanese War, U.S. opinion openly favored the Japanese. But all was forgotten when Russia joined the Allied cause on the outbreak of World War I. The United States was the first country to recognize the Provisional Government that took over after the czar's abdication in March 1917.

"The Cold War was an artificial conflict initiated and aggressively pursued by a dictatorship..."

The seven decades of U.S.-Russian hostility that followed the Bolshevik coup d'etat were the result not of a conflict of interests but of the peculiar needs of Russia's conquerors, the Soviet ruling elite. The Bolsheviks seized power in Russia not to reform their country but to secure a base from which to launch a worldwide revolution. They never thought it possible to establish a socialist society in a single country, least of all their own, where four-fifths of the inhabitants were peasants rather than Marx's industrial workers. To remain in power, they needed revolutions to break out in the industrialized countries of the West, by which they meant in the interwar years principally Germany and Britain, and after World War II, the United States. The Cold War was an artificial conflict initiated and aggressively pursued by a dictatorship that invoked to its people phantom threats to justify its illegitimately acquired and lawlessly enforced authority. No concessions to the communist regime could attenuate its hostility because its very survival depended on it: as in the case of Nazi Germany, belligerency and expansionism were built into the system.

Indeed, as soon as the Communist party fell from power, the government that succeeded it abandoned all pretense that the country faced threats from without. If the Soviet regime required international tension, its democratic successor needs peaceful relations with other countries so that it can cut military spending and attract foreign capital. It is clearly in Russia's interests to be on the best of terms with the rest of the world, especially the United States.

Fighting the Culture

Yet self-interest has to contend with a political culture based in traditions of empire-building and reliance on military power for stature rather than security. For, unfortunately, Russia has not made a clean break with its Soviet past.

The bloodless revolution of 1991 that outlawed the Communist party, oversaw the peaceful dissolution of the Soviet Union, and installed democracy is in many respects incomplete. The new coexists with the old in an uneasy symbiosis. No fresh elites have emerged: the country's political, economic, military, and cultural institutions are run by ex-communists who cannot shed old mental habits. The Duma, the lower house of parliament, is dominated by communists and nationalists equally suspicious of the West and equally determined to reclaim for Russia superpower status. Unlike the Bolsheviks, who on coming to power promptly obliterated all the symbols of the overthrown czarist regime, Russia's democrats have left in place the myriad memorials glorifying their predecessors without substituting pervasive symbols of their own.

Russia is torn by contradictory pulls, one oriented inward, hence isolationist, the other imperialist. The population at large, preoccupied with physical survival, displays little interest in foreign policy, taking in stride the loss of empire and the world influence that went with it. People pine for normality, which they associate with life in the West as depicted in foreign films and television programs. Depoliticized, they are unresponsive to ideological appeals, although not averse to blaming all their troubles on foreigners. But for the ruling elite and much of the intelligentsia, accustomed to being regarded as citizens of a great power, the country's decline to Third World status has been traumatic. They are less concerned with low living standards than the loss of power and influence, perhaps because inwardly they doubt whether Russia can ever equal the West in anything else. Power and influence for them take the form of imperial splendor and military might second to none.

In contrast to the Western states, which acquired empires after forming nation-states, in Russia nation-building and empire-building proceeded concurrently. Since the seventeenth century, when Russia was already the world's largest state, the immensity of their domain has served Russians as psychological compensation for their relative backwardness and poverty. Thus the loss of empire has been for the politically engaged among them a much more bewildering experience than for the British, French, or Dutch. Unable to reconcile themselves to the loss, they connive in various ways to reassert control over the separated borderlands and regain superpower status for the motherland.

The situation in today's Russia is highly volatile. There are really two Russias. One is led by the younger, better-educated, mostly urban population that is eager to break with the past and take the Western route; the new deputy prime minister, Boris Zemtsov, is a representative spokesman for this constituency. The other Russia is made up of older, often unskilled, preponderantly rural or small-town citizens, suspicious of the West and Western ways and nostalgic for the more secure Soviet past; their principal mouthpiece is the head of the Communist party of the Russian Federation, Gennadi Zyuganov.

At present the pro-Western contingent runs the country, but it is by no means firmly in the saddle. In the first round of the June 1996 presidential election, incumbent Boris Yeltsin received the most votes (35 percent), but had the anti-liberal opposition combined forces it would have decisively defeated him: Zyuganov won 32 percent of the vote, the extreme nationalist Vladimir Zhirinovsky nearly 6 percent, and the authoritarian Aleksandr Lebed over 14 percent, to produce a theoretically absolute majority of 52 percent. Three years ago, when asked what they thought of communism, 51 percent of Russians polled said they had a positive image of it and 36 percent a negative one. (It is, however, indicative of the prevailing confused mood that fewer than half those who expressed a positive attitude toward communism wanted to see it restored.) The popular base of democracy in the country is thus thin and brittle; the political climate can change overnight. Countries like Russia, lacking in strong party organizations and loyalties, are capable of swinging wildly from one extreme to another, often in response to a demagogue who promises quick and easy solutions.

"Russia bears a heavy burden of history which has taught its people better how to survive than how to succeed."

For Russians, the road to a civil society is long and arduous because they have to overcome not only the communist legacy but also that of the czars and their partner, the Orthodox Church, which for centuries collaborated in instilling in their subjects disrespect for law, submission to strong and willful authority, and hostility to the West. Russia bears a heavy burden of history which has taught its people better how to survive than how to succeed.

Their present striving for what they conceive of as normality is further hampered by a mindset formed in a harsh rural environment that bred suspicion of anyone who did not belong to the community and demanded social leveling within it. (Although the majority of the Russian population lives in cities, the bulk of city dwellers are first- or second-generation peasants who have never been truly urbanized.) As anthropologists have noted, peasants, dependent on a fluctuating but unchanging Nature, tend to believe that the good things in life, such as hunting grounds or farmland, are available only in finite quantities. Having had no opportunity to learn that an economic milieu that enables some to profit more than others can, in the end, benefit all, numerous Russians, like others of the same background, resent anyone more affluent or distinguished than themselves because they believe that such affluence and distinction are purchased at their expense. This attitude impedes both the evolution of market institutions and friendly relations with foreigners. It will come as a surprise to Americans that many Russians, possibly the majority, believe that U.S. aid and investments are a ploy to acquire their country's resources at liquidation prices.

An Empire Reclaimed

Moscow acknowledged the sovereign status of the former Soviet republics, but it is a recognition that comes from the head, not the heart. The patrimonial mentality embedded in the Russian psyche, which holds that everything inherited from one's forefathers is inalienable property, works against accepting the separation of the borderlands as a fait accompli. It prompts Moscow to strive for their gradual economic, political, and military "reintegration" with Russia—which, given the disparity in their respective size and population, can only mean reducing the former republics once again to the status of clients. In this endeavor the government is abetted by the Orthodox Church, which claims authority over all Orthodox Christians of what was once the Soviet Union.

In December 1991, immediately after the dissolution of the U.S.S.R., Moscow created the Commonwealth of Independent States, ostensibly to enable the former Soviet republics to resolve common problems by common consent. In time, ten of the 15 republics joined the CIS, some enrolling of their own free will, others under duress. In 1992, at Moscow's insistence, CIS members signed a mutual security treaty, which in effect entrusted the defense of their territories to the only military force on hand, the Russian army.

Despite the declared objectives of the CIS covenant and its security treaty, Moscow has used the documents, especially the latter, as excuses to meddle in the affairs of the borderlands. At first the preferred technique was economic pressure, which Russia had at its disposal because it owns the bulk of the industries of the defunct Soviet Union as well as the principal developed energy resources. Such pressure became less effective when foreigners began to pour capital investment into the other former republics. The fledgling states have further enhanced their economic independence by signing commercial treaties with each other and friendly neighbors like Poland and Turkey.

The main instrument of "reintegration" today is the Russian army, and this is worrisome because its formidable officer corps is society's most embittered and vindictive group. Anyone who spends an hour with Russian generals cannot but feel the intensity of their resentment against the West as well as against their own democratic government for reducing to the status of a negligible force the army that defeated Nazi Germany and was acknowledged by the U.S. military as a peer. The dethroned Communist party nomenklatura has adapted to the new era by appropriating some of the state's wealth and continuing to manage much of the rest. But the generals, dependent on government allocations, have had no such opportunity, and they seethe with humiliation both personal and professional. Most analogies between contemporary Russia and Weimar Germany fall wide of the mark, but parallels between the general officers of the two are striking: one sees the same sense of degradation and thirst for revenge. As in Weimar Germany, civilian authorities in Russia exert only nominal control over the military; the Ministry of Defense has a single civilian executive.

Although Russia's armed forces are demoralized and starved for money, their command structure remains largely intact and extends over most of what was once the Soviet Union. With the exception of the three Baltic states and Azerbaijan, Russian troops are deployed in every one of the ex-Soviet republics: 24,000 in Tajikistan, 15,000 in Turkmenistan, 5,000 in Uzbekistan, and so on. In Armenia, which has traditionally relied on Russia for protection from Turkey and other Muslim neighbors, Moscow has secured a 25-year basing right for its troops, in return for which it sent Armenia $1 billion worth of military equipment. The ostensible mission of these Russian expeditionary forces is to defend the former republics' borders and protect their ethnic Russian residents. In reality, they also serve as the vanguard of Russia's imperial drive. Moscow interprets the terms of the mutual security treaty as giving it license to intervene militarily in any CIS country where, in its judgment, the commonwealth's security is threatened. Russian troops guarding the border between Tajikistan and Afghanistan have engaged in desultory clashes with Muslim fundamentalist forces. A Russian general stationed in Central Asia declared recently that if hard-line Islamist Taliban units from Afghanistan menaced Tajikistan, his troops would intervene. Thus a modified Brezhnev Doctrine is still in force: Moscow regards any country that was once part of the Soviet Union as falling within the sphere of its security interests. Decolonization has been quite halfhearted.

Georgia is a classic case of Moscow's use of military power for imperial objectives. Moscow overcame Georgia's reluctance to join the CIS by inciting a 1992 rebellion of the Abkhaz minority inhabiting the northwestern region of the country. With Russian political and military backing, the Abkhazians expelled 200,000 ethnic Georgians and declared independence. Unable to quell the rebellion, Tbilisi was forced to request aid from Moscow, which consented to provide it so long as Georgia joined the CIS and acquiesced to 15,000 Russian troops on its territory, along with a Russian "peacekeeping" force in Abkhazia. As soon as Tbilisi met these conditions, the Abkhaz rebellion abated. President Eduard Shevardnadze's efforts to rid his country of the putative Russian peacekeepers have so far proved unavailing. Russian forces guard Georgia's land and sea borders with Turkey; since other troops are stationed on Armenia's western border, Russia has direct access to Turkey along the old Soviet frontier.

Moscow's encroachments on the sovereignty of its onetime dependencies present a serious potential threat to East-West relations. The situation is not entirely clear-cut, since the West tacitly recognizes all lands that were once part of the Soviet Union as Russia's legitimate sphere of influence while insisting that Russia respect the sovereignty of the separated republics. If the past is any guide, in the event of an overt conflict between Russia and another of the former republics, the European allies are unlikely to go beyond expressions of regret. The United States, however, is almost certain to react more harshly, especially if the victim of Russian intimidation is Ukraine or one of the countries adjoining the Caspian Sea—the former because of its geopolitical importance, the latter because of those oil-rich states' potential contribution to the world economy.

The existence of petroleum in the Caspian region has been known since antiquity; in late czarist Russia Baku was the center of the empire's oil production. Since 1991 Western companies have engaged in intensive exploration around the Caspian, which has led to the discovery in Turkmenistan, Azerbaijan, and Kazakstan of oil reserves estimated to be at least as large as those of Iraq and perhaps equal to those of Saudi Arabia. International consortia are pouring hundreds of millions of dollars into the three former republics to extract the oil and natural gas and ship them to world markets. Direct foreign investment in the three countries nearly equals that in Russia.

"Russia's claim to be a world power has traditionally rested on military prowess..."

Having lost these assets, Russia for the time being contents itself with pressing its claim to their transport, demanding that all oil from the Caspian region be sent by pipeline across Russian territory to the Black Sea port of Novorossiysk. This damaged pipeline runs through Chechnya, which for years has been torn by ethnic strife. For security reasons, as well as to prevent Moscow from using the pipeline for political or economic blackmail, the oil-producing republics and their foreign backers prefer an alternate route running across Azerbaijan and Georgia to the Black Sea and from there to the Mediterranean coast of eastern Turkey. The issue is a matter of keen competition between Russia and foreign oil firms, in which the other republics concerned, for both economic and political reasons, lean toward the latter.

Dreams of the Generals

Many influential persons in Russia want to regain not only the empire but the status of superpower. Russia cannot attain the latter objective by economic means, which in the modern world confer such rank; its partial inclusion in the Group of Seven is little more than a public relations ploy to compensate it for its forced acquiescence to the expansion of NATO into Eastern Europe. Russia's claim to be a world power has traditionally rested on military prowess, and the temptation is to resort to this expedient once again.

It is common knowledge that Russia's armed forces are destitute and demoralized. Officers drive taxis; soldiers engage in crime for the money. There is so much draft-dodging that officers are believed to constitute half of military personnel. While some generals find the situation intolerable and virtually threaten mutiny, the more far-sighted view it as a temporary setback that they can exploit to revamp the armed forces. Their ambition is to lay the groundwork for a military establishment so effective that its mere presence will guarantee Russia what they deem its rightful place among nations.

That projected force differs greatly from Russia's traditional army, which relied on masses of foot soldiers storming enemy positions without regard to casualties. For one thing, Russia no longer commands unlimited manpower. The death rate exceeds the birthrate; the percentage of babies with genetic defects is well above normal. Nor is there money to rebuild and maintain a large standing force, let alone switch to an all-volunteer army, which President Yeltsin mentions from time to time. Apart from these constraints, Russia's strategists have absorbed the lessons of the Persian Gulf War, which conclusively demonstrated the superiority of modern weapons technology over conventional forces. They were awed by the Americans' ability, before the battle was even joined, to disable Iraq's large and well-equipped army through the electronic suppression of its military communications network, cutting off forces in the field from the command. They were no less impressed by precision missiles' ability to strike and destroy key enemy installations. Those lessons have persuaded them to abandon Russian canon and adopt what American military theorists have designated the revolution in military affairs.

Russia's new military doctrine, approved by the Yeltsin government in 1993, following U.S. practice calls for a shift in defense allocations from procurement to research and development. Hoover Institution Fellow Richard F. Staar estimates that 1997 expenditures on high-technology R&D will account for 40 percent of the defense budget. Drawing on Russia's excellent scientific talent in the field of military technology, the new doctrine projects designing, with the help of supercomputers imported from the United States, prototypes of directed-energy weapons, electronic warfare equipment, and stealth aviation. Naval weaponry is to be emphasized as well. Russia recently established an Academy of Military Sciences to study "military futurology" so as to anticipate developments among potential enemy nations and thus insure itself against shocks like Operation Desert Storm. Such a program can be carried out with the limited funds currently allocated the armed forces. First Deputy Defense Minister Andrei Kokoshkin boasts that it will enable Russia to produce weapons "that have no equivalent in the world."

Until they have designed the new military hardware and secured sufficient funds to procure it—a period of between ten and 20 years, in their estimation—Russian generals intend to rely on the nuclear deterrent. They have revoked Brezhnev's 1982 "no-first-use" pledge and, in view of the superiority of NATO 's conventional forces, adopted NATO 's own flexible response strategy, formulated when Soviet conventional forces enjoyed the upper hand.

Of what use will such a modernized force be to Russia? The new military doctrine speaks of protecting Russia's "vital interests," but these are nowhere defined, an omission that reflects widespread confusion in the country about its place in the world. Certainly, apart from restoring to Russia the prestige of a great power, the new force will enable it to insist on a sphere of influence in adjacent regions, thereby again becoming a leading player on the global stage.

Even in its present reduced state, Russia still has the world's longest frontier, bordering Europe and East Asia, neighboring on the Middle East, and even touching North America. Its capacity for exploiting instabilities along its borders is therefore undiminished. Historically, whenever it has suffered setbacks in one sector of its frontier, Russia has shifted attention to the others. The pattern seems to be repeating itself: feeling rebuffed by Europe, Moscow is turning to the Middle East and East Asia. Yeltsin declared in May that to counter the "Western alliance's expansion plans" his administration has designated the integration of the CIS and the strengthening of ties with China its principal foreign policy goals. Moscow is also cultivating Iran and the other fundamentalist Muslim states. Given the interest of Western powers in Caspian oil and the desire of former Soviet republics in that region to escape Russian pressures for dissolution in the CIS by drawing closer to Turkey, a new political alignment appears to be emerging along Russia's southern frontier. With it, a new East-West geopolitical fault line, running somewhere across Central Asia and the Caucasus, seems to be opening up.

"...Russia still has the world's longest frontier, bordering Europe and East Asia..."

The Choice

It is impossible at this time to foresee which path Russia will choose, pro-Western or anti-Western. The country's political structures are too fragile and the mood of its people too volatile for predictions. Russia's true national interests demand a pro-Western alignment and integration into the world economy. The ambitions and emotional needs of Russia's elite, however, pull in the opposite direction: away from the global economic order dominated by the industrial democracies and toward reliance on military power as well as rapprochement with countries that for one reason or another are hostile to the West. The latter course is alluring because catching up with the West militarily would be much easier for Russia than catching up economically.

Yet it would be an error of historic proportions if Russia threw away the chance of becoming a genuine world power to pursue the illusion of power based on the capacity to threaten and coerce. Russia was acknowledged as a superpower during the Cold War not by virtue of economic might, technological leadership, or cultural achievement, but solely because it possessed weapons capable of wreaking universal destruction—in other words, because of its ability to blackmail the world. The hollowness of Russian claims to superpower status became apparent immediately after the collapse of the Soviet Union: having abandoned its adversarial posture in order to carry out long overdue internal reforms, Russia stood revealed as a second-class power, dependent on foreign loans and exports of raw materials.

The next few years will confront Russia with a supreme test. Can the nation realize its aspirations through internal reconstruction and international cooperation, or will it once again seek to make its mark by resorting to military force and exploitation of international tensions?

Each year that Russia continues as a partner of the West strengthens the forces that favor development over expansionism. A younger generation aspiring to be Western gradually replaces the older one mired in nostalgia for the Soviet past. A business class emerges that has little use for militarism, along with a new breed of politicians who cater to an electorate more concerned with living standards than imperial grandeur.

The choice will be made by the Russians themselves; the West can influence the decision only marginally. The situation calls for a subtle policy that mixes toughness with understanding of Russian sensitivities. No special favors should be granted. They only whet the appetites of nationalists who interpret undeserved concessions to mean that the world is so anxious to bring Russia into the international community that it is prepared to show boundless tolerance for its behavior. Moscow should not be allowed to increase its forces in the country's southern regions in violation of the 1990 Conventional Forces in Europe Treaty, or to bully its erstwhile republics and ex-satellites. The world must not acquiesce to a new Brezhnev Doctrine.

At the same time, Western leaders should consider ways of avoiding actions that, without any real bearing on their countries' security, humiliate Russians by making them keenly aware how impotent they have become under democracy. These leaders should consider whether extending NATO to Eastern Europe to forestall a putative military threat to the region is worth alienating the majority of politically active Russians, who see the move as permanently excluding their country from Europe and giving it no alternative but to seek allies in the east. The ambiguity of a "gray zone" between Russia and the present members of NATO would actually help assure Russia that even if it is not politically and militarily part of Europe, it is also not categorically excluded. Projected joint military exercises of forces from the United States and the Central Asian nations scheduled for September in Kazakstan and Uzbekistan are certain to be perceived in Moscow as a deliberate provocation: what purpose do they serve? Assistance of any kind, no matter how well-meaning, must take into account Russian people's suspicions of the motives behind it, irrational as these may be. Immense patience and empathy are required in dealing with Russia's halting progress toward democracy; failure to display them only helps anti-Western forces.

Is Russia then still an enemy? It is not and it ought not to be. But it might become one if those who guide its destiny, exploiting the political inexperience and deep-seated prejudices of its people, once again aspire to a glory to which they are not yet entitled save by the immensity of their territory, meaningless in itself, vast mineral resources that they cannot exploit on their own, and a huge nuclear arsenal that they cannot use. Russia could again become an adversary if, instead of building their country from the ground up after seven decades of destruction such as no nation in history has ever inflicted on itself, its leaders once again were to seek to escape the difficulties facing them through self-isolation and grandstanding. I fear that if it fails to confront reality and tries to make up for internal shortcomings by posturing on the global stage, Russia may not be given another chance.

Shortsighted[4]

After the failed Communist coup in August 1991, America decided that true democracy had finally come to Russia. But that was far from true, because the old Soviet *nomenklatura,* including Boris Yeltsin, was still in place.

The brief period of liberal Government, under Prime Minister Yegor Gaidar, ended in May 1992. When he was replaced some months later by Viktor Chernomyrdin, Russia regressed to a replica of the old Soviet system, with different titles. The bureaucracy, the absence of civil society, the existence of the old Soviet monopolies all created obstacles for people who wanted to live differently or start their own businesses.

"Russians feel abandoned by America."

To the United States, however, it was a new Russia, and its policy toward Russia changed drastically. In the Soviet period, Washington followed a two-pronged approach. While maintaining relations with the Soviet leaders, it communicated with the people directly—through radio broadcasts and the United States Embassy in Moscow. In the late 1980's, Ambassador Jack Matlock turned the embassy into something like a club, where we could meet, discuss ideas and issues and learn about America.

That is why Americans had an unlimited credit of trust in Russia in the early 90's; Americans had not confused the Government with the people. But then, suddenly, America seemed to recognize only the Government.

This simplistic approach to Russia is typical of some American attitudes: there are good guys and bad guys. The good guys had won. Let's move on. In the Soviet period, American mass media blasted poor living conditions in Russia. Wages not being paid! Corrupt politicians! It's the Evil Empire! Now nothing seems to arouse American outrage on behalf of the Russian people. Wages not being paid? Corrupt politicians? It's a democracy—no problem.

But you can't have a democracy by fiat. More than ever, Russians need to hear about life in a democracy. Yes, in 1991 and 1992 we needed money, and we will be forever grateful to the American taxpayers for their timely help. Today Russia needs intellectual, moral and political support, and that requires a deep understanding of what is going on.

Russians feel abandoned by America. We cannot understand why, if we have followed all your advice, we still face a profound economic decline. American economic advisers assumed that whatever was good for America had to be good for Russia. Inflation and the budget deficit were serious problems for the

---

[4] Article by Grigory Yavlinsky from *New York Times Magazine,* Je 8, '97. Translated from Russian by Antonina W. Bouis. Copyright © 1997 The New York Times Company. Reprinted with permission.

United States. Somehow, that became the focus of American advice to us: stabilize inflation, balance your budget and all will be well. But the two countries are completely different.

The Soviet Union's economy was created by central planning. To create an effective market economy, we have to resolve the problems that America faced *and* we also have to change the monopolistic structures, implement private-property rights and have real privatization.

Here are the questions I would like to ask an American economic expert. How did you deal with the robber barons and cartels during the Progressive Era? How did Theodore Roosevelt implement an effective tax system? How did you develop competition? This is what Russia really needs to know.

Instead, we were told to stabilize inflation. And then, of course, "re-elect Yeltsin." So what happened? Russia re-elected Yeltsin and the West expanded NATO. What message does that send? Few Russians think that NATO is being expanded because you want to attack us. But it is a sign that you do not believe that Russia will become a democracy in the near future. You are expanding NATO because 100,000 people were killed in Chechnya, because we have an unpredictable leadership, because we have corruption, because there are enormous failures in economic reform.

You should say so openly. I know that an enormous investment of time and money has been spent by the government, by the private sector, by foundations and universities in promoting the myth that Russia has achieved democracy. It would take great courage to admit that the taxpayers' money was wasted. But it is always better to be honest.

Russians used to rely on America for the truth, for validation of their own perceptions of reality in Russia. When President Clinton came to Russia, the Russian people expected to hear something like this: "We Americans understand the difficulties you are facing. America has been through the Depression, has dealt with corruption and crime. Please do not think that corruption and crime are normal attributes of democracy." Instead all they saw was unstinting praise for the Government, which the people no longer trust.

Reform is possible and reform is necessary. Do not give up on Russia. Tell the truth to us and to yourselves. It is the false political picture of what is going on in Russia that is creating the climate for business failure. American businesspeople are coming here with the notion that they can do business, as if Russia were California, Michigan or Texas. They find instead that they are expected to give bribes. They become frustrated and leave. Or they pay the bribes, which is bad for them and bad for Russia.

Russian businesspeople are in the same fix. Today, to be successful, a Russian must be a close friend or relative of a high-ranking official. In Boston, a businessperson may not even know the names of the local bureaucrats. That is my dream model for Russians—that they simply not know who the governor is.

An Unhealthy Russia[5]

Russia is dying, its largest doctors' organization said yesterday, warning that the population was shrinking at a rate not seen in peacetime and accusing the government of failing in its legal duty to provide health care.

"Russia is losing its main state asset—its citizens," the Russian Pirogov Congress of Physicians said in a resolution after a three-day meeting of more than 1,700 doctors.

The resolution, quoted by the Interfax news agency, decried the "unprecedented peacetime decline in the Russian population."

Statistics have found that the country is losing about a million of its 150 million people every year, as the death rate outstrips the birth rate by 1.6 times. A third of those dying are of working age.

Hardships since the Soviet Union collapsed have damaged health, and state medical care for ordinary people has declined.

Men in particular, who also suffer from high levels of alcoholism, have seen their average life expectancy sink to 58, at least 15 years fewer than men in Western Europe.

The doctors sent a letter to Prime Minister Viktor Chernomyrdin arguing that the government was in breach of its constitutional obligation to provide free health care.

They resolved to take the issue to the state prosecutor and Constitutional Court.

---

5 Article from the *Boston Sunday Globe* Je 8 '97. Copyright © 1997 Reuters. Reprinted with permission.

The End of the Beginning: The Emergence of a New Russia[6]

Thanks, Chris [Warren Christopher], to you, to Bill Perry, and to David Hamburg for the chance to return to Stanford, where I spent quite a bit of time in the late 1960s and early 1970s. In those days I had an academic pretext for hanging around this campus—something to do with multiarchival research on early 20th-century Russian history at the Hoover Institution. But that was a cover story. My real mission was to court a Stanford under-graduate. I'm courting her still, and she's here with me today, looking at me somewhat askance and hoping I'll get on with this speech.

I also want to thank Chris and Bill for the chance to work at their sides for four years. That work was far-ranging, fascinating, and often—I can admit this because I'm among friends—fun. Among the most important of the many enterprises on which we worked was the one that you are discussing at this conference: the design and construction of a new security architecture in Europe—one that recognizes and encourages the full and vigor-ous participation of a new and reforming Russia.

It is about Russia that I would like to speak to you this evening. I believe Russia is at a turning point. Let me explain that asser-tion by doing something that I've heard Bill Perry do on any number of occasions—by quoting Winston Churchill. In November 1942, just after the British victory over General Rommel in North Africa, Churchill said, "Now is not the end. It is perhaps not even the beginning of the end. But it is perhaps the end of the beginning."

Churchill was saying that the Battle of El Alamein was a hope-ful moment. But he was also warning that the war would go on for a long time. He was exhorting a combination of confidence, patience, and fortitude.

The parallel I'm suggesting is this: Like Britain in 1942, Russia in 1997 is still in the throes of a titanic struggle. We Americans have a huge stake in how that struggle turns out. Our goal, like that of many Russians, is to see Russia become a normal, mod-ern state—democratic in its governance, abiding by its own con-stitution and by its own laws, market-oriented and prosperous in its economic development, at peace with itself and with the rest of the world. That, in a nutshell, is what we mean—and more to the point, what many Russians mean—by the word *reform*.

The forces complicating, impeding, and often opposing Russian reform include various demons of Russian history. We

---

[6]Speech delivered by Deputy Secretary of State Strobe Talbott at Stanford University, Stanford, CA on September 19, 1997.

all know the litany of experiences from Russia's past that cast a shadow over its future: subjugation for nearly three centuries to the Golden Horde from the East, followed by four centuries of imperialist expansion combined with vulnerability to invasion from the West. Internally, Russia long ago adopted an autocratic order. Along the way, it missed the advent of the modern nation-state in the 16th century, the Enlightenment in the 18th, and the Industrial Revolution of the 19th. Those blank spots prefigured the tragedy of the 20th. The Bolshevik coup d'etat plunged the old Russia into misery, brutality, isolation, and confrontation with the outside world.

Against that background, the new Russia faces a particularly difficult set of challenges. Like every country on Earth, Russia wants to be strong and secure. But how should it define strength and security? I'll rephrase the question using Joe Nye's terminology: What is the optimum mixture of hard power and soft power appropriate to today's world?

"The Bolshevik coup d'etat plunged the old Russia into misery, brutality, isolation, and confrontation with the outside world."

All states face some version of this issue. But for Russia—as Churchill might put it—the political quandary is wrapped in an existential dilemma. It is an issue not just of what Russia wants to do, but of what Russia wants to be. It's a matter of how Russia will define statehood itself. Will it be in terms of Russia's specialness and separateness? Or will it be in terms of those heritages and interests it has in common with the rest of the world, particularly with Europe and the West?

The Russians themselves often call this "the question of questions." They have been grappling with it for a very long time—for hundreds of years. The search for an answer was underway during the Middle Ages in the rivalry between the absolutism and isolation of Muscovy on the one hand and, on the other, the openness and trading culture of Novgorod. In the 19th century, the issue was at the core of the schism between the Slavophiles and the Westernizers. Then along came Lenin and Stalin. With their claim of championing an internationalist ideology, they forcibly suppressed expressions of ethnic and national identity. In their place arose the idea that Ukrainians, Kazaks, Armenians, Karelians, Chukchis, and 100 other nationalities were evolving into a new species—homo sovieticus. By Brezhnev's time, this notion was the object of much lip-service—but of much more muffled ridicule. Soviet man was everywhere on posters and pedestals, but nowhere in real life. That myth died an unmourned death with the Soviet Union itself.

Now that Russia is again Russia rather than the metropole of an empire or the headquarters of a global movement, the old debate rages anew. What is Russia? The 19th- and early 20th-century literary and philosophical combatants—Chadaayev, Solovyev, Berdyayev—are back in fashion, their works selling briskly in the bookstores along the Arbat and Kuznetsky Most. Last year, Rossiskaya Gazeta ran an essay contest to see who could come up with the best statement of "the Russian national idea." President Yeltsin has established a blue-ribbon commission on the same subject. It's hard to sit for long at a kitchen table with friends in Moscow or St. Petersburg without someone agonizing aloud about where Russia belongs and where it is headed. Needless to say, there's more than a little intellectual wind in these debates, but how they play out in Russian politics—and in Russian policy, especially foreign policy—does matter to us.

We are not neutral bystanders. There is no doubt where our own national interest lies: Quite simply, we want to see the ascendancy of Russia's reformers, those who look outward and forward rather than inward and backward for the signposts of national revival. A Russia that reflects their aspirations is likely to be part of the solution to the world's many problems. Conversely, a Russia that erects barriers against what it sees as a hostile world and that believes the best defense is a good offense—such a Russia could be, in the 21st century just as it was in much of the 20th, one of the biggest of the problems we and our children will face.

There is nothing preordained about the outcome of this clash of alternative futures. But there is reason for hope that the latter-day Westernizers will prevail over the latter-day Slavophiles. Let me explain why.

During most of the first term of the Clinton Administration, we were witnessing what might be called the beginning of the beginning; that is, the first phase of Russia's rebirth and its self-liberation from Soviet communism. That phase is now drawing to a close. It has been a period of opportunity as well as of uncertainty and even danger. I suspect I speak for Chris, Bill, Chip [Blacker], Ash [Carter], Liz [Sherwood], and other veterans of the first term who are here this evening when I say that all of us came to work more than once with the bracing sense that everything in Russia was up for grabs—that Russia itself was teetering on the brink of regression or chaos.

That danger has not disappeared altogether, but it has diminished, and—like Britain after El Alamein—Russia may have turned the tide; it may be on the brink of a breakthrough. It has happened with a constellation of several events, of which I'd like to single out four.

First, in domestic politics, there was the presidential election 14 months ago. With Boris Yeltsin's victory over Gennady Zyuganov, the communist electoral tide began to recede from its high-water mark.

Second, in the economy, after 5 years of virtual free fall, Russia's gross domestic product seems finally, in 1997, to be stabilizing and may be registering a real upturn. That achievement, combined with the government's success in slaying the beast of hyperinflation, means that Russia can focus more on taking advantage of its immense human and natural resources to build a world-class market economy.

Third, in relations between Moscow and the regions, the bell-wether event was the pact signed May 12 that ended the war in Chechnya. For all the ambiguity in the terms of that agreement and for all the suspense over its implementation, it represented a recognition, however belated, that the federation cannot and should not be held together by brute force; a recognition that tanks, artillery, and bombers are not legitimate or, in the final analysis, efficacious instruments of governance.

And **fourth,** in relations with the West, there was the signing of the NATO–Russia Founding Act in May, which I look forward to discussing with many of you in tomorrow morning's session of this conference.

While none of these developments is decisive, each is significant in its own right. Moreover, there is a synergy among them—the whole is more than the sum of its parts. Together they may mark a takeoff point in post-Soviet Russia's evolution as a modern state.

"...Russians today can be more confident than a year ago that their country will make it..."

This is not to say that Russian reform has scored a knockout blow against crime; corruption, the uglier manifestation of nationalism and the other forces arrayed against it; or that the Russian economy is home free; or that old Soviet attitudes and habits are gone forever. But it is to say that Russians today can be more confident than a year ago that their country will make it—not just as a safe, secure, unitary state, but as a law-based, democratic society, increasingly integrated with the growing community of states that are similarly constituted and similarly oriented.

The key word here—the key concept—is integration. It is crucial to our foreign policy, in general, since it captures the imperative of working with other states to revitalize and, where necessary, create mutually reinforcing international organizations and arrangements to ensure peace and prosperity in an increasingly interdependent world. Integration is also key to our policy toward Russia in particular, since Russia's attainment of its most worthy aspirations will depend in large measure on its ability and willingness to integrate—that is, to participate in, contribute to, and benefit from the phenomenon of globalization.

The initial signs are auspicious. The new Russia has already gone a long way toward repudiating the old Soviet Union's delusions that autarky and self-isolation are even options for a modern state. Russia today plays an active role in organizations of which it was a founding member, such as the UN and the OSCE. It is also knocking at the door of those from which it has been excluded. Over the past two years, it has become a member of the ASEAN Regional Forum and the Council of Europe, agreed to join the Paris Club, and it has strengthened its ties to the European Union.

We are not just letting this happen—we are helping make it happen. We are doing what we can to ensure that the international community is as open as possible to Russia. That's why we pushed in Denver for the expansion of the G-7 agenda to become the Summit of the Eight. That's also why, in Helsinki, President Clinton and President Yeltsin set a joint goal to work toward Russian accession in 1998 to the World Trade Organization and to launch a dialogue in Paris that will accelerate Russia's admission to the OECD.

Then there's the Asia-Pacific Economic Cooperation forum. When Secretary Albright and the other APEC ministers meet in November in Vancouver, they will be setting the criteria for new members, and we will support Russia's admission to APEC as it meets those standards.

Let me here offer a general proposition. Russia's membership—even its aspiration for membership—in these bodies is welcome in and of itself, since all of them enshrine the premise that the modern state should be part of an international order that is based on certain common principles. One of the most fundamental of those principles is that there are limits to the role and writ of the state, particularly with regard to its resort to force, both in its internal regime and in its external behavior. Since that is a principle that runs very much against the grain of Russian tradition, under Czars and commissars alike, it is one that we would like to see the new Russia associate itself with in every way possible.

However, integration is not an end in itself; it is a means to an end. Now that Russia is an eager joiner, the issue remains what kind of member is Russia going to be? How will it fit in? Will it play by the rules?

There is still a lot of skepticism on this point that resonates in our national debate about Russia and U.S. policy. Many experts and commentators start from a presumption of guilt about Russia's strategic intentions. They nurture a suspicion that Russians are predisposed genetically, or at least historically, to aggression and imperialism.

I believe that's the wrong way to think about the issue. The right way is the one Ian Buruma articulated in his book, *The Wages of Guilt*. He was writing about two other great nations—Germany and Japan—whose peoples were, not so long ago, feared, and hated, as inherently militaristic. "There are," said Buruma, "no dangerous peoples; there are only dangerous situations, which are the result, not of laws of nature or history, or of national character, but of political arrangements."

Our purpose in working with Russia should be to fashion the right political arrangements; in other words, to weave beneficial relationships and devise incentives that will encourage Russia to continue its democratic progress and that will yield material benefits to the Russian people.

The idea that the North Atlantic Treaty Organization (NATO) can be part of that larger structure and that larger strategy is, to put it mildly, not self-evident to all Americans, including, I'm sure, some of you who are participating in this conference. And it is certainly not self-evident to all Russians.

Part of the problem here is perceptions—old perceptions. Stereotypes evaporate slowly. just as many of our own experts and commentators cling to Cold War prejudices about Russians and what makes them tick, so many Russians have fixed in their minds a Cold War image of NATO. I'm convinced that this disagreement is manageable. Indeed, we now have a mechanism for managing it.

One week from today, Secretary Albright and her 15 alliance colleagues will sit down at the UN with Yevgeny Primakov for the first ministerial meeting of the NATO–Russia Permanent Joint Council. This new institution has real promise. It can help ensure that Europe is never again divided and that a democratic Russia plays its rightful role in that new Europe.

"...Russia is now attempting to end the decade-old war in Nagorno-Karabakh."

But in order to live up to its potential, the Permanent Joint Council must be more than a talk shop. It must identify new ways and places for NATO and Russia to work together in maintaining peace, combating common threats, and dismantling the vestiges of the Cold War, especially the lingering fears and suspicions that exist on both sides of the old Iron Curtain—and on both sides of the new international boundaries that used to be the internal; that is, inter-republic borders of the USSR.

That brings me to the most salient issue of Russian foreign policy for Russians and the rest of the world alike, which is how Russia relates to those new independent states that were until only 6 years ago part of the Soviet Union and, as such, subject to Russia's domination. In this regard, too, there have recently been some developments that are favorable and encouraging—though by no means conclusive.

One was President Yeltsin's landmark visit to Kiev in May, which put Russia's relations with Ukraine on a more equitable and predictable footing. Another is the way that Russia is now attempting to end the decade-old war in Nagorno-Karabakh. This year, Russia has joined diplomatic forces with the United States and France under the aegis of the OSCE. This willingness on Russia's part to internationalize rather than attempting to monopolize the management of security along its periphery augurs well for the chances of equitable settlements to other conflicts in Moldova, Georgia, and Tajikistan.

Let me say a few words about the Baltics, which represent an especially acute challenge. In our analysis, we need to bear in mind—and in our diplomacy, we need to balance—two factors. One is the Balts' anxieties about Russian motivations and their legitimate desire to join Western institutions, including the European Union and NATO. The other factor is Russia's fear and loathing at the prospect of the Balts' fulfilling those aspirations.

Quite bluntly, Russians need to get over their neuralgia on this subject: They need to stop looking at the Baltic region as a pathway for foreign armies or as a buffer zone, not just because such "oldthink" offends and menaces the Balts but because it doesn't make sense, since there are no would-be aggressors to be rebuffed.

In the final analysis, Russia will have to make that adjustment itself, by its own lights and for its own reasons. But we and our European partners can help. One way is to make the idea of commercial, political, environmental, and other forms of collaboration among the states along the littoral of the Baltic Sea a centerpiece of our own activity there—and an important part of our dialogue with Russia as an important regional power.

Our message to Moscow here is this: If you Russians insist on looking to the 13th century for models applicable to the 21st, then you should dwell less on the image of Alexander Nevsky defeating the Swedish knights on the ice and think instead in what might be called "Hanseatic" terms; that is, think about the Baltics not as an invasion route inward, but as a gateway outward.

This is a version of what Peter the Great, the patron figure of the Westernizers, had in mind when he opened Russia's window to the West nearly 300 years ago. In fact, St. Petersburg is an obvious candidate for participation in a revival of the Hanseatic concept.

So, too, might be Novgorod and Kaliningrad, the former Konigsberg, both of which were associated with the original Hanseatic League. In fact, Kaliningrad is an especially tantalizing case, at least historically. Those of us who labor in the thickets of CFE—the Conventional Forces in Europe talks—tend to think of Kaliningrad as the headquarters of the Russian 11th Guards Army with its 850 tanks and 100 combat aircraft. But it is also one corner of what is now Russia that did experience the Enlightenment. It's where Immanuel Kant lived, taught, and set forth several principles of international law intended to bind like-minded republics into a community of "civil states" that could enjoy what he called "perpetual peace."

That said, we all recognize how far this theory is from reality in that neighborhood. Few places on earth have seen as little peace of any kind as Russia and its environs. But here again, I reiterate: There is reason for optimism. In addition to the ones I've already mentioned, I'd like, in conclusion, to add one more. It's generational—or, to be even more blunt, biological. The dynamic of what is happening in Russia today is not just Westernizers versus Slavophiles; it is also young versus old—and the young have a certain advantage in at least that dimension of the larger struggle between the old and the new.

Let me illustrate the point this way: Nearly four years ago, in a televised town meeting at Ostankino television station, President Clinton put a question to the Russian people—and to the Russian leadership—his own version of the question of questions:

How will you define your role as a great power?

he asked.

> Will you define it in yesterday's terms, or tomorrow's?
> Russia,

he said,

> has a chance to show that a great power can promote
> patriotism without expansionism; that a great power can
> promote national pride without national prejudice...I
> believe the measure of your greatness in the future will
> be whether Russia, the big neighbor, can be the good
> neighbor.

Chris and I were both there when the President delivered that
message, and we were both struck that his very youthful audience—an audience representing Russia's future—burst into
applause. They not only thought the President was asking the
right question; they clearly liked his proposed answer.

Perhaps the single-most significant and hopeful statistic I've
seen is this: Although 65% of those Russians over the age of 65
think things got worse over the last year, 60% of those under 35
think things got better. So among the positive trends underway
in Russia is perhaps the most basic one of all, the one represented by the actuarial tables.

Hence, to the extent possible, our policy toward Russia should
be geared toward the younger citizens of Russia who will decide
who they are, where they belong, how they relate to Europe and
to the outside world. The essence of our policy, in short, is: give
them time—give them time to consolidate the reforms that constitute the good news of the past few years; give them time to
beat back the forces that have generated the bad news; give them
time to work out their identity and destiny in ways that will not
only best serve a modern Russia's real interests but that will also
be, to the greatest extent possible, compatible with our interests
as well.

In other words, we need to make sure we have a policy toward
Russia that contains an indispensable feature: strategic patience.
That means a policy not just for coping with the issue or the crisis of the moment or the week or even of the season, or for getting through the next summit meeting; rather, it means a policy
for the next century—which, by the way, begins in 2 years, 3
months, 11 days, and 4 hours.

So the timing of this conference could not be better. Nor could
the agenda be more germane and the participants more appropriate. Thank you again, Chris, Bill, and David, for helping our
nation grapple with what is, for us, also a question of questions—how to understand and deal with Russia—and for helping
make sure that we come up with the right answer of answers.

II. NATO Expansion

Editor's Introduction

The North Atlantic Treaty Organization, or NATO, was founded in 1949 to safeguard against aggression by the Soviet Union, which, along with the United States, had emerged after World War II as one of the world's two superpowers. The original member nations of NATO were Belgium, Canada, Denmark, France, Great Britain, Iceland, Italy, Luxembourg, the Netherlands, Norway, Portugal, and the United States; Greece and Turkey joined NATO in 1952, West Germany in 1955, and the former East Germany, after reunification, in 1991. The agreement reached by the original member nations was that they would respond to aggression against one member as an aggression against all. With the dismantling of the Soviet Union, in 1991, some observers called into question the role of NATO—and they began to do so with greater urgency in the mid-1990s, with the proposed expansion of NATO to include the formerly Communist nations of Poland, Hungary, and the Czech republic by the end of the 1990s. This section comprises essays that argue either for or against such expansion, on which the United States Senate must vote in the spring of 1998, as this volume is being prepared.

In "Toward a Secure Europe," her article in *Current History*, Jane M. O. Sharp points out that the discussion about NATO enlargement leaves out any mention of the war-ravaged states of the former Yugoslavia, a crucial issue for European security. She therefore maintains that NATO should be expanded in order to oversee more easily the aspects of the Dayton agreement (the peace plan for the former Yugoslavia) that have yet to be implemented. On the subject of NATO's original purpose, Sharp writes, "The optimists in Washington and Bonn may be correct that [Russian president Boris] Yeltsin will turn out to be a democrat, but there is no evidence of it on the arms control front. There, as in Chechnya, Yeltsin has so far been closer to Leonid Brezhnev than Gorbachev."

Likewise, the writer for *National Review* regards Russia as still being a potential adversary, lamenting NATO's having "tripped over itself to give Russia reassurances" after talk of NATO expansion. The author of this piece further finds it regrettable that "the generation that now governs us, formed by the Vietnam experience, sees the Alliance of the Western democracies as a Cold War relic—something to apologize for." NATO is, the writer feels, "something to be preserved *and expanded*, not apologized for—or neutered" [emphasis mine].

In a 1997 statement given before the Senate Foreign Relations Committee and reprinted in the State Department publication *Dispatch*, U.S. secretary Madeline K. Albright discussed what she viewed as three reasons for strengthening NATO: to counteract a potential return to the intra-European animosity of cenuries past; to be able to cope better with current troubles in the Balkans; and to protect against potential threats from outside Europe, from "rogue states with dangerous weapons."

On the other side of the coin, Jonathan Dean contributed to the *Washington Monthly* an article unmisleadingly titled "The NATO Mistake." Dean expresses the belief that President Bill Clinton has failed to put forth a convincing reason for NATO expansion—and that the true reason, unspoken because a crisis would erupt if it were revealed, is "to counter future Soviet aggression." Expansion is unnecessary, in Dean's opinion, because it will take "a decade or more" before Russian military strength is a threat to "far superior NATO," if Russia's performance in the war against Chechnya is any indication. As for countering Russian aggression in the future, Dean believes that there is a better alternative: "an improved Partnership for Peace Program."

The writer of an editorial for the *New York Times* also feels that the reasons for NATO expansion have not been made clear, and that enlargement is not only unnecessary but a grave mistake. The author of this piece agrees with Dean that years would be required for Russia to regain its military strength—and points out that it is "hard to see" what benefits Poland, Hungary, and the Czech republic could bring to NATO in terms of either military might or financial resources. The writer argues further that presenting the current NATO as insurance against potential Russian aggression "can only strengthen the anti-democratic forces in Russia." Also, the editorial attacks some of the other propositions that have surfaced during discussions of NATO enlargement, including the building of a "global NATO" and the broadening of the organization's mission to encompass not only defense of the United States and Europe but of "common American and European interests anywhere in the world."

Toward a Secure Europe[1]

During the cold war, European security was thought to depend in large part on maintaining a stable military balance between two adversarial alliances: the United States–led North Atlantic Treaty Organization (NATO) and the Warsaw Treaty Organization, dominated by the Soviet Union. Relations between the two blocs fluctuated between tension and détente, but diplomatic contacts were always maintained to make sure the cold war did not erupt into actual warfare.

Arms control diplomacy was an important factor in maintaining stability during these years. The pace was plodding and progress incremental, and the goals were modest: to build confidence and trust between potential adversaries. Deep cuts in military forces through negotiation were not anticipated, though reductions were sometimes achieved by unilateral actions. Agreements took years, even decades, to conclude and usually reflected—rather than affected—the state of East-West relations.

Mikhail Gorbachev changed all this when he assumed the leadership of the Communist Party of the Soviet Union in 1985. He used arms control as a tool to alter relations not only between the Soviet Union and the West, but also between the Soviet Union and its Warsaw Pact allies. Gorbachev was impatient with the pace of traditional diplomacy, and with the preoccupation of his military staff with codifying parity with NATO and preventing the intrusive inspection of Soviet territory.

Gorbachev's first innovation was to allow foreign inspectors onto Soviet territory to verify the confidence- and security-building measures (CSBMS) negotiated at the 1986 Conference on Security and Cooperation in Europe (CSCE) meeting in Stockholm. This new openness also facilitated the conclusion in 1987 of the Soviet-American treaty banning intermediate-range nuclear forces.

Gorbachev was especially impatient with the long-running NATO-Warsaw Pact negotiations on Mutual and Balanced Force Reductions (MBFR) that had been under way in Vienna since 1973 with no tangible result. He believed the Soviet economy required deep cuts in military spending and suggested that instead of building up to parity, NATO and the Warsaw Pact states would do better to build down. Specifically, Gorbachev said that whichever side was ahead in a particular category of weapons should be the one to make reductions. Gorbachev put this idea into practice in December 1988 at the United Nations when he announced unilateral withdrawals of Soviet troops from Central Europe.

---

[1]Article by Jane M. O. Sharp, director of the defense and security program at the Institute for Public Policy Research and senior research fellow at the Center for Defense Studies at King's College, London, from *Current History* magazine 96/608:130-34 Mr '97. Copyright © 1997 Current History, Inc. Reprinted with permission.

Gorbachev's proposals rendered the MBFR talks redundant. More purposeful talks began in March 1989. These produced the Conventional Forces in Europe (CFE) treaty, in November 1990, which set equal ceilings for NATO and the Warsaw Pact in tanks, armored combat vehicles, artillery larger than 100mm caliber, combat aircraft, and helicopters in a series of five zones. Four of these zones are nested like a *matryoshka* doll to permit free movement of forces away from but not toward Central Europe. A fifth or "flank zone" surrounds the four nested zones. CFE mandated the destruction of some 50,000 pieces of treaty-limited equipment during a three-year reduction period between 1992 and 1995, and established a regime of inspections and exchanges of information designed to remove the threat of surprise attack by making each alliance transparent to the other.

"...Gorbachev and his foreign minister, Eduard Shevardnadze, did not have the Soviet military's backing for their conciliatory overtures to the West."

NATO and the Central European members of the Warsaw Pact judged CFE an unambiguous success and gave Gorbachev much of the credit. The problem was that Gorbachev and his foreign minister, Eduard Shevardnadze, did not have the Soviet military's backing for their conciliatory overtures to the West. The Soviet General Staff did not veto the signing of CFE, but it did its best to sabotage the treaty and evade its provisions. Senior Soviet military officers resented CFE because it mandated the destruction of more equipment by Warsaw Pact members than by NATO. As the Warsaw Pact and the Soviet empire collapsed, CFE became even more humiliating, codifying Russian inferiority with NATO, although Russia remained the most powerful state in Europe. German unification, plus the desire of all the former European members of the Warsaw Pact to join NATO, exacerbated Russia's sense of loss.

Article V and Russia's "Extraordinary" Circumstances

CFE provides for the convening of "extraordinary conferences" should the treaty require adaptation. Three such conferences were held during the early 1990s: in 1991 to settle disputes over Soviet data on military equipment; in 1992 to adjust to the dissolution of the Soviet Union; and in 1993 to note the separation of the Czech and Slovak republics. In September 1993, Russia asked NATO to convene a fourth extraordinary conference to revise Article V of the treaty, which sets limits for the flank zone.

Russia claimed, with some justification, that since the breakup of the Soviet Union, Article V had become discriminatory with respect to Russia and Ukraine, the only state parties whose territories straddled more than one treaty zone. Thus Russia and Ukraine were subject not only to numerical limits—as were all state parties—but also to geographic restrictions within their own sovereign territory. NATO was reluctant to revise the zonal aspect of the treaty, even though the United States, Germany, and the United Kingdom expressed some sympathy for the Russian predicament. Had NATO dealt with the flank problem when

Russia first raised it in 1993, all might have been well. However, the problem was allowed to fester until 1995, by which time Russia had moved even more equipment into the flank to conduct its war against the secessionist republic of Chechnya. Most NATO states were by then reluctant to make any concessions on Article V, lest they seem to condone Russian brutality in the Caucasus.

The result was that the CFE reduction period ended in November 1995, with Russia in violation of two key provisions: Article V and a politically binding commitment of June 1991 to destroy the equipment moved east of the Urals by the Soviet Union just before the treaty's signing in 1990.

In May 1996, at the first five-year review conference of CFE, the United States persuaded the other CFE parties not only to turn a blind eye to Russian noncompliance, but also to redefine the zones in Russia's favor. The United States was anxious to make NATO enlargement more palatable to Russia and to shore up Russian President Boris Yeltsin's reelection prospects. Not surprisingly, this pleased General Pavel Grachev, the Russian defense minister, who saw the NATO concessions as vindicating Russian demands to revise the flank ceilings. Many Europeans, however, feared that acquiescence in Russian violations set a dangerous precedent. Several CFE parties were also irritated by what was essentially a bilateral United States–Russian deal at the expense of the security interests of small states contiguous with or close to Russian territory. These included Norway and Turkey in NATO, as well as the former Soviet states of Moldova, Georgia, Ukraine, Azerbaijan, and Armenia. Some nonparties to CFE were also upset by the final document of the review conference, notably the three Baltic states: Estonia, Latvia, and Lithuania.

The Impact of NATO Enlargement

Two issues dominate the debate about adapting CFE to the new political realities in Europe: how NATO enlargement will affect CFE, and whether CFE limits should be harmonized throughout Europe.

During 1995, senior Russian Foreign Ministry spokesmen articulated seven conditions that would make NATO enlargement more palatable to Russia: no forward-based nuclear weapons and troops; no hasty enlargement to upset the 1996 Russian elections; and no NATO exercises on former Warsaw Pact territory. Russia was also not to be permanently excluded from NATO, new NATO members should remain (as France and Spain then were) outside NATO'S integrated military command, and the CFE treaty should be revised. When Yevgeny Primakov replaced Andrei Kozyrev as foreign minister in January 1996, he emphasized the "no nukes, no troops" conditions, but also spoke of no forward movement of NATO infrastructure onto the territory of new NATO states. Russia also argued that the CSCE'S successor, the Organization for Security and Cooperation in Europe (OSCE), should replace NATO as Europe's main security organization.

NATO adopted manifestly conciliatory policies toward the former Warsaw Pact states, including all the former Soviet republics, once the pact and the Soviet Union collapsed in 1991, but NATO could brook no outside interference in the running of its internal structures. An obvious way to assuage some of Russia's hostility to enlargement, however, was to pay more attention to requests to modify CFE. In mid-January 1997, OSCE agreed that the CFE state parties should open negotiations in Vienna to modify the treaty. Without making specific promises or proposals, NATO agreed to review the following issues: the bloc-to-bloc structure of CFE; how NATO enlargement would affect CFE ceilings; the possibility of putting excess equipment into secure storage rather than destroying it all; and the possible extension of the scope of CFE to cover new states.

France and Russia, who were the strongest advocates of national (versus group) ceilings, had not by late 1996 offered any specific proposals on how national ceilings would work. In London, skeptical British officials asked how national limits would apply in the different zones and, in particular, how they would apply to United States holdings in Europe, since United States territory is not within the CFE area.

Negotiating Beyond Dayton

In the debate about NATO enlargement, few suggest the admission of any of the former Yugoslav republics, except perhaps Slovenia. The question then arises as to what, if any, security guarantees can be offered to the region. Some suggest that NATO could extend its Partnership for Peace (PFP) program to form a virtual protectorates. Others think the United States should offer bilateral guarantees. Another possible means to gain a greater sense of security for states aspiring to post-first-wave NATO membership would be to join the CFE regime before joining NATO. For the former Yugoslav states, much will depend on the success of the post-Dayton arms control agreements.

The arms control provisions in the December 14, 1995, Dayton (Paris) peace agreement for Bosnia and Herzegovina are to be found in Annex 1-B, which deals with regional stabilization. Articles II and III require the parties to negotiate CSBMs. Article IV mandates the parties to negotiate a subregional arms control agreement limiting the same five categories of heavy weaponry as in the original CFE treaty. Article V stipulates that OSCE will assist the parties in negotiating a regional arms control regime "in and around the former Yugoslavia."

In late January 1996, the former warring parties in Bosnia negotiated on schedule a series of CSBMs modeled on those negotiated throughout Europe under the OSCE's predecessor, the CSCE. Inspections and exchanges of information were conducted during 1996 under the supervision of OSCE. Some of the post-Dayton CSBMs go further than those in the OSCE regime by restraining military deployments in certain areas, withdrawing heavy weapons to cantonments, and banning the reintroduction of foreign forces.

On June 14, 1996, a subregional agreement was signed that limits five categories of weapons on the basis of a 5:2:2 ratio among Serbia and Montenegro (which make up the rump Yugoslavia), Bosnia and Herzegovina, and Croatia. Within Bosnia the ratio of agreed limits between the Muslim-Croat Federation and Republika Srpska (Serb Republic) is 2:1. The five categories consist of battle tanks, armored combat vehicles (ACVs), attack helicopters, artillery larger than 75 mm caliber, and combat aircraft.

The subregional agreement provides for a 16-month reduction period and protocols for destruction and inspection. Under pressure from the Contact Group, the reduction period was front-loaded, meaning that by the end of 1996, 40 percent of the reduction liability should have been met for aircraft, helicopters, and artillery, and 20 percent of the liability for tanks and ACVs. The initial idea was to implement as much of the agreement as possible during the term of the NATO-led Dayton Implementation Force (IFOR). In mid-December 1996, however, NATO agreed to deploy a follow-on force to IFOR over an 18-month period between January 1997 and June 1998; among other things, the force will be responsible for supporting the implementation of arms control agreements.

By December 1996, it appeared that Croatia and Serbia had met the target to cut 40 percent of their excess aircraft, helicopters, and artillery and 20 percent of their excess tanks and ACVs. Neither the Serb Republic nor the Muslim-Croat Federation was believed to be in compliance. The main difficulty for the federation was not a dispute about its overall reduction obligations, but problems associated with the merger of the Muslim and Croat armies. Despite a document providing for joint command that Presidents Alija Izetbegovic and Kresimir Zubak signed in early October 1996, at the end of the year the armies remained separate and neither could agree who was responsible for destroying which pieces of excess equipment. With respect to the Serb Republic, there was still a large discrepancy in declared holdings of equipment, with the Bosnian Serbs claiming invalid and unreasonable exemptions. Another problem was that the Bosnian Serbs resisted cutting excess treaty-limited equipment as long as the United States continued to train and equip the federation armies.

Train and Equip Derailed?

"Train and Equip"" is the less controversial title for the "Arm and Train" program the United States promised the Bosnian government during the Dayton negotiations. The fact that no mention of the program appears in the language of the peace agreement reflects American sensitivity to the opposition of most of the NATO allies. The United States nevertheless promised to implement Arm and Train, despite allied opposition, because President Bill Clinton needed a more capable Bosnian army to justify the withdrawal of United States troops from IFOR by the end of 1996.

Transatlantic differences on Train and Equip recall intra–NATO differences on the arms embargo during the war in Bosnia. While paying lip service to the embargo on all the former Yugoslavia republics, in 1994 the Clinton administration gave a green light to arms shipments to Croatia and Bosnia from a number of Muslim countries, including Iran, Turkey, Saudi Arabia, and Malaysia.

"...Poland strives to maintain good relations with all NATO governments..."

While there was a strong legal case for lifting the embargo against Bosnia when its independence was recognized in April 1992, and subsequently a strong moral argument for giving Bosnia the means to defend itself against the better-armed Serbs, all suggestions of arming the Bosnians were strongly opposed by almost every European country, especially the United Kingdom and France, which provided the bulk of ground troops for the UN peacekeeping force in the country.

These differences continued after the war. Rather than lift the arms embargo on the former Yugoslav states—as it was permitted to do after conclusion of the Dayton peace agreement in late 1995—the European Union adopted in February 1996 a policy of maintaining an embargo on arms shipments to any part of the former Yugoslavia as long as either UN or NATO troops remain on the territory. Transatlantic differences about the program also put the Polish government in a difficult position in the summer of 1996. As an aspirant to NATO, Poland strives to maintain good relations with all NATO governments, but on this question was forced to choose between the United States and the West Europeans. When the Clinton administration tried to persuade Poland to supply some of its excess T-72 tanks to the Bosnian army, Poland refused (despite a generous United States offer of compensation), citing its desire to stand in solidarity with the rest of Europe in not supplying arms to any of the former warring factions.

The least provocative aspect of Train and Equip is the imposition of Western-style political-military relations in Bosnia, and the imposition of defensive as opposed to offensive postures. The more troublesome aspect is the training of Bosnians to use offensive United States equipment. The training has been contracted out to a United States company, Military Professional Resources, Inc., which also trained the Croatian army during the war.

The two main problems with Train and Equip are that it undermines Bosnian Serb interest in the subregional agreement and hinders prospects for the integration of Bosnia and Herzegovina. if the Western democracies are serious about those aspects of the Dayton peace agreement that seek stability through a single, integrated, multiethnic and multiconfessional Bosnia, there will have to be a greater effort to encourage reconciliation between the Muslim-Croat Federation and Serb Republic. Train and Equip goes in the opposite direction, toward permanent partition. Too many commitments have been made by President Clinton to the Bosnian government and to the United States Congress to cancel the program. One solution, however, might be to offer the training element of Train and Equip to the Serb Republic and the federation on an equal basis. If there is to be an integrated Bosnia, the separate Croat, Muslim, and Serb armies in Bosnia must eventually train together. This will be more easily achieved, and with more democratic political-military relations, under NATO supervision.

Article V of Annex 1-B of the Dayton agreement commits the parties to seek a wider Balkan arms control regime. This could include not only former Yugoslav states like Slovenia and Macedonia, but also Albania and the Balkan states that are parties to the original CFE agreement: Turkey and Greece as well as Romania and Bulgaria (and perhaps Hungary, although Hungary likes to avoid being labeled a Balkan nation).

Expanding the subregional agreement throughout the Balkans will be problematic, not only because the region has some fuzzy edges, but also because three Balkan parties to CFE (Bulgaria, Romania, and Greece) announced that they will not be subjected to tighter limits in a new treaty. Much will depend on the negotiations to adapt CFE that began this January. If the CFE regime embraces the former Yugoslav states, there may be no need for a separate Balkan arms control regime beyond the June 1996 subregional agreement.

Transparency and the Clouded Future

Peace in Europe depends as much on political stability and economic prosperity as on arms control arrangements. The enlargement of both NATO and the European Union eastward is thus the most important way to share the benefits of the Western security community. But this is a necessarily slow process requiring difficult adjustments and restructuring. In the shorter term, arms control diplomacy can play an important role in building trust and confidence between former warring factions, not only in the former Yugoslavia, but perhaps also in the former Soviet Union. In addition to curbing offensive military equipment, the main benefit in recent agreements like the CFE treaty and the post-Dayton subregional agreement is the increased transparency of military force postures and defense planning, which in turn helps to build trust and confidence.

The question mark hanging over the future of European arms control is the behavior of Russia, and the example that Russia sets for other former Communist states such as Serbia. Western governments (especially the United States and Germany) continue to give President Boris Yeltsin the benefit of the doubt despite his record: CFE violations, the war against Chechnya, hostility to

NATO enlargement, and gross mismanagement of the Russian economy. The optimists in Washington and Bonn may be correct that Yeltsin will turn out to be a democrat, but there is no evidence of it on the arms control front. There, as in Chechnya, Yeltsin has so far been closer to Leonid Brezhnev than Gorbachev. The smaller European countries are hoping that Western leaders will stop rewarding bad behavior in Moscow and begin to demand higher standards from Russia in meeting its international obligations.

Helsinki Illusions[2]

President Clinton met with Boris Yeltsin in Helsinki to end the conflict over NATO enlargement. Russia wants to head it off but, failing that, to extract the maximum "compensation" from the West. Accordingly, Russia has been on a year-long tantrum, threatening the West (including the Central Europeans and Balts) with dire consequences if NATO enlargement should proceed. It was a bluff, but it has paid off.

NATO has tripped over itself to give Russia reassurances— pledging that no nuclear weapons will be moved eastward; ditto no substantial NATO troops; reopening treaties on strategic and conventional arms to give the Russians a break. But the worst came at Helsinki. Mr. Clinton has now all but promised Russia a seat at the G-7 economic summits, agreed to dangerous limits on U.S. anti-missile defenses in the name of the 1972 ABM Treaty, and given Russia a virtual seat in NATO councils.

The last is the most serious. As Henry Kissinger pointed out in a stinging critique, the generation that now governs us, formed by the Vietnam experience, sees the Alliance of the Western democracies as a Cold War relic—something to apologize for. It was the "mirror image of the Warsaw Pact," our President opined in his Helsinki news conference. Thus, its "profound transformation" is required. Letting the fox into the chicken coop will do that, for sure. A new NATO—Russia council is being formed, in which Russia will be a full member, not merely an occasionally invited guest.

Mr. Clinton assures us that Russia will have "a voice, not a veto," in Alliance deliberations. But Yeltsin's foreign-policy advisor, Dmitri Ryurikov, had a clearer picture. In a Moscow interview, Ryurikov insisted that President Yeltsin "acts on the assumption that if our country has a voice, it will have the right to block decisions that are unacceptable to it," adding wryly, "otherwise, there is no sense in having a voice."

What can be done? At a minimum, the Russians, having been the beneficiary of such largesse, must call off their campaign against a larger NATO. This means no more bullying of their neighbors—especially the Balts or Ukraine. They've been bought off; let them stay bought.

Beyond this, the U.S. Senate has to look for ways to undo some of the damage. The agreement on missile defense is essentially a treaty amendment, which requires Senate approval. Even the NATO—Russia "charter" can be fixed somewhat, if the Senate, when the time comes to vote on new NATO members, reaffirms some basic principles about the Alliance: that the North Atlantic

---

[2]Article from *National Review* 49:16-17 Ap 21 '97. Copyright © 1997 by National Review, Inc. Reprinted with permission.

Council (not any new NATO—Russia council) remains the supreme forum for Alliance deliberation and decisions, and that nothing shall interfere with the Alliance's right to defend its members by any means necessary.

The Atlantic Alliance is something to be preserved and expanded, not apologized for—or neutered.

NATO Expansion: Beginning the Process of Advice and Consent[3]

Chairman Helms, Senator Biden, members of the committee: It is with a sense of appreciation and anticipation that I come before you to urge support for the admission of the Czech Republic, Hungary, and Poland to NATO.

Each of us today is playing our part in the long, unfolding story of America's modern partnership with Europe. That story began not in Madrid, when the President and his fellow NATO leaders invited these three new democracies to join our alliance, nor eight years ago when the Berlin Wall fell, but a half-century ago, when your predecessors and mine dedicated our nation to the goal of a secure, united Europe.

It was then that we broke with the American aversion to European entanglements—an aversion which served us well in our early days, but poorly when we became a global power. It was then that we sealed a peacetime alliance open not only to the nations which had shared our victory in World War II, but to our former adversaries. It was then that this committee unanimously recommended that the Senate approve the original North Atlantic Treaty.

The history books will long record that day as among the Senate's finest. On that day, the leaders of this body rose above partisanship, and they rose to the challenge of a pivotal moment in the history of the world.

Mr. Chairman, I believe you are continuing that tradition today. I thank you for your decision to hold these hearings early, for the bipartisan manner in which you and Senator Biden are conducting them, and for the serious and substantive way in which you have framed our discussion.

I am honored to be part of what you have rightly called the beginning of the process of advice and consent. And I am hopeful that with your support, and after the full national debate to which these hearings will contribute, the Senate will embrace the addition of new members to NATO. It would be fitting if this renewal of our commitment to security in Europe could come early next year, as Congress celebrates the 50th anniversary of its approval of the Marshall Plan.

As I said, and as you can see, I am very conscious of history today. I hope that you and your colleagues will look back as I have on the deliberations of 1949, for they address so many of the questions I know you have now: How much will a new alliance cost, and what are its benefits? Will it bind us to go to

---

[3]Speech by Secretary of State Madeleine K. Albright before the Senate Foreign Relations Committee, Washington, DC on October 7, 1997.

war? Will it entangle us in faraway quarrels?

We should take a moment to remember what was said then about the alliance we are striving to renew and expand today.

Senator Vandenberg, Chairman Helms' extraordinary predecessor, predicted that NATO would become "the greatest war deterrent in history." He was right. American forces have never had to fire a shot to defend a NATO ally.

This committee, in its report to the Senate on the NATO Treaty, predicted that it would

> free the minds of men in many nations from a haunting sense of insecurity, and enable them to work and plan with that confidence in the future which is essential to economic recovery and progress.

"The threat of nuclear war has sharply diminished."

Your predecessors were right. NATO gave our allies time to rebuild their economies. It helped reconcile their ancient animosities. And it made possible an unprecedented era of unity in Western Europe.

President Truman said that the NATO pact

> will be a positive, not a negative, influence for peace, and its influence will be felt not only in the area it specifically covers but throughout the world.

And he was right, too. NATO gave hope to democratic forces in West Germany that their country would be welcome and secure in our community if they kept making the right choices. Ultimately, it helped bring the former fascist countries into a prosperous and democratic Europe. And it helped free the entire planet from the icy grip of the Cold War.

Thanks in no small part to NATO, we live in a different world. Our Soviet adversary has vanished. Freedom's flag has been unfurled from the Baltics to Bulgaria. The threat of nuclear war has sharply diminished. As I speak to you today, our immediate survival is not at risk.

Indeed, you may ask if the principle of collective defense at NATO's heart is relevant to the challenges of a wider and freer Europe. You may ask why, in this time of relative peace, are we so focused on security? The answer is, we want the peace to last. We want freedom to endure. And we believe there are still potential threats to our security emanating from European soil.

You have asked me, Mr. Chairman, what these threats are. I want to answer as plainly as I can.

First, there are the dangers of Europe's past. It is easy to forget this, but for centuries virtually every European nation treated virtually every other as a military threat. That pattern was broken only when NATO was born and only in the half of Europe NATO covered. With NATO, Europe's armies prepared to fight beside their neighbors, not against them; each member's security came to depend on cooperation with others, not competition.

That is one reason why NATO remains essential, even though the Cold War is over. It is also one reason why we need a larger NATO, so that the other half of Europe is finally embedded in the same cooperative structure of military planning and preparation.

A **second** set of dangers lies in Europe's present. Because of conflict in the Balkans and the former Soviet Union, Europe has already buried more victims of war since the Berlin Wall fell than in all the years of the Cold War. It is sobering to recall that this violence has its roots in the same problems of shattered states and hatred among ethnic groups that tyrants exploited to start this century's great wars.

Finally, Mr. Chairman, and most important, we must consider the dangers of Europe's future. By this I mean direct threats against the soil of NATO members that a collective defense pact is designed to meet. Some are visible on Europe's horizon, such as the threat posed by rogue states with dangerous weapons that might have Europe within their range and in their sights. Others may not seem apparent today in part because the existence of NATO has helped to deter them. But they are not unthinkable.

Within this category lie questions about the future of Russia. We have an interest in seeing Russian democracy endure. We are doing all we can with our Russian partners to see that it does. And we have many reasons to be optimistic. At the same time, one should not dismiss the possibility that Russia could return to the patterns of its past. By engaging Russia and enlarging NATO, we give Russia every incentive to deepen its commitment to democracy and peaceful relations with neighbors, while closing the avenue to more destructive alternatives.

We do not know what other dangers may arise 10, 20, or even 50 years from now. We do know enough from history and human experience to believe that a grave threat, if allowed to arise, would arise. We know that whatever the future may hold, it will be in our interest to have a vigorous and larger alliance with those European democracies that share our values and our determination to defend them.

We recognize NATO expansion involves a solemn expansion of American responsibilities in Europe. It does not bind us to respond to every violent incident by going to war, but it does oblige us to consider an armed attack against one ally an attack against all and to respond with such action as we deem necessary, including the use of force, to restore the security of the North Atlantic area.

As Americans, we take our commitments seriously and we do not extend them lightly. Mr. Chairman, you and I do not agree on everything, but we certainly agree that any major extension of American commitments must serve America's strategic interests.

Let me explain why welcoming the Czech Republic, Hungary, and Poland into NATO meets that test.

First, a larger NATO will make us safer by expanding the area in

Europe where wars simply do not happen. This is the productive paradox at NATO's heart: By imposing a price on aggression, it deters aggression. By making clear that we will fight, if necessary, to defend our allies, it makes it less likely our troops will ever be called upon to do so.

Now, you may say that no part of Europe faces any immediate threat of armed attack today. That is true. And I would say that the purpose of NATO enlargement is to keep it that way. Senator Vandenberg said it in 1949:

> [NATO] is not built to stop a war after it starts, although its potentialities in this regard are infinite. It is built to stop wars before they start.

It is also fair to ask if it is in our vital interest to prevent conflict in central Europe. There are those who imply it is not. I'm sure you have even heard a few people trot out what I call the "consonant cluster clause," the myth that in times of crisis Americans will make no sacrifice to defend a distant city with an unpronounceable name, that we will protect the freedom of Strasbourg but not Szczecin; Barcelona, but not Brno.

Let us not deceive ourselves. The United States is a European power. We have an interest not only in the lands west of the Oder River, but in the fate of the 200 million people who live in the nations between the Baltic and Black Seas. We waged the Cold War in part because these nations were held captive. We fought World War II in part because these nations had been invaded.

Now that these nations are free, we want them to succeed, and we want them to be safe, whether they are large or small. For if there were a major threat to the security of their region, if we were to wake up one morning to the sight of cities being shelled and borders being overrun, I am certain that we would choose to act, enlargement or no enlargement. Expanding NATO now is simply the surest way to prevent that kind of threat from arising and, thus, the need to make that kind of choice.

Mr. Chairman, the **second** reason why enlargement passes the test of national interest is that it will make NATO stronger and more cohesive. The Poles, Hungarians, and Czechs are passionately committed to NATO and its principles of shared responsibility. Experience has taught them to believe in a strong American leadership role in Europe. Their forces have risked their lives alongside ours from the Gulf War to Bosnia. Just last month, Czech soldiers joined our British allies in securing a police station from heavily armed Bosnian Serb extremists.

I know you have expressed concern that enlargement could dilute NATO by adding too many members and by involving the alliance in too many missions. Let me assure you that we invited only the strongest candidates to join the alliance. And nothing about enlargement will change NATO's core mission, which is and will remain the collective defense of NATO soil.

At the same time, it is important to remember that NATO has

always served a political function as well. It binds our allies to us just as it binds us to our allies. So when you consider the candidacy of the Czech Republic, Hungary, and Poland, Mr. Chairman, I ask you to consider this: When peace is threatened somewhere in the world, and we decide it is in our interest to act, here are three nations we have been able to count on to be with us. In the fight against terror and nuclear proliferation, here are three nations we have been able to count on. In our effort to reform the UN, here are three nations we have been able to count on. When we speak out for human rights around the world, here are three nations we will always be able to count on.

Here are three nations that know what it means to lose their freedom and that will do what it takes to defend it. Here are three democracies that are ready to do their dependable part in the common enterprise of our alliance of democracies.

Mr. Chairman, the **third** reason why a larger NATO serves our interests is that the very promise of it gives the nations of central and eastern Europe an incentive to solve their own problems. To align themselves with NATO, aspiring countries have strengthened their democratic institutions. They have made sure that soldiers serve civilians, not the other way around. They have signed 10 major accords that taken together resolve virtually every old ethnic and border dispute in the region, exactly the kind of disputes that might have led to future Bosnias. In fact, the three states we have invited to join NATO have resolved every outstanding dispute of this type.

"...a larger NATO will make America safer, NATO stronger, and Europe more peaceful and united."

I have been a student of central European history, and I have lived some of it myself. When I see Romanians and Hungarians building a genuine friendship after centuries of enmity; when I see Poles, Ukrainians, and Lithuanians forming joint military units after years of suspicion; when I see Czechs and Germans overcoming decades of mistrust; when I see central Europeans confident enough to improve their political and economic ties with Russia; I know something remarkable is happening.

NATO is doing for Europe's east precisely what it did—precisely what this committee predicted it would do—for Europe's west after World War II. It is helping to vanquish old hatreds, to promote integration, and to create a secure environment for economic prosperity. This is another reminder that the contingencies we do not want our troops to face—such as ethnic conflict, border skirmishes, and social unrest—are far more easily avoided with NATO enlargement than without it.

In short, a larger NATO will make America safer, NATO stronger, and Europe more peaceful and united. That is the strategic rationale. But I would be disingenuous if I did not tell you that I see a moral imperative as well. For this is a policy that should appeal to our hearts as well as to our heads, to our sense of what is right as well as to our sense of what is smart. NATO defines a community of interest among the free nations of North

America and Europe that both preceded and outlasted the Cold War. America has long stood for the proposition that this Atlantic community should not be artificially divided and that its nations should be free to shape their destiny. We have long argued that the nations of central and astern Europe belong to the same democratic family as our allies in Western Europe.

We often call them "former communist countries," and that is true in the same sense that America is a "former British colony." Yes, the Czechs, Poles, and Hungarians were on the other side of the Iron Curtain during the Cold War. But we were surely on the same side in the ways that truly count.

As Americans, we should be heartened today that so many of Europe's new democracies wish to join the institutions Americans did so much to build. They are our friends, and we should be proud to welcome them home.

We should also think about what would happen if we were to turn them away. That would mean freezing NATO at its Cold War membership and preserving the old Iron Curtain as its eastern frontier. It would mean locking out a whole group of otherwise qualified democracies simply because they were once, against their will, members of the Warsaw Pact.

Why would America choose to be allied with Europe's old democracies forever but its new democracies never? There is no acceptable, objective answer to that question. Instead, it would probably be said that we blocked the aspirations of our would-be allies because Russia objected. And that, in turn, could cause confidence to crumble in central Europe, leading to a search for security by other means, including costly arms buildups and competition among neighbors.

We have chosen a better way. We have chosen to look at the landscape of the new Europe and to ask a simple question: Which of these nations that are so clearly important to our security are ready and able to contribute to our security? The answer to that question is before you today, awaiting your affirmation.

I said at the outset, Mr. Chairman, that there are weighty voices on both sides of this debate. There are legitimate concerns with which we have grappled along the way, and that I expect you to consider fully as well. Let me address a few.

First, we all want to make sure that the costs of a larger NATO are distributed fairly. Last February, at the behest of Congress and before the alliance had decided which nations to invite to membership, the Administration made a preliminary estimate of America's share. Now that we have settled on three candidates, we are working with our allies to produce a common estimate by the December meeting of the North Atlantic Council. At this point, the numbers we agree upon as 16 allies are needed prior to any further calculations made in Washington.

I know you are holding separate hearings in which my Pentagon colleagues will go into this question in detail. But I will say this: I am convinced that the cost of expansion is real but affordable. I am certain our prospective allies are willing and able to pay their share, because in the long run, it will be cheaper for them to upgrade their forces within the alliance than outside it. As Secretary of State, I will insist that our old allies share this burden fairly. That is what NATO is all about.

I know there are serious people who estimate that a larger NATO will cost far more than we have anticipated. The key fact about our estimate is that it is premised on the current, favorable security environment in Europe. Obviously, if a grave threat were to arise, the cost of enlargement would rise. But then so would the cost of our entire defense budget.

In any case, there are budgetary constraints in all 16 NATO democracies that will prevent costs from ballooning. That is why the main focus of our discussion, Mr. Chairman, and in our consultations with our allies, needs to be on defining the level of military capability we want our old and new allies to have in this favorable environment and then making sure that they commit to that level. We should spend no more than we must but no less than we need to keep NATO strong.

Another common concern about NATO enlargement is that it might damage our cooperation with a democratic Russia. Russian opposition to NATO enlargement is real. But we should see it for what it is: a product of old misperceptions about NATO and old ways of thinking about its former satellites in central Europe. Instead of changing our policies to accommodate Russia's outdated fears, we need to encourage Russia's more modern aspirations.

This means that we should remain Russia's most steadfast champion whenever it seeks to define its greatness by joining rule-based international institutions, opening its markets, and participating constructively in world affairs. It means we should welcome Russia's decision to build a close partnership with NATO, as we did in the NATO–Russia Founding Act.

But when some Russian leaders suggest that a larger NATO is a threat, we owe it candor to say that is false—and to base our policies on what we know to be true. When they imply that central Europe is special, that its nations still are not free to choose their security arrangements, we owe it candor to say that times have changed and that no nation can assert its greatness at the expense of its neighbors. We do no favor to Russian democrats and modernizers to suggest otherwise.

I believe our approach is sound and producing results. Over the past year, against the backdrop of NATO enlargement, reformers have made remarkable gains in the Russian Government. We have agreed to pursue deeper arms reductions. Our troops have built a solid working relationship on the ground in Bosnia. Russia was our partner at the Summit of the Eight in Denver, and it has joined the Paris Club of major international lenders.

What is more, last week in New York we signed documents that should pave the way for the Russian Duma to ratify the

START II Treaty. While this prospect is still by no means certain, it would become far less so if we gave the Duma any reason to think it could hold up NATO enlargement by holding up START II.

As you know Mr. Chairman, last week, NATO and Russia held the first ministerial meeting of their Permanent Joint Council. This council gives us an invaluable mechanism for building trust between NATO and Russia through dialogue and transparency.

I know that some are concerned NATO's new relationship with Russia will actually go too far. You have asked me for an affirmation, Mr. Chairman, that the North Atlantic Council remains NATO's supreme decisionmaking body. Let me say it clearly: It does, and it will. The NATO–Russia Founding Act gives Russia no opportunity to dilute, delay, or block NATO decisions. NATO's allies will always meet to agree on every item on their agenda before meeting with Russia. And the relationship between NATO and Russia will grow in importance only to the extent Russia uses it constructively.

> *"The NATO–Russia Founding Act gives Russia no opportunity to dilute, delay, or block NATO decisions."*

The Founding Act also does not limit NATO's ultimate authority to deploy troops or nuclear weapons in order to meet its commitments to new and old members. All it does is to restate unilaterally existing NATO policy: that in the current and foreseeable security environment, we have no plan, no need, and no intention to station nuclear weapons in the new member countries, nor do we contemplate permanently stationing substantial combat forces. The only binding limits on conventional forces in Europe will be set as we adapt the CFE treaty, with central European countries and all the other signatories at the table, and we will proceed on the principle of reciprocity.

Another important concern is that enlargement may create a new dividing line in Europe between a larger NATO and the countries that will not join in the first round. We have taken a range of steps to ensure this does not happen.

President Clinton has pledged that the first new members will not be the last. NATO leaders will consider the next steps in the process of enlargement before the end of the decade. We have strengthened NATO's Partnership for Peace program. We have created a new Euro-Atlantic Partnership Council, through which NATO and its democratic partners throughout Europe will shape the missions we undertake together. We have made it clear that the distinction between the nations NATO invited to join in Madrid and those it did not is based purely on objective factors—unlike the arbitrary line that would divide Europe if NATO stood still.

Among the countries that still aspire to membership, there is enthusiastic support for the process NATO has begun. Had you seen the crowds that cheered the President in Romania in July, had you been with me when I spoke to the leaders of Lithuania and Slovenia, you would have sensed how eager these nations are to redouble their efforts.

They understand a simple fact: With enlargement, no new democracy is permanently excluded; without enlargement, every new democracy would be permanently excluded. The most important thing the Senate can do to reassure them now is to get the ball rolling by ratifying the admission of the first three candidates.

Mr. Chairman, a final concern I wish to address has to do with Bosnia. Some have suggested that our debate on NATO enlargement simply cannot be separated from our actions and decisions in that troubled country. I agree with them. Both enlargement and our mission in Bosnia are aimed at building a stable undivided Europe. Both involve NATO and its new partners to the east.

It was our experience in Bosnia that proved the fundamental premise of our enlargement strategy: There are still threats to peace and security in Europe that only NATO can meet. It was in Bosnia that our prospective allies proved they are ready to take responsibility for the security of others. It was in Bosnia that we proved NATO and Russian troops can work together.

We cannot know today if our mission in Bosnia will achieve all its goals, for that ultimately depends on the choices the Bosnian people will make. But we can say that whatever may happen, NATO's part in achieving the military goals of our mission has been a resounding success. Whatever may happen, our interest in a larger, stronger NATO will endure long after the last foreign soldier has left Bosnia.

We can also say that NATO will remain the most powerful instrument we have for building effective military coalitions such as SFOR. At the same time, Bosnia does not by itself define the future of a larger NATO. NATO's fundamental purpose is collective defense against aggression. Its most important aim, if I can paraphrase Arthur Vandenberg, is to prevent wars before they start so it does not have to keep the peace after they stop.

These are some of the principal concerns I wanted to address today; I know you have many more questions, and I look forward to answering them all.

This discussion is just beginning. I am glad that it will also involve other committees of the Senate, the NATO Observers' Group, and the House of Representatives. Most important, I am glad it will involve the people of the United States, for the commitment a larger NATO entails will only be meaningful if the American people understand and accept it.

When these three new democracies join NATO in 1999, as I trust they will, it will be a victory for us all, Mr. Chairman. And on that day, we will be standing on the shoulders of many.

We will be thankful to all those who waged the Cold War on behalf of freedom, to all those on both sides of the Iron Curtain who believed that the goal of containment was to bring about the day when the enlargement of our democratic community would be possible.

We will be grateful to all those who championed the idea of a larger NATO—not just President Clinton or President Havel or President Wałesa, but Members of Congress from both parties who voted for resolutions urging the admission of these three nations. We will owe a debt to the Republican members who made NATO enlargement part of their contract with America.

Today, all of our allies and future allies are watching you for one simple reason. The American Constitution is unique in the power it grants to the legislative branch over foreign policy, especially over treaties. In this matter, Mr. Chairman, members of the committee, you and the American people you represent are truly in the driver's seat.

That is as it should be. In fact, I enjoy going to Europe and telling our allies: "This is what we want to do, but ultimately, it will be up to our Senate and our people to decide." I say that with pride because it tells them something about America's faith in the democratic process.

But I have to tell you that I say it with confidence as well. I believe that when the time comes for the Senate to decide, Mr. Chairman, you and I and the American people will stand together. For I know that the policy we ask you to embrace is a policy that the Administration and Congress shaped together, and I am certain that it advances the fundamental interests of the United States.

Thank you very much.

The NATO Mistake[4]

This July, the 16 leaders of the North Atlantic Treaty Organization's member nations will convene in Madrid for a special summit meeting. In between the customary public photo-ops and back room shmoozing, they will take a bold and unprecedented step: this year they will formally invite at least three, and possibly five, Eastern European countries to begin the process of joining the NATO club. The invitation of former Warsaw pact nations to join the very alliance they had opposed for four decades will mark a watershed event in NATO's history. But what is really remarkable is that almost no one thinks it is a good idea. The Eastern European countries are only interested in entering NATO insofar as doing so integrates them into Western Europe; their real preference would have been membership in the European Union. The Western European NATO members are, for the most part, following the United States' lead. Thus responsibility for NATO expansion falls squarely with the Clinton administration. Without the administration's continual pressure on the American bureaucracy and on the European NATO states, the project would have died a natural death in the NATO Council.

Clinton has yet to articulate a single reason for his drive to expand NATO that is compelling enough to override its clear downside. But ever since Clinton's 1994 announcement that "the question is no longer whether NATO will take on new members, but when and how," it has become increasingly difficult to turn back. And once adopted, a big multilateral project like NATO enlargement tends to take on a life of its own; it is tough to stop because doing so would be very costly to the prestige of governments that have supported it.

But why did the Clinton administration push for NATO expansion in the first place?

Misreading History

The administration's first mistake was its misapplication of historical analogy, which led it to harbor an exaggerated fear of Russia's threat to European security and to believe that a weak Eastern Europe must inevitably elicit aggressive behavior from both Russia and Germany. For one thing, administration analysts overlooked the far-reaching changes that have taken place in Germany. And they misread the future prospects for Russia. In short, the administration fell victim to what philosopher Karl Popper called historicism, a process that converts distinctive historical events into general laws of historical inevitability ruling future policy.

---

4 Article by Jonathan Dean, former U.S. arms control ambassador and adviser to the Union of Concerned Scientists, from *The Washington Monthly* 29:35-7 Jl/Ag '97. Copyright © 1997 The Washington Monthly Company. Reprinted with permission.

Of course, administration officials never actually came out and declared that their intention was to counter future Russian aggression. They knew that revealing such an analysis of the future would precipitate an immediate crisis. Consequently, the disease for which NATO enlargement was to be the remedy was never fully diagnosed in public. Instead, fear of Russian aggression as a motive for NATO enlargement was translated into a bland desire to promote democracy in Eastern Europe—a goal which the Western countries were already supporting with other programs. The explanation for enlarging NATO most frequently stated by the Clinton administration officials was "instability" in Eastern Europe. In a March 1995 *Foreign Affairs* article, Assistant Secretary of State Richard Holbrooke claimed political instability of the newly established democracies of Eastern Europe as the main grounds for rapid Western action to bolster them. In an article written 18 months earlier, Ronald Asmus, Richard Kugler and Stephen Larrabee, three Rand Corporation analysts who played a central role in selling NATO enlargement within the administration, argued that East-Central Europe was littered with "potential mini-Weimar republics" who were "experiencing a wave of instability and conflict generated by virulent nationalism."

Yet the argument that NATO must expand rapidly to save tottering Eastern European democracies was and is far from compelling. There was conflict and instability in former Yugoslavia, but by 1995, when the NATO enlargement project went into full gear, this was being contained by NATO forces. Poland, Hungary, and the Czech Republic, who were the main candidates for NATO membership, were not perfect democracies. However, they had democratic constitutions. Most had had two or even three nationwide free elections. All were making progress in free market economies.

Meanwhile, the missing part of the argument for NATO enlargement—the reason why administration leaders believed the project was urgent—was obvious to everyone: Russia. Russia's leader, Boris Yeltsin, an unhealthy alcoholic, had used artillery against his own parliament in October 1993. In late 1993, the supporters of democracy and reform were reduced to a minority of 25 percent in Duma elections that brought in a majority of communists and extreme nationalists. There was fighting in the republics surrounding Russia, in most cases involving Russian forces. In December 1994, the Russian military entered Chechnya in a bloody, brutal attempt to end secession.

Many administration analysts concluded from these developments that Russia would collapse, sending streams of refugees westward or, more likely, that it would become involved in a new European war. A single sentence of his *Foreign Affairs* article reveals Holbrooke's underlying concern: "And for Germany and Russia," instability in Central and Eastern Europe "has historically been a major contribution to aggressive behavior." In other words, World War III would have the same genesis as World

Wars I and II, the tendency of two large imperialistic countries to expand at the cost of weak neighbors between them.

Administration analysts had made a wholly pessimistic analysis of the future of Russia (and of Germany as well) and had decided that Eastern Europe must be saved from possible aggression by Western action while there was still time. As the reference to Weimar revealed, NATO enlargement was for them a mental recreation of the struggle with Hitler—moved eastward. NATO enlargement was a panicked administration reaction to a potential crisis which, if it had any real existence, had passed after the Russian military was defeated in Chechnya, Russia had the common sense to make peace, Yeltsin was re-elected in free elections in 1995, and then survived serious heart surgery.

Of course, Russia still has its dangers, but it is lumbering on toward a rough democracy and a crude capitalism. The chance for a positive outcome is there in the long run. And even if the analysis of possible future conflict with Russia were correct, the administration's method of isolating Russia outside an expanding NATO was and is the wrong way to deal with the problem.

"...Russia still has its dangers, but it is lumbering on toward a rough democracy and a crude capitalism."

A Substitute for Action

The second reason for the administration's drive to expand NATO was its conviction that doing so would preserve NATO's (and consequently the United States's) key role in Europe while allowing the United States to avoid intervention in Bosnia. Again, this calculation backfired.

With the end of the cold war, the Clinton administration was keenly concerned about America's position in Europe. After nearly half a century of playing the dominant role in European security, the U.S. role seemed at an end. How could American influence in Europe be maintained? The Conference for Security and Cooperation in Europe was too weak a structure. There, the U.S. was only one of 53 members, without the primacy it had in NATO from the outset. The transatlantic structure of liaison with the European Union was also still too weak. So it had to be NATO.

But NATO was in trouble. Since mid-1991, conflict had raged in former Yugoslavia. However, following the example of the Bush administration's decision not to intervene in Yugoslavia, Clinton held back. In the meanwhile, public criticism of NATO mounted both in the U.S. and Europe. Here was the world's most powerful military alliance, victorious in the cold war, whose forces were still costing over $200 billion a year, reorganized and ready for a fight, but standing on the sidelines while some of its own soldiers were being humiliated by armed Serb and Croat bands as a result of the restrictions of a neutral role under UN command.

Sen. Bob Dole said NATO's absence from Bosnia conveyed the impression that the NATO alliance had outlived its usefulness. NATO Secretary General Manfred Wörner said that failure to handle the Bosnia crisis would seriously damage NATO. In a much noted speech in June 1993, Senator Lugar argued that, "NATO had to go out of area (western Europe) or out of business." In an article published at the time of the January 1994 summit, Secretary of State Warren Christopher declared that "a NATO that does not adapt itself to the new security challenges facing Europe risks being pulled apart by the centrifugal forces of apathy and parsimony as budget-conscious governments in the West respond to an increasingly skeptical public." Secretary Christopher had laid out a primary motive for NATO enlargement: there was a real risk that NATO would be brought low if it did not remain relevant to Europe's security problems. In the administration's analysis, if NATO went into decline, so would U.S. leadership in Europe. If, in turn, NATO could not act in Bosnia because of the administration's own self-imposed strictures, then let it at least justify itself by extending its membership eastward. NATO enlargement was a bureaucratic response to institutional crisis.

There is great irony in the fact that NATO enlargement was undertaken as a kind of bureaucratic surrogate for NATO involvement in Bosnia. If the Clinton administration had come earlier to the overdue decision to intervene in Bosnia, the world would then have seen, as it did two and a half years later when Clinton finally did step in, that NATO continued to have a valuable function. The need to justify NATO by eastward expansion would have been subsumed in the drama of Bosnia, and the enlargement project might never have been advanced as a serious administration program.

Finally, in sponsoring NATO enlargement, the Clinton administration had an obvious partisan political motive. In the presidential race with Sen. Bob Dole, Dole was absolutely sure to criticize the administration for inaction on international security issues, especially NATO, exploiting President Clinton's vulnerabilities from his lack of military experience and his opposition to the Vietnam War. In particular, NATO enlargement was of direct interest to Polish and Eastern European voters in key areas of the Midwest. Faced by this possible attack, the Clinton administration preempted it and took the subject of NATO enlargement as its own cause. President Clinton's only foreign policy speech of the 1996 presidential campaign was on the NATO issue; it was given in Detroit in October 1996. Senator Dole's subsequent charge that the administration was not doing enough for NATO enlargement had no impact.

What Next?

NATO remains an indispensable organization for coordinating the security policy of the world's richest and most powerful countries in North America and Europe. It should be retained. NATO's capacity for organizing peacekeeping missions, attested in Bosnia, should also be retained. Moreover, there is a residual need for NATO as a defensive alliance to insure against possible Russian misbehavior. But, as the miserable performance of the Russian military in Chechnya showed, it will take a decade or more before Russia's conventional forces can become any threat to far-superior NATO. Now, the main risks and dangers from Russia are in the nuclear field. But the U.S. is in a position to deal with these risks bilaterally, preferably through further mutual disarmament. There is no need to enlarge NATO for this purpose.

Of course, now that it has embarked on a policy of NATO expansion, it will be tough for the United States to pull back. But if Clinton wants to avoid the trap fallen into by previous presidents like Lyndon Johnson—who, for fear of losing face, failed to pull out of Vietnam even when it became apparent that the United States was losing the war—Clinton should take the courageous step of placing NATO enlargement on hold while an alternative is considered. This alternative would consist of an improved Partnership for Peace program, already underway, of the Charter relationship between Russia and NATO, recently signed in Paris, and of return to enlargement of the European Union as the main means of integrating Eastern European countries into Western Europe. Negotiations for enlargement of the European Union are beginning. They will take a long time to come to fruition. But there is plenty of time for them. Despite the administration's claims, there is no crisis in Eastern Europe.

If, despite the fact that this alternative program represents a safer, more constructive course, invitations for a first group of candidate states are extended in July this year and the enlargement is, in fact, ratified by the legislatures of the 16 NATO countries, the administration should do some serious homework. It should develop a credible, detailed, 20-year program for the admission to NATO of all eligible European states, including Russia. This approach should provide realistic prospects of NATO membership to excluded candidates like the Baltic States and to Ukraine. It would give time for the Russian polity to settle down while keeping open a convincing, real prospect that NATO will ultimately become a truly all-European organization for European security.

The NATO Debate Begins, Badly[5]

Though the Senate has barely begun consideration of NATO's eastward expansion plans, the discussion has already drifted into troubling territory. Because the Clinton Administration has offered no compelling security justification for enlargement, a variety of dubious rationales are being advanced. The confusion should be a warning that the Administration's scheme for NATO lacks a core organizing principle.

The most disturbing articulation of NATO's purpose comes from Senator Jesse Helms, the chairman of the Foreign Relations Committee. Mr. Helms would frame NATO expansion partly as a means to isolate Russia. That cold-war approach is likely to boomerang.

Russia no longer presents a military or political threat to Europe. It is a nascent democracy with a struggling market economy and a hollow conventional military force. Even under the most alarming political realignment in Moscow, it would take Russia years to reconstitute its military machine. Positioning NATO today as an alliance against a potential Russian threat can only strengthen the anti-democratic forces in Russia.

Another proposition would radically expand NATO's purpose from the territorial defense of Europe to the defense of common American and European interests anywhere in the world. That is a startling idea, with all sorts of implications. A NATO claim to conduct military operations in the Middle East, Asia or Africa would certainly be a surprise to countries in those regions. It might also alarm Americans, who thought the Atlantic alliance merely obliged them to come to the defense of European democracies.

The idea of a global NATO is supported by two veterans of President Clinton's first-term Cabinet, Warren Christopher and William Perry, both instrumental in designing the expansion into Eastern Europe. Though their notion seems improbable and imperial, it warrants discussion at some point. The coalition of European and Middle Eastern nations that fought alongside America in the Persian Gulf war offers a model for the kind of military cooperation the two men seem to have in mind.

But the very audacity of their idea makes it a mismatch for the enlargement plan now before the Senate, which would add Poland, Hungary and the Czech Republic to NATO by the end of the decade. It is hard to see what relevance the admission of three or more Eastern European nations would have to NATO activity in the Middle East or the Far East. The countries have neither the money nor the military forces to make a meaningful

---

[5]Editorial from the *New York Times,* O 16 '97. Copyright © 1997 The New York Times Company. Reprinted with permission.

contribution to such operations.

It was unnerving to hear the global NATO idea casually discussed at the Foreign Relations Committee hearing by Senators Richard Lugar and John Ashcroft and Secretary of State Madeleine Albright, as though it were just another idea floating about the Capitol. Its acceptance would mark a tectonic shift in international affairs and require the negotiation of an entirely new NATO charter.

Other equally inappropriate security constructs are bound to appear in the weeks ahead because there is no sensible and suitable military reason to expand NATO eastward at this time. The plan is a poor substitute for the economic and political integration of Europe that ought to be taking place under the leadership of the European Union.

As the Senate weighs expansion, which must be approved by a two-thirds majority to become effective, it should concentrate on practical security questions, and related matters like the unknown costs of enlargement. It ought not to dwell on the prophecies of Jesse Helms or expansive theories about the global projection of American power.

III. How Viable Are the "New" States?

Editor's Introduction

With the virtual death of communism in Eastern Europe in the early 1990s and the collapse of the Soviet Union in 1991, many countries—former USSR satellites as well as semi-independent Eastern bloc nations—found themselves struggling to form new identities. These struggles are political, economic, and even cultural in nature. For example, in 1995, in the former Eastern-bloc nation of Poland, five years after Lech Wałesa led his country away from communism, the ex-communist Alexander Kwasniewski wrested the presidency from the Solidarity leader—only to see Solidarity triumph again in 1997.

But with more than 30 political parties vying for power in Poland, Solidarity's long-term leadership is by no means certain. The former Soviet countries Ukraine and Belarus continue to grapple internally, as well as with Russia, over the extent of their independence—a debate that touches on the very language that Ukrainians speak. Meanwhile, the former East Germany is attempting to adapt to a free-market economy. The aim of this section, then, is to examine several of the "new" independent nations that came into existence in the early 1990s, with a view toward their viability as independent, free, economically self-sustaining entities.

This section looks at nations individually. In his article "Tinderbox," reprinted from *Forbes*, Paul Klebnikov declares Ukraine, a nation of 52 million people, to be "riven between those who want reunion with Russia and those who want to remain independent," and he warns that this is "not a dispute likely to be settled amicably."

The desire of some to reunite with Russia has to do with the country's economic picture; privatization is progressing slowly, basic necessities such as heat are in short supply, and many see reunification as the solution to these problems. Ukraine, Klebnikov explains, is a well-armed nation with a large standing army, and a civil war there—which would inevitably involve Russia, still very much tied to Ukraine economically—would spell disaster. As problematic as the state of Ukrainian independence is, John Edwin Mroz and Oleksandr Pavliuk, in their article "Ukraine: Europe's Linchpin" (originally published in *Foreign Affairs*), see the country as playing a key role in the maintenance of European security, and the writers warn of the danger of Ukraine's falling back under complete Russian control. The writers also paint a somewhat more optimistic picture of the Ukrainian economy than does Klebnikov.

Two articles, Radek Sikorski's "Belarus in Winter" (from *National Review*) and Ustina Markus's "Imperial Understretch: Belarus's Union with Russia" (from *Current History*), examine Belarus—whose president, Alexander Lukashenko, unlike Ukrainian president Leonid Kuchma, wants to reunite with Russia. Sikorski argues that it is in the interests of the West to maintain close ties with Belarus and to support its continued independence—because many of that country's people, if not its leader, are nationalistic, and because "independent Belarus is a good litmus test of Russian behavior and a potential buffer, if Russia were to go nasty," in Sikorski's words. Markus argues that reunification is unlikely simply because Russia has nothing to gain by reuniting with Belarus, noting that "many observers...dismissed the Belarusian-Russian [integration] agreement as a publicity stunt designed to boost [Russian president Boris] Yeltsin's standing with conservative voters," who desire the reintegration of all former Soviet states.

The former East Germany differs from the other nations under discussion here, in that we examine its ability to succeed not as a nation newly independent from another nation but as a formerly separate and Communist entity now united with a free-market democracy. In "The Transition from Communism to Capitalism in East Germany," from *Society*, Rüdiger Pohl points out the contradictory impressions created by (1) the encouraging economic growth in eastern Germany; (2) the significant level of unemployment there; (3) the growing number of entrepreneurs in eastern Germany, and (4) the lack of trade among its various regions—while maintaining that the "dynamic development of economic activity in eastern Germany reflects an economic transformation that is heading toward success."

In a *World Press Review* piece, "Getting Kazak Oil to Market," Sander Thoenes and Anthony Robinson look at the international deals that the former Soviet state of Kazakhstan has been able to make because of the oil in its western region. Finally, a *Boston Sunday Globe* article by David Filipov provides a portrait of the war-torn former Soviet satellite Azerbaijan.

Tinderbox[1]

Even with the fighting in the former Yugoslavia stopped, at least for now, the world may not have seen the end of turmoil in Eastern Europe. Watch Ukraine. This former member country of the Soviet Union, the size of France, with 52 million people, is riven between those who want reunion with Russia and those who want to remain independent. It is not a dispute likely to be settled amicably.

The problem is not just political; it's economic as well. The economies of Russia and Ukraine are intertwined, and separating them is a lot harder than just drawing boundaries. Under Soviet rule, Russia was Ukraine's principal market and the main supplier of its oil. Lacking that old guaranteed market and short of hard currency, Ukraine is a basket case economically.

Nowhere is this clearer than in Ukraine's primary port, Odessa. The city has a glorious past. Its tree-lined boulevards speak of a time when it was the center of the world's grain trade and one of the wealthiest cities in Europe. That wealth is gone. Last winter—the harshest in recent memory—energy shortages plunged the city into freezing darkness for two hours each day. Lacking the hard currency to pay Russia for oil, Odessa could not run its generators full time. Its enormous ports, which handled 85 million metric tons of goods the year before independence, handled just 51 million tons last year.

Yet this is a potentially rich land. In World War II, Ukraine, with huge deposits of coal and iron ore, was the big prize for Hitler's panzers. Its farms, sitting on some of the richest soil in the world, made it the bread basket of Europe.

But politics trumps economics. Potentially rich, Ukraine is poor. Since independence, coal and steel output has fallen by about 40%. Factories have gone without capital spending for years. Ukrainian agriculture now produces only enough to feed the population.

Ukraine's capital, Kiev, shows none of Russia's post-communist vitality: no traffic jams, few foreign cars, no new construction, no new wealth. Foreign exchange coffers are virtually empty.

The European Union does not need Ukrainian wheat, and the world is already awash in steel. Ukraine's ports have lost much of their Russian trade. Faced with cumbersome tariffs and regulations, Russian trading companies prefer to bypass Ukraine and ship through ports in Russia or the Baltic states.

Ukraine lags far behind Russia in abandoning socialism. Because of opposition from both the old communists and many

---

[1]Article by Paul Klebnikov from *Forbes* 158/6:158+ S 9 '96. Reprinted by permission of Forbes Magazine © 1996.

nationalists, privatization in Ukraine is proceeding at a snail's pace. Some of the country's most attractive assets are still government owned. These include Azovstal, one of the best steel mills in the former Soviet Union, and Chernomorflot, the enormous Black Sea shipping fleet. The investment law has been changed four times since 1992, and taxes sometimes take up to 93% of companies' profits.

"Without foreign investment, we won't be able to pull ourselves out of our economic crisis," Ukrainian President Leonid Kuchma tells *Forbes*. But foreign investment in Ukraine has totaled only $1 billion over the past five years, less than the aid doled out by Western nations. While Kuchma says he wants foreign investment, local politics makes it unwelcome.

Reintegration with Russia would alleviate many of these problems, but the electorate is of two minds on the subject. In March 1991 over 70% of Ukrainians voted in a referendum to stay in the Soviet Union. Eight months later, after the Soviet Union was dissolved anyway, 92% of Ukrainians voted to approve their new independence. Now they seem to be changing their minds again.

One survey for the Kiev Center for Political Research & Conflict Studies found that 30% of Ukrainians want to merge with Russia and another 50% want closer economic, political or military ties. President Kuchma is firmly in the independence camp. "Independent Ukraine is an obstacle to the rebirth of the Russian empire," he declares.

But a lot of Ukrainians see things differently. "What imperialism?" asks Alexander Lukianchenko, former deputy governor of the coal-mining region of Donetsk. "Considering that 85% of the population here speaks Russian, we have no feeling of suffering from Russian imperialism."

But then Yugoslavs all speak pretty much the same language. Like Yugoslavia, Ukraine has a long tradition of ethnic strife and borders that were fixed arbitrarily by communist leaders decades ago. In 1954, for example, Soviet Premier Nikita Khrushchev simply gave the lush Crimean peninsula to Ukraine as a present to commemorate the 300-year union between Russia and Ukraine. Now the population of Crimea wants to return to Russia.

Ukrainians are ethnically almost indistinguishable from Russians. But languages and culture differ—about to the degree that Portugal differs from Spain. But not all Ukrainians are Ukrainian. There are a lot of Russians, too. If you go by the number of people who prefer to speak Russian rather than Ukrainian, that's 55% of the population. The Russian-speakers inhabit the richer eastern part of the country and the Black Sea coast; the Ukrainian-speakers are concentrated in the more rural west.

Given their tenuous support, it would make sense for Ukrainian nationalists to be accommodating, but they are not.

They push President Kuchma to suppress Russian speakers. The Ukrainian language has, since independence, become dominant in television, radio and the schools. Both groups cling as stubbornly to their distinct tongues as the groups in the old Yugoslavia have clung to their ethnic identities.

Independence has deepened the gulf between the two groups. In Odessa, *Forbes* copped a ride with Sergei, a retired factory worker who supplements his meager pension with taxi fares. "What have we gained from independence?" snorts Sergei. "Nothing good, that's for sure." What irks Sergei most is television. Up until last year Russian-speakers in Ukraine could watch Moscow TV, which serves up relatively entertaining fare. Now Moscow has been banished to a weak third channel, hardly visible in most places; the only available choice is turgid, Ukrainian-language programming.

For Russian-speakers economic injury is being added to political insult. The coal mines, steel mills and engineering companies of Russian-speaking eastern Ukraine may be inefficient, but they account for the vast majority of the country's export earnings and tax revenues. Where does the money go? To subsidize the poorer, Ukrainian-speaking regions of the west.

This summer has seen a series of acrimonious strikes by coal miners in the Donetsk region. Ukrainian Prime Minister Pavlo Lazarenko blamed the Russian-speaking coal miners for a bomb that narrowly missed him in Kiev in July.

If tensions increase, Russia can hardly avoid being drawn into the quarrel. Russia has a stranglehold on Ukraine's economy. It still accounts for 46% of Ukraine's trade, and it supplies almost all Ukraine's energy.

So desperate is Ukraine to break its dependence on Russian energy that it has kept the dangerous Chernobyl nuclear plant open. It has also been trying to line up financing to build a $1 billion oil terminal in Odessa so it can import oil from the Middle East. "We can't survive on just one pipeline [through Russia]," President Kuchma explains. But so far investors have shown little interest.

Russian President Boris Yeltsin's government has refrained from either squeezing Ukraine economically or fanning the simmering ethnic flames in the eastern part of the country. But Russia is now a democracy, and the Russian president cannot ignore the pleas of the Russian-speakers in Ukraine if they ask for his help.

Could the problem be solved by splitting off the Russian-majority areas and uniting them with Russia? Over the dead bodies of Ukrainian nationalists. "We will use force to protect Ukraine's national integrity!" vows Dmitro Korchinsky, a nationalist leader who heads the paramilitary organization UNSO.

If it comes to fighting, Ukraine is not helpless. As late as 1991 Ukraine boasted a huge standing army (720,000 men) and the third-largest nuclear arsenal in the world (1,800 warheads). The last of the Ukrainian nukes was decommissioned in June, but there are still enough arms around to equip several enormous armies. A civil war with the threat of foreign intervention is the last thing that Ukraine needs. But it was the last thing the former Yugoslavia needed too.

Ukraine: Europe's Linchpin[2]

Five years after independence, Ukraine watches the nationalist turn in neighboring Russia with unease bordering on alarm. Much of the Russian political spectrum, obsessed with reclaiming great power status and reuniting the former Soviet republics, recognizes that Ukraine is the key to its plans and openly espouses reabsorption. President Boris Yeltsin, instrumental in the 1991 dissolution of the Soviet Union, has, in his quest for votes, adopted much of the nationalist agenda; he has dismissed his Western-oriented foreign minister, Andrei Kozyrev, cracked down on the rebellion in Chechnya, and pursued formal union with Belarus. Continued progress in Ukraine toward democracy and free markets will be more difficult no matter who triumphs in Russia's presidential election in June. A victory for Gennadi Zyuganov, the Communist Party boss and the leading presidential contender, would give Ukraine's communists a second wind and could well throw Ukraine back into the instability that preceded reform.

"An independent, democratic, and reform-oriented Ukraine can provide a model for Russia's development..."

With a landmass equal to France, a population of 52 million, a location at the crossroads of Europe and Asia, large agricultural and high-tech industries, and extensive natural resources, Ukraine is crucial for the stability of the continent, and uncertainty there would reverberate throughout Europe. An independent, democratic, and reform-oriented Ukraine can provide a model for Russia's development, prevent the emergence of the Commonwealth of Independent States (CIS) as a political and military alliance under Moscow's control, and promote stability in Central and Eastern Europe. The next year's events in Ukraine will determine whether the continent continues on its path toward integration or faces a new confrontational divide.

Regardless of the outcome of Russia's presidential contest, Ukraine has ample reason to suspect Moscow's long-term intentions. Russia has refused to negotiate the exact borders between the two states. The Duma has not annulled its 1993 resolution declaring Sevastopol a Russian city, nor has it canceled its order to review the 1954 transfer of Crimea from Russia to the Ukraine. Most recently, it proclaimed illegal the dissolution of the Soviet Union. In fact, many Russians believe that Ukraine's leaders, not its people, have been the impediment to closer relations, if not union, between the two countries.

But a majority of Ukrainians would not voluntarily agree to union with Russia. Ukrainians in the country's west have long associated domination by Moscow with political oppression and economic decline. Despite forces in eastern Ukraine that favor reintegration, nationalist sentiment has grown throughout the

---

[2]Article by John Edwin Mroz, president of the Institute for EastWest Studies, and Oleksandr Pavliuk, a program associate in the Institute's European Security Program, from *Foreign Affairs* 75:52-62 My/Je '96. Copyright © 1996 by the Council on Foreign Relations, Inc. Reprinted with permission.

rest of the country. The prospect of again being a provincial out-
post of Moscow does not appeal to Ukrainians, who contrast that
scenario with improving conditions in neighboring countries like
Poland, Hungary, and the Czech Republic. Ukrainians in the eastern, Russified areas have demonstrated in the two elections since
independence that they will vote for the candidate best able to
improve their economic situation. Thus in 1991 a majority of the
eastern region voted to secede from the Soviet Union because an
independent Ukraine seemed to offer better economic opportunities, but in 1994 a majority, judging that the Russian economy
had improved and was clearly in better shape than their own,
opted for a candidate who endorsed closer ties with Russia. With
few exceptions, reintegration with Russia is in the interests of
neither the new Ukrainian political elite nor much of the commercial class. In a recent set of interviews, Ukrainian entrepreneurs, many of whom are personally pro-Russian, argued that
Ukrainian sovereignty protects the country's emerging business
community from the rich, powerful capitalists of Russia.

Ukraine desires normal relations with Russia, but attempts to
force it back under Moscow's thumb would further alienate its
already suspicious population. Aggressive Russian efforts might
lead to civil war in Ukraine, accompanied by an overwhelming
refugee crisis and ecological disasters.

Missiles Into Plows

Since winning election as president of Ukraine in 1994, Leonid
D. Kuchma has focused on the single greatest security threat to
Ukraine—the near-collapse of its economy. Kuchma has been
surprisingly successful, and Ukraine now has a fighting chance
of following Central European countries' example and creating a
viable market economy. He has also worked hard to bind
Ukraine to Europe while maintaining normal relations with
Russia. Kuchma's presidential campaign concentrated on closer
ties with Russia and the introduction of Russian (his native language) as Ukraine's second official language, and thus his stress
on economic reform and relations with Europe is astounding.
Though a former director of the world's largest missile factory,
Kuchma has convinced his countrymen to relinquish their
nuclear weapons, creating goodwill with the West. Most important, he has turned out to be a staunch defender of Ukraine's
independence and sovereignty.

Kuchma's persistence has brought financial stabilization within reach. Inflation in 1995 decreased to roughly 150 percent, an
enormous improvement over the 4,000 percent hyperinflation of
just two years before. Total trade volume in 1995 grew by 32 percent, as trade with the West rose by 40 percent. For the first time
in 60 years, Ukraine exported grain, reminding the world that it
once was, and can again become, the breadbasket of Europe.

By securing the support of many voters in western Ukraine
who had originally been against him, Kuchma has bridged the

gap between the country's Russian-populated eastern half and
its more nationalist west, restoring unity to the country and dis-
pelling the specter of instability. Any significant shift in the
course of reform would ruin his coalition, restrain economic
growth, and split the country once again. Mindful of such dangers, Kuchma and his able prime minister, Yevhen Marchuk,
have pursued radical economic reforms vigorously, despite
resistance from powerful groups more interested in accumulat-
ing personal power and wealth than nation-building. The forces
of opposition—the post-Soviet bureaucracy, the leftist-dominat-
ed parliament, the industrial and agricultural lobbies—have
relentlessly attacked Kuchma and Marchuk's policies. Group
and corporate interests often prevail in economic decisions, and
corruption remains a serious problem, though less daunting
than in Russia.

In 1995, following a pattern common to East European
economies in transition, Ukraine's GDP declined, although at
a lower rate than in past years. Total industrial production
decreased by 11.5 percent and the production of consumer goods
by 19.1 percent. Perhaps most disquieting was the sluggishness
of privatization; less than 10 percent of the 8,000 targeted large
and medium-size enterprises went into private hands in 1995.
The government, which has been disappointingly indecisive in
this regard, announced in March that it will speed up the privatization of 400 of these companies through international tender.
Ukraine's difficulties in delivering on its commitments led the
International Monetary Fund (IMF) in January to postpone the
fourth tranche of a standby loan.

Despite its size, agricultural potential, and key location,
Ukraine has failed to attract major investors. Kuchma claims that
the economy requires about $40 billion in private investment,
but it received only $750 million between 1992 and 1995. He told
New York investors last October that in 1994 direct foreign
investment per capita was $12 in Ukraine versus $670 in
Hungary, $319 in the Czech Republic, $298 in Estonia, and even
$27 in Russia. The country's confusing tax laws and its failure to
allow private property have combined with its economic instability to scare away many investors. Meanwhile, internal sources
of financing remain very limited. A significant portion of the new
Ukrainian business elite is parasitic and reluctant to invest in the
Ukrainian economy. If Ukraine is counting on increased Western
financial assistance and investment, it must take the necessary
steps, such as large-scale privatization, banking sector reform,
and capital market development. Unless Western investors bring
their capital to Ukraine, disappointment may lead ordinary
Ukrainians—like their Russian fellows—to harbor anti-Western
sentiments.

Ukraine's mixed economic performance has caused foreign
investors to be cautious, but some remain optimistic because of
the country's political stability and commitment to democracy.

The international community has applauded Kiev for its handling of the Crimean secession, which for several years seemed sure to spark serious regional conflict. Kuchma and Yeltsin displayed true statesmanship in defusing a potentially violent eruption there last year. Similar leadership will be required to complete negotiations over the Black Sea fleet. While many CIS countries have retreated from democracy, Ukraine has compiled a solid track record, particularly in its treatment of its national minorities. It was the first member of the CIS to enjoy a peaceful, democratic transfer of presidential power. In its transition, Ukraine has avoided violence, and its army has not been dragged into domestic political quarrels, let alone projected its power beyond the country's borders. Despite heated debates and political tension, strong leadership and democratic compromise have characterized Ukraine's politics since Kuchma's election. The June 1995 Constitutional Agreement between the president and the parliament, for example, temporarily resolved a serious deadlock by regulating the division of power between the legislative and executive branches, while setting out a procedure for the adoption of a new constitution. Last fall Ukraine became the second CIS country, after Moldova, to be admitted to Europe's "democratic club," the Council of Europe.

"...Ukraine is the only country in the former Soviet Union that has not adopted a new constitution since independence..."

Still, Ukraine is the only country in the former Soviet Union that has not adopted a new constitution since independence, and Kuchma's June deadline will prove tough to meet. Many observers expect him to prevail by the end of the year, but his constant battles with the leftist forces in parliament provide skeptics with enough evidence to adjudge the current political situation fragile. As coal miners strike and religious tensions fester, Kuchma's opponents can easily exploit social unrest. Most of Ukraine's domestic and foreign policy dilemmas stem from the nation's tenuous unity. Its size, cultural diversity, and weak tradition of statehood seriously complicate its transition.

Walking a Tightrope

Kuchma's foreign policy aims to balance gradual but steady integration into Europe's political and economic structures with constructive, friendly relations with Russia. While many other Central European countries have declared their desire for admission into NATO, Ukraine has firmly committed itself to nonalignment. It has participated in NATO's Partnership for Peace program and now publicly seeks a special relationship with the alliance, parallel to that which Russia has demanded; it is a reluctant member of the CIS and has time and again refused to sign the 1992 Tashkent collective security agreement. Just as it has combated anti-Russian sentiment in its western region, the Ukrainian government has done its best to avoid anti-NATO paranoia, present in other CIS countries, in its eastern half.

Both Russia and the West have hailed Kuchma's success in persuading his country to abandon nuclear arms, even though many

Ukrainians still view the decision as harmful to the country's long-term national security. Once the third-largest nuclear power and owner of the third-largest conventional force in Europe, Ukraine voluntarily transferred its tactical nuclear stocks to Russia in 1992 and started to remove and destroy its strategic nuclear weapons in 1994. Ukraine has already reduced its conventional forces from 800,000 to 500,000.

Internal economic weakness makes Ukraine susceptible to outside pressures and has complicated Kuchma's foreign policy. The prime example of this vulnerability is Ukraine's dependence on Russia for energy. Russia supplies 80 percent of Ukraine's gas, and Ukraine has accumulated an energy debt of $4 billion, making energy Russia's most effective lever over the country. Gazprom, Russia's gas monopoly and a powerful lobby, has threatened to close the pipeline to Ukraine unless it pays its bill. At one point, in exchange for debt relief, Gazprom unsuccessfully maneuvered for stakes of between 35 and 50 percent in 15 of Ukraine's most profitable and strategic national enterprises.

Reducing this dependence on Moscow has become Ukraine's top priority. It has made some progress toward this goal by commercializing its oil import business, restructuring its debt, and using IMF standby loans to pay its gas bills. But the energy problem still awaits a comprehensive solution, and Russia has objected to some of Ukraine's stopgap measures. Last February, for instance, Ukraine found itself on the edge of an energy collapse: coal miners' strikes coincided with Gazprom's decision to stop dealing with Ukraine's commercial gas importers and with Moscow's decision to disconnect Ukraine from its electricity system. Until the energy problem is addressed, Ukraine will remain a weak state, vulnerable to Russian pressure.

Opposed to Ukraine's independence in 1991 and preoccupied with Russia in 1992 and 1993, the West has since become a significant supporter of Ukraine and its transition to a market economy. While serving briefly as prime minister three years ago, Kuchma criticized Western policy, saying that "on the map of world leaders, Ukraine does not even exist. They are indifferent [to] whether Ukraine is independent or not." Ignored by the West, Ukrainian policymakers lacked the confidence to pursue difficult decisions on nuclear disarmament and economic reform, and the West's focus on Russia further aggravated Kiev's sense of insecurity and made Ukrainian-Russian relations even more tense. That initial delay in formulating a clear Western policy has been responsible in part for Ukraine's tortoise-like progress toward capitalism.

A discernible Western policy first emerged in 1994. Vladimir Zhirinovsky's strong showing in the Duma elections of December 1993 and Russia's subsequent great power posturing sent the first warning signals to the West. The election of Kuchma, then deemed pro-Russian, shocked the West out of its lethargy. Relations between the West and Ukraine have since improved substantially. Last summer British Foreign Secretary Malcolm Rifkind called Ukraine "a strategic pivot in Europe" that would determine the future prosperity and security of the continent. Even Russophile France has started to pay more attention to Ukraine. And American officials have stated that a free and independent Ukraine is "a vital strategic interest of the United States." Ukraine's accession to the Nuclear Nonproliferation Treaty and its launching of economic reforms prompted security assurances and financial support from Western governments and international institutions. Western assistance, pushed largely by Canada, the United States, and Germany, made possible Kuchma's macroeconomic reforms.

"Nobody wishes to shut Chernobyl more than the Ukrainians..."

The latest figures show that since Kuchma began his reform program in late 1994, the World Bank and the IMF have committed a total of $3.4 billion in loans, $1.5 billion of which is slated for 1996. This year the European Union (EU) will provide $250 million, the European Bank for Reconstruction and Development $80 million, the United States $170 million, and the Export-Import Bank of Japan $180 million. Russia's rescheduling of $3 billion of Ukraine's energy arrears is another reason for the improvement in Ukraine's economic situation.

Since 1992 American and German firms have invested the most in Ukraine, $202.8 million and $129.6 million respectively. The EU's support strategy for the country, adopted in November 1994, marked an important step. It included trade concessions, accelerated political dialogue, and a framework for industrial, financial, and scientific cooperation. Particularly important was the signing and implementation of the interim agreement that gave Ukraine most-favored-nation trading status with the EU. Significantly increasing Ukrainian exports to the EU, the agreement helps Ukraine avoid becoming shackled to the CIS, which accounted in 1995 for 55 percent of Ukraine's exports and 57 percent of its imports. Current plans would admit Ukraine to the EU's single market after 1998.

The Chernobyl nuclear reactor remains an irritant in relations between Ukraine and the Group of Seven industrialized nations. Ukraine's leaders believe that Western demands to close the plant ignore the social and political consequences of doing so without addressing Ukraine's overall energy situation. Nobody wishes to shut Chernobyl more than the Ukrainians, who will continue to suffer from the 1986 meltdown for many years to come. Yet by producing 40 percent of the country's energy, instead of their usual 25 percent, Chernobyl and the five other Ukrainian nuclear power plants prevented an energy crisis last winter. The recent memorandum of understanding between Ukraine and the Group of Seven may have diminished some of these misunderstandings; the memorandum stipulated the terms for decommissioning the Chernobyl nuclear station by 2000 but unfortunately did not discuss its funding.

Staying the Course

Ukraine's future lies within European structures, and the West should not slow this process. The West should adopt a double staircase approach—one for market reforms and one for political and security issues. Each Ukrainian step upward would be met by an appropriate and symmetrical step by the West. For example, were Ukraine to accelerate privatization and agricultural reform and further strengthen financial stabilization, Western institutions would expand assistance. Similarly, on the political level, Ukraine needs to resolve its constitutional stalemate. In return, the West would increase technical and financial support to the Ukrainian parliament and train larger numbers of Ukrainians for public administration and the judiciary.

The West can bolster Ukraine's security through strong, sustained economic support, with particular assistance in the energy sector. Under the leadership of the World Bank and the EU, Western and Ukrainian experts should develop an expanded energy strategy, beyond the EU's useful 1994 action plan for Chernobyl, which offered Ukraine a large aid package in exchange for timely closure of the flawed nuclear plant. Rationalizing Ukraine's oil refining capacity would by itself dramatically decrease the country's consumption; Ukraine loses some 40 percent of its crude during refining, but that figure can easily be cut to as low as 2 percent. The construction of an oil port at Odessa, currently blocked by hard-line local officials, would open Ukraine to Middle Eastern oil. Technologies that convert coal into gas would also make a significant difference. Western experts could help Ukraine develop a contingency plan in case of an energy crisis. As Ukraine transforms its agriculture industry, converting its large state-run farms into a cooperative farming system, the West can make sure Ukraine avoids Bulgaria's error of splitting such farms into units too small for international marketing.

On the security side, while encouraging Kiev to cooperate extensively within the Partnership for Peace, NATO should negotiate a treaty that would guarantee Ukraine's neutrality. Given Ukraine's location and history, it must be a bridge, not a buffer, between Russia and Europe. Its market economy and democratic system could become a positive model for, and the single greatest influence on, Russia. Despite some antagonism, Russians regard Ukrainians as closer to them than any other nationality, except the Belarusans. Ukraine's failure would strengthen Russia's authoritarian tendencies and leave Europe substantially less secure.

Moscow must overcome its ambivalence about Ukraine and recognize how much the country can contribute to Russia's own development as well as to the stability of Europe. The economic and cultural ties between Ukraine and Russia are strong; the two countries enjoy a natural interdependence. Forty-six percent of

Russian trade within the CIS goes to Ukraine, which is also the world's largest importer of Russian gas and oil. As democratic, free-market societies, these neighbors would soon enjoy a prosperity long denied their people. If Russia learns to live with Ukraine as an independent state, it will have overcome the most critical element behind several centuries of imperialism.

As for the rest of the former Soviet world, Ukraine increasingly determines whether the CIS remains a loose economic association or becomes a tight political and military confederation under Moscow's control. Ukraine leads the CIS nonaligned group, which also includes Moldova and Azerbaijan, in opposition to the creation of any supranational bodies or military and political mechanisms, and the CIS countries know that without Ukraine, a new Soviet Union is impossible. As Belarus merges with Russia, Ukraine's position becomes even more significant. While avoiding the institutionalization of the CIS as a security arrangement, Ukraine should pursue economic cooperation with Russia and the other states of the former Soviet Union.

The independence of Ukraine has fundamentally altered the status of the other Central and East European countries. For the first time in modern history, these countries find themselves separated from Russia. An independent and democratic Ukraine between Russia and the Czech Republic, Poland, and Hungary lays the groundwork for stability in Eastern Europe by fostering lower perceptions of threat and a greater sense of security in Prague, Warsaw, and Budapest. A new iron curtain in Europe is impossible if Ukraine enjoys a positive relationship with both the West and Russia. The West should encourage Ukraine to cooperate more extensively with the Central and East European states and urge it to join the Central European Free Trade Agreement.

Support that treats Ukraine as important in its own right will bolster reform-minded decision-makers and political forces there. It will help assure the success of reform in Ukraine and make Ukraine a model for Russia and the rest of the CIS. Given its strategic position, an independent and healthy Ukraine will indeed be the linchpin of stability in post-communist Europe.

Belarus in Winter[3]

Scientists have recently established the theoretical possibility of time travel, and you don't have to be an astrophysicist to know that they are right. A slow train from Warsaw to Minsk, the capital of Belarus, will do. You board in bustling, neo-capitalist Warsaw in the mid 1990s and you disembark in Brezhnev's Soviet Union in the mid 1970s. Comrade Lenin still beckons from statues, a bronze Felix Dzerzhinsky still faces the KGB headquarters, red stars still adorn the caps of militiamen and soldiers. Switch on the television, and Communist Party hacks will harangue you for hours. For those who miss the good old days of the Cold War, this is the perfect destination for a nostalgia tour.

In Belarus the dream of Soviet social engineers, the breeding of Soviet Man, succeeded. Soviet Man was supposed to be hard-working, ahistorical, fiercely devoted to the class struggle, and, whatever his nationality, Russian-speaking. I encountered one specimen on a collective farm outside of Minsk. His face was unshaven and tired of toil and vodka. Beneath his flat forehead, characteristic of the species, his eyes were dull and apprehensive. "Will you vote in the parliamentary elections?" I asked.

"Of course," he replied emphatically. "You have to support authority."

I caught sight of another the following day, coming out of a voting station. He was middle-aged, in a fake fur black coat. "How did you vote?" I enquired.

"For the Communists, naturally."

"Why?"

"Because the Communists will take all those democrats in hand and bring back order," he thundered. "Without order, there is no prosperity, and without prosperity, there is no culture." Soviet Man is far from extinct.

In fact, the most Soviet of Belarus's Soviet Men is the president himself, Alexander Lukashenko, a former collective-farm manager. His public persona is that of a mad peasant crossed with Colonel Qaddafi: ranting, unpredictable, self-contradictory. He had recently issued a decree stating that Soviet-era history textbooks should be brought back into use in schools. Belarusian children would no longer have their minds poisoned with such slanders as the history of the purges, or the 1930s man-made famine, and could instead exult in the miracles of five-year plans. When it transpired that the old textbooks had been trashed and the children would be getting a glimpse of the truth for a little longer, Lukashenko denied ever signing such an order.

---

[3]Article by Radek Sikorski, *National Review*'s roving correspondent. He observed the Belarusian parliamentary elections as a guest of the British Helsinki Human Rights Group. From *National Review* 48:28+ F 12 '96. Copyright © 1996 National Review, Inc. Reprinted with permission.

Lukashenko's oft-repeated ambition is to consign the country's four-year-old independence to oblivion. His big idea has been to unite his country with Russia. The ostensible reason is that the country has few natural resources, so it might be advantageous to acquire raw materials and energy at subsidized, internal Russian prices. The real agenda is that in such a neo-Soviet Union, it would make good PR sense to appoint a non-Russian president, so as to deflect charges of Russian imperialism. Who better than a man who paid his dues with his own country's independence? Unfortunately, Lukashenko's courtship of Moscow has so far been unrequited. Even Vladimir Zhirinovsky, not exactly an opponent of Soviet restoration, has dismissed him as "a goatherd."

"Reformist governments in Central Europe may have suffered the pain of economic adjustment, but those countries have now been rewarded with growth."

Much as in the European Community, a customs union with Russia was to lead to a currency union, but, again, Moscow balked. Belarus is even poorer than Russia, and its market reforms have barely started. A currency union would have amounted to a never-ending Russian subsidy to a bankrupt enterprise. After much soul-searching, Russia refused to pay the price. This decision, or rather lack of it, may prove to be momentous. If it means that the Russian establishment has at long last learned to count money, and is no longer willing to sacrifice Russia's prospects for the sake of imperial illusions, then Russia's neighbors should not be the only ones to rejoice.

Meanwhile, the Belarusian economy is in free fall: most enterprises are working a curtailed week; the backlog of unpaid wages fluctuates between three and six months; the average pension suffices for little more than bread and salt; hard-currency reserves are running out. Reformist governments in Central Europe may have suffered the pain of economic adjustment, but those countries have now been rewarded with growth. Belarus has yet to find out the price of not carrying out reform. When the inevitable day of reckoning arrives for Belarus the recession that usually accompanies structural adjustment will begin from a much lower base.

For the moment, Lukashenko's control still holds, helped by the results of the elections I observed. They were not rigged, not exactly. It is just that the spending limit on the campaign was $50 per candidate, not enough even to photocopy leaflets with one's manifesto to hand to each voter in the constituency. Opposition candidates were virtually barred from the mass media, which remain largely government-owned. As for the "independent" candidates, on closer inspection many proved to be representatives of the president's own power structures. In the military garrison which I visited as an observer, where 100 per cent of registered voters had already gone to the polls by 2 P.M., the candidate turned out to be, quite by accident, a colonel from the divisional staff. I was not surprised that the final count gave no seats to the opposition Belarusian National Front.

But pushing the opposition out of the moderating ambience of parliament, like banning historic national symbols, may prove to be a mistake in the long run. The Belarusian economy is already so bad that even the official, Soviet-era trade unions, which had for years been perfectly happy to act as transmission belts from the Party to the masses, are beginning to get fidgety. They have recently forced the government to increase the minimum wage and promise to pay salaries more promptly. Since the government is unlikely to be able to fulfill its promises, their demands will no doubt escalate.

Does all this mean that the West should write Belarus off as a basket case? Quite the contrary. First, while Belarusian national identity may have been badly mauled by decades of Russification and Sovietization, it is reviving. Belarusian may not be widely spoken in the streets, but hundreds of thousands of people pay a premium to read non-government Belarusian newspapers, which have to be printed in Lithuania and arrive late. My fellow Western observers were struck by how different Belarusians were from most Russians they had met. Politeness seems to be a national characteristic. And with the Belarusian Orthodox Church now also developing a mind of its own, the building blocks of national identity are coming into place.

Second, independent Belarus is a good litmus test of Russian behavior and a potential buffer, if Russia were to go nasty. The key country in the region is of course Ukraine, with its 50 million people (Belarus has 10 million) and a serious army. Nevertheless, whoever wanted to start rebuilding the empire would first have to consolidate control over Minsk. Resistance in Belarus could scotch the project before more harm was done.

Third, strengthening Belarusian independence would be good for reformers, both in Belarus, and in Russia. Russia does not need another millstone around its neck, and Belarus, if made to swim on its own, might well begin to make it. If Belarus's government ceased to pursue suicidal policies, the country might at last begin to take advantage of its position astride highways and pipelines between Russia and the West.

The West should adopt a dual strategy. Despite Moscow's rebuffs, President Lukashenko still seems hell-bent on acting out the role of the last of the Soviets, but there are already whispers of dissatisfaction in his entourage. The customs union with Russia, for example, far from helping Belarus, stokes up inflation. Contrary to expectations, Russian brother Slavs charge Belarus almost the full world price for oil and energy. Given Lukashenko's unpredictability, I would not put it past him to appear one day on national television and declare that sidling up to Russia had been an elaborate hoax, that he has in fact been a fierce Belarusian patriot all along, and that Belarusian independence is a sacred cause after all. The West should encourage such a tendency by periodically reaffirming that once reform begins, the usual credits and trade concessions will flow.

At the same time, we must not desert Belarus's patriots and

democrats, men like Zenon Pozniak (who publicized the grave of 300,000 of Communism's victims at Kurpaty) or Adam Maldhis (who helped to preserve the Belarusian language even at the height of Khrushchev's persecutions). The resurgence of former Communists all over Central and Eastern Europe makes them look hopeless, but Sakharov, Wałesa, and Havel all once seemed more so. Justice and truth are not on the side of the old Party hacks, however much money they now spend on laundering themselves into respectability. Neither is biology. Eventually, a new generation will come to rule Belarus. You can already see it in the few Minsk nightclubs. Like the Nineties generation the world over, it is English-speaking and Internet-connected, and would rather talk business than politics. It will not accept the likes of Lukashenko forever.

Imperial Understretch:
Belarus's Union with Russia[4]

Belarus has been the most strident among the former Soviet republics in seeking to preserve its ties with Russia and re-create some type of union. To this end Belarus has signed a number of agreements, the most recent and comprehensive of which is the Treaty on the Formation of a Community. But for all the fanfare surrounding the signing of the agreement, it is uncertain whether it, like previous, unimplemented agreements, will actually bring the two countries closer together. Moreover, although Russia is often accused of harboring imperial ambitions, in the case of Belarus it has been Moscow that has stalled on closer integration with Minsk.

Differing Motives

The basic problem with any of the plans for integration between Russia and Belarus is that their motives for integration, and visions of it, are at odds. Economically, Belarus is looking to Russia for a bailout. Unfortunately for Belarus, Russia is not interested in providing it. Politically, Belarusian President Alexander Lukashenko envisages a union between the two states in which he would have equal status with Russian President Boris Yeltsin. Russia, however, assumes it will have the dominant political role, and that its smaller neighbor will follow Russia's lead in foreign affairs and economic policy. These differences were illustrated during a visit to Moscow by Lukashenko in October 1995, when he proposed creating a unified state that would be led by the Russian president one year, and by the Belarusian president the next. A further feature of the unified state would be the automatic cancellation of Belarus's energy debts to Russia and a continuing supply of Russian oil and gas to Belarus at reduced prices. Russian Prime Minister Viktor Chernomyrdin looked visibly stunned when told of the proposals, and coolly told Lukashenko, a former collective farm chairman, that Russia and Belarus were not collective farms.

A number of other differences have also emerged as obstacles to integration. When the recent treaty of the community was to be signed, a number of articles appeared in the Russian media warning against closer ties with Belarus because of the threat it would pose to democracy in Russia. The extensive censorship in Belarus and Lukashenko's public praise of Hitler as an example of a strong leader were cited as evidence of the undesirability of such a relationship.

---

[4]Article by Ustina Markus, analyst at the Open Media Research Institute in Prague, Czech Republic, specializing in Ukraine and Belarus, from *Current History* magazine 95:335-9 O '96. Copyright © 1996 Current History, Inc. Reprinted with permission.

The media also noted that Russia and Belarus have completely different economic policies. The private sector in Russia makes up 65 percent of the economy, and prices have been freed on most consumer goods. In contrast, the private sector accounts for only 15 percent of Belarus's economy, and Lukashenko wants to ban private land ownership altogether. In the dominant state sector, prices and wages are still set by the government, and the president even issued a decree bringing banks back into the government's fold and setting bank employees' wages.

Belarusian opponents of the integration accords are concerned that Belarus could be swallowed up by its larger neighbor and lose its independence and national identity. They hold that any economic benefits are illusory. Russia is pushing forward with economic reform faster than Belarus. It is raising energy prices to world levels for its own consumers, so it is unrealistic to expect it to continue selling gas and oil to Belarus at a subsidized rate. Ultimately, they argue, a union would only make Belarus a tariff-free transit route for Russian goods to Europe.

"Russia is pushing forward with economic reform faster than Belarus."

Along with resistance on the part of nationally minded Belarusians, the country's russophone president has himself been an obstacle to the implementation of such accords. Lukashenko was not a member of the nomenklatura before becoming president, but had worked as a political officer in the border guard and collective farm chairman before his election. While the abrasive populist may have won the hearts of average Belarusian peasants, who view him as one of their own, other political leaders, including Yeltsin and Chernomyrdin, treat him with barely disguised disdain.

Yet another impediment to integration has been Belarusian concerns over military obligations. Belarusians worry that integration could mean Belarusian servicemen would have to serve in conflict zones in Chechnya or Tajikistan. Thus, when Belarus signed the Commonwealth of Independent States (CIS) collective security pact in January 1994, an amendment was added stipulating that Belarusian soldiers would not serve outside of the country unless parliament expressly permitted it. This clause was unacceptable to Moscow.

The Sum of Its Contradictions

The Treaty on the Formation of a Community was signed in an elaborate ceremony in Moscow on April 2, with Russian Orthodox Patriarch Aleksei 11 giving his blessing to the accord. Despite the strong emotions the accord evoked, the document itself is little more than a declaration of intent on the part of Russia and Belarus to integrate. The exact nature of the integration is unclear since there are a number of contradictions in the text. in addition, the treaty does not provide the bodies that are to implement the process with any binding powers. The vagueness is not unique. Previous documents signed by the two countries have failed to include any precise timetables or binding commitments on integration.

Article 1 of the treaty calls on Russia and Belarus to set up a politically and economically integrated community that will allow them to pool their material and intellectual resources to improve living standards. After this the contradictions begin.

Article 2 says the community will be based on principles of democracy. Almost no one believes Belarus is a democracy Article 3 says both sides will coordinate their foreign policies; article 16 says they will establish their relations with foreign states independently. Articles 4, 5, and 6 specify time frames for the integration, yet the only action that must be achieved by the end of the specified time frames is the formulation of measures to carry out integration.

Article 7, which calls for the creation of a unified monetary, credit, and budget system between Russia and Belarus and conditions for the introduction of a common currency by the end of 1997, is entirely unrealistic. According to Grigori Yavlinsky, the leader of Russia's reformist Yabloko faction, any talk of a joint budget is "nonsense," since Russia itself has so far failed to come up with a "sensible" budget.

Articles 9 through 14 discuss the role of the Supreme Council and Parliamentary Assembly of the community. The impotence of these overseeing bodies becomes apparent when the accord states that any decisions by the Supreme Council are to be made on the basis of unanimity, with each party having one vote. Because of the two countries' conflicting interests on so many major issues, the council will likely reach agreement only on the most mundane matters. In addition, since the chairmanship of the Supreme Council is to be rotated between Russia and Belarus every two years, it is difficult to imagine that Moscow agreed to allow the chairman to have any binding or overriding powers. Moreover, Belarus calling the shots over Russia for two years is implausible—despite some dubious opinion polls emanating from Belarus claiming to show that many Russians would vote for the Belarusian president to be their president.

A History of Unimplemented Agreements

Given the track record of previous Russian-Belarusian integration agreements, the Treaty on the Formation of a Community is unlikely to live up to its stated purpose. The fate of the CIS is a reminder of why such agreements between the former Soviet republics fail. Within a year of the signing of the CIS agreement, it became clear that the group was not working to facilitate economic interactions between the former republics or to coordinate their foreign policies. Each state was pursuing its own interests, and any economic accords that were implemented were agreed to on a bilateral basis. Belarus's amendments prohibiting the use of Belarusian troops in foreign actions that were made part of the CIS collective security pact were a strong indication that the republic is aware of its own interests, and is prepared to protect them.

The agreement on monetary union Belarus and Russia signed in April 1994 was partly a political gesture by Russia in support of former Belarusian Prime Minister Vyacheslav Kebich in his bid for the Belarusian presidency in the July 1994 elections. Like all other Russian-Belarusian integration agreements, it provided for the stationing of Russian troops at Belarusian bases free of charge, even though the troops have no connection with monetary union or fiscal policy. The agreement itself was an unrealistic document, providing no timetable for uniting the Belarusian and Russian currencies. Given that the two countries were following monetary policies that were completely at odds with each other, it must have been apparent to Kebich and the Russian leaders that the agreement would never get off the ground. Belarus was continuing to print money and issue credits to pay wages and subsidize its agricultural and industrial sectors—policies that were leading to hyperinflation. In addition, it continued to drag its feet on freeing prices on consumer Belarus goods. Russia, meanwhile, had managed to rein in inflation, had effectively freed prices on most consumer goods, and was making headway in privatizing state enterprises.

The strongest arguments against the union from the Russian side came from former Deputy Prime Minister Yegor Gaidar and former Finance Minister Boris Fedorov. Both resigned in January 1994, citing opposition to the economic union with Belarus as one of the reasons for leaving office. Fedorov pointed out that the inflation rate in the two countries differed vastly: in Russia it was 8 percent per month at that time, while in Belarus it was running at 40 percent. Less than two months after Kebich lost the race to Lukashenko, Chernomyrdin informed the new president that there would be no monetary union.

Lukashenko was not put off by Moscow's lack of interest in creating an economic union with Belarus. Unwilling to implement market reforms that would free prices, cut subsidies to unprofitable firms, and privatize state enterprises—all of which would create unemployment—the new president continued to pin his hopes on a union with Russia to solve the country's economic problems and ensure cheap energy supplies. In February 1995 it appeared that Lukashenko had some success when Yeltsin signed an agreement on a customs union with Belarus. Like the agreement on monetary union, the new accord allowed for the stationing of Russian troops in Belarus at two early-warning missile bases without charge. It also envisaged open borders and called for the two countries to coordinate their tariff policies.

Opposition to the new agreement could be found in both Russia and Belarus. Russians argued it would prove costly to them, while the Belarusian opposition felt free borders were the first step toward the virtual integration of Belarus into Russia. As it turned out, both sides had little to fear. Just as the monetary union had not been fulfilled, the customs union made little real progress. Half a year after the signing of the customs union,

Belarus had still not brought its legislation into line with Russia's, and each side complained that the other had not lifted tariffs on imports.

Because the agreements elicited so much opposition at home, Lukashenko held a referendum on integration with Russia at the same time as parliamentary elections in May 1995. The referendum was deemed not to have taken place under free and democratic conditions since the press was heavily censored before the vote; moreover, the state-controlled media only promoted integration. On the referendum ballot itself, the question regarding Russia was worded somewhat benignly, asking only if people were for "economic integration" with Russia. Not surprisingly, more than 80 percent voted yes. Lukashenko interpreted this as support for straightforward integration with Russia.

Despite the Belarusian referendum results, Moscow did not rush forward to integrate with Belarus. Russian hard-liners such as Vladimir Zhirinovsky and former Duma member Konstantin Zatulin sent congratulatory messages on the referendum results, and it was suggested that Russia hold a similar referendum on integration with Belarus during its parliamentary elections in December 1995. This did not happen, and Lukashenko continued to criticize Russia for not implementing the customs agreement.

While Yeltsin and Chernomyrdin refrained from drawing up any more binding documents, the Russian media printed stories critical of Lukashenko's dictatorial regime and generally ridiculed the Belarusian president. Lukashenko's chief ideologist, Uladzimir Zamyatalin, sent a note to the Duma at the end of the year demanding that it order the press to stop writing derogatory stories about Lukashenko. He was told that Russia did not engage in the same censorship practices as Belarus.

The Electoral Catalyst to Integration

Not until this Russian presidential election year were any further moves made to draw up an integration agreement. On New Year's Day 1996, Lukashenko announced that he had spoken with Yeltsin by phone and that the Russian president had agreed to a "zero option" on the cancellation of their mutual debts. Such an agreement made little sense since most of the money Belarus owed Moscow was due to the gas and oil entity Gazprom, which had nothing to gain from absolving Belarus of its debts. The only explanation for the acceptance of such a deal is the Russian government's close connection to Gazprom; the monopoly probably received government concessions in exchange for the debt cancellation.

In February, Lukashenko traveled to Russia, where he and Yeltsin signed a number of agreements, including the zero option, which canceled Belarus's $1.27 billion debt to Russia for gas and credits in exchange for Belarus's cancellation of Russia's $914 million debt for stationing Russian troops in Belarus (including environmental damage they caused) and compensation for the nuclear weapons removed from Belarus. The two presidents also discussed building a highway from Russia to Kaliningrad through Belarus. The talks were not greeted with enthusiasm by Poland, since part of the corridor would cross through its territory. Despite assurances from Russia and Belarus that they posed no threat to Poland, Warsaw remained wary. At the same time, nationalists in Belarus were concerned that their country was to become a transit route for Russian troops in Kaliningrad.

As the Russian presidential election day neared, the integration process picked up speed. For his part, Lukashenko made every effort not to let the opportunity be derailed. In mid-March he called a meeting and told Belarusian officials to look into ways of speeding up the integration process. That month he fired Miklai Halko, the editor-in-chief of the largest Belarusian daily, *Nardnaya gazeta*, allegedly because he was unhappy that the paper had carried criticism of his efforts to integrate with Russia. Soon after, at his instruction, the left-dominated Belarusian parliament voted to debate the issue of closer integration with Moscow.

"...as many as 40,000 people demonstrated in Minsk against integration in Minsk."

While Lukashenko was making every effort to ensure that an integration agreement was signed, nationalist forces in Belarus began to stir. On March 24, as many as 40,000 people demonstrated in Minsk against integration in Minsk. The demonstration was largely peaceful, although a few protesters were reportedly beaten by security troops. In order to quash any further protests, Lukashenko issued arrest warrants for the leader of the nationalist opposition Belarusian Popular Front, Zenon Poznyak, and its spokesman, Sergei Naumchik. The two went into hiding and have made their way to the United States, where they applied for political asylum in July.

On March 29 the leaders of Belarus, Kazakstan, Kyrgyzstan, and Russia signed an agreement in Moscow to further economic and humanitarian integration within the context of the CIS. This agreement effectively created a customs union between the four pro-CIS states. The document contains the same loose wording as other integration agreements, making its implementation unlikely. Its signing was interpreted as the result of short-term political considerations rather than a real intention by the four to integrate.

A Publicity Stunt?

The integration agreement between Russia and Belarus won overwhelming support in the Russian State Duma, where deputies voted 320 to 8 for a resolution in its favor on April 5. In May, the Belarusian Supreme Soviet ratified the document by a vote of 166 to 3, with 1 abstention. The same month, both houses of the Russian Federal Assembly overwhelmingly ratified it.

On the day the treaty was signed, there was another anti-integration demonstration of between 20,000 and 30,000 people in

Minsk. The turnout was impressive, given the number of security troops stationed throughout the city and the fact that the protest had not been officially sanctioned. The size and persistence of demonstrations since then indicate that there is a committed opposition to integration with Russia within the country that can act as an obstacle to the implementation of the accord.

The political context in which the accord was signed casts further doubt on how seriously Russia wants to integrate with Belarus. The signing took place as presidential elections loomed in Russia and a Communist hard-liner, Gennadi Zyuganov, was favored to win over the incumbent. Under pressure to score political points with the electorate, Yeltsin drew up a peace plan for Chechnya, signed the agreement on closer integration with Kazakstan, Kyrgyzstan, and Belarus, announced he would travel to Kiev to sign the long-delayed agreement on friendship and cooperation with Ukraine, and announced plans to sign the integration agreement with Belarus—all in the space of one week. Many observers simply dismissed the Belarusian-Russian agreement as a publicity stunt designed to boost Yeltsin's standing with conservative voters.

A number of influential politicians in both countries reacted negatively to the treaty. Belarusian parliamentary deputy Stanislav Bahdankevich put the agreement down to political propaganda, saying Yeltsin needed it for his election campaign and that Lukashenko was covering up the fact that he had not managed to live up to any of his campaign promises. In Russia, Yavlinsky's kindest word about the agreement was to call it "strange." *Literaturnaya gazeta* said that Russia would suffer economic losses from every article in the agreement, and warned that the customs union envisaged in the accord would cost Russia $1.2 billion each year.

While there is little doubt that Yeltsin was making political capital out of the accord by presenting himself to the Russian electorate as the reintegrator of the former Soviet states, it is uncertain how forcefully he will pursue such a course now that he has been reelected. The conflicting expectations Russia and Belarus have for any integration agreements were immediately apparent. Russian Central Bank chairman Sergei Dubinin assured Russians that there were no financial risks involved, while Lukashenko told Belarusians that the treaty ensured subsidized energy supplies from Russia. The contradictory statements appeared on television on the same day. Should the accord prove costly to Russia, it is unlikely Moscow will continue to follow through with the process since numerous opinion polls have shown Russians are unwilling to bear hardships for the sake of reintegration.

In addition, Russia's primary interests in Belarus have been the right to keep troops stationed at the country's early-warning missile bases and the ability to maintain an avenue for exports, including energy, to the West. The troops are there, and the construction of a gas pipeline through Belarus, bypassing Ukraine, is slowly being realized. if Belarus has little to offer economically beyond that, it is likely economic integration will go no further. The expansion of NATO to include Poland could act as an impetus to expand military cooperation with Belarus. At the moment, however, Russia appears content with the use of the early-warning bases and is uninterested in financing the Belarusian armed forces.

Although the Executive Committee of the community was formed the same month the integration agreement was signed and met regularly over the next three months, problems between Russia and Belarus quickly appeared. In June the Russian press began reporting that Belarus had stopped delivering its nuclear missiles to Russia. Although Belarus has assured Moscow that it will finish handing its remaining nuclear missiles over to Russia by the end of the year, Moscow clearly was not pleased with the suspension. Another indication of the rocky relations between Moscow and Minsk was Lukashenko's refusal to endorse Yeltsin in the run-up to the first round of the Russian elections; he was the only CIS president who refused to back Yeltsin. In response, Yeltsin remarked that he had been forced to give his Belarusian colleague a few lessons in democracy at a CIS meeting prior to the elections.

A month after Yeltsin's reelection, Lukashenko began criticizing Russia for not implementing the customs union agreement and for failing to cancel Belarus's energy debt. When Russian Deputy Prime Minister Aleksei Bolshakov visited Minsk in July, Lukashenko asked Moscow to impose tariffs on practically all imported consumer goods in order to protect Belarusian producers from competition from cheaper imports. Because the measure would run counter to the demands of international financial organizations, Moscow only promised to talk about it. This bodes ill for the implementation of the community treaty.

Despite the disagreements and stumbling blocks, it cannot be ignored that the treaty was passed by enormous margins in the Russian and Belarusian legislatures, and that Lukashenko does find common ground on the issue with some of the more extreme Russian politicians, such as Zhirinovsky. Thus, it is possible that consensus between some politicians in the two countries may be reached on integration. What is unsettling is that if Lukashenko does make some deal on integration, it is likely to be with elements in Russia that are not concerned with his dictatorial rule or lack of progress in economic reform. Agreement with more moderate leaders is less likely.

The Transition from Communism to Capitalism in East Germany[5]

Soon after the fall of the Berlin Wall, a mining engineer from Mansfelder Land who had little money but lots of ideas set up a recycling company. Today he can be found describing the dynamic development of his business to others at the industrial association—the fairy tale career of an eastern German entrepreneur and an example of the forces that have made eastern Germany the fastest growing region in all of Europe. The construction of a vibrant market economy is now in full swing.

Euphoria and Disillusionment

But anyone who wants to assess the economy of eastern Germany at the present time—five years after the introduction of German—German monetary union—should not judge it solely in terms of the initial euphoria of unification or the later widespread disillusionment. It is much more important to assess the true economic situation. Here, however, we find a complex picture with conspicuous contrasts. Respectable economic growth stands in stark contrast to a definite trend toward structural unemployment, and the crystallization of a healthy entrepreneurial class stands in stark contrast to serious difficulties in penetrating inter-regional markets. Despite extensive state financial aid, a lack of equity capital remains a serious hurdle. Despite high levels of investment activity in both the private and public sectors, substantial deficits continue to be registered in the field of public infrastructure. The transformation of the failed communist German Democratic Republic (GDR) economy into a market economy does not represent a normal process of structural change but is tantamount to building a totally new economy. Even after five years, this process is not yet complete. The processes of dismantling old structures and building new ones are still taking place side by side. The process of dismantling—factory closures, job losses in declining industries, relocation away from structurally weak areas, the loss of sales markets—is certainly no longer as dramatic as it was during the first two or three years after reunification, but it is not yet over. The process of reconstruction—setting up new businesses, creating and modernizing jobs in flourishing industries, the dynamic expansion of successful contributions, opening new markets—is also taking place at the same time.

[5]Article by Rüdiger Pohl, president of the Institute for Economic Research in Halle, head of the Berlin Institute for Empirical Economic Research, and a former member of the "Council of the Five Wise Persons," from *Society* 33/4:62-5 My/Je '96. Copyright © 1996 by Transaction Publishers; all rights reserved. Reprinted with permission.

To be sure, balancing the successes of the transformation process against the remaining deficiencies does not produce an overall assessment of the economic situation. In western Germany there are also differentials, various gradations between rich and poor, prosperous and declining industries, dynamic and stagnant regions, successful and unsuccessful enterprises, employed and unemployed. Drawing up an economic balance sheet for eastern Germany calls for a yardstick other than differentiation. Essentially, it involves an appraisal of the growth process as it now is, five years after monetary union. At the very beginning, the need to catch up and the euphoria of unification, followed by the massive transfers of funds from western Germany, gave rise to an economic dynamism that, by its very nature, could not last. Now, in the second half of the 1990s, the question arises as to whether the growth process can yet be described as "self-sustaining." An analysis of this criterion is extremely difficult, as difficult as it is important. Certainly, the existence of self-sustaining development would mean that the growth process in eastern Germany could continue without significant state financial aid. This would assume sufficient competitiveness on the part of eastern German enterprises. However, economic activity should also have to have a certain breadth; in other words, it should not remain restricted to a few products, sectors, or regions but should make adequate use of available resources, particularly the available labor potential.

"...the question arises as to whether the growth process can yet be described as 'self-sustaining'..."

The central thesis of this analysis is that the dynamic development of economic activity in eastern Germany reflects an economic transformation that is heading toward success. Be that as it may, five years after monetary union this process cannot yet be described as "self-sustaining" because eastern German enterprises are not yet competitive enough. Any appraisal of the economy in eastern Germany must take into account the greatest shortcoming that has arisen from the transformation process—a shortcoming that will stay around for the foreseeable future: the problem of underemployment. While the economic process remains non-self-supporting, there will be an ongoing need for special economic policy support. However, the prospect of growth without special support measures must show itself gradually.

Growth Forces Continue to Prevail

It is inevitable that any examination of the last five years of economic development in eastern Germany will also give rise to questions about possible alternatives. Should monetary union have been organized and implemented differently? Did the privatization strategy make sense? Did the solution of the ownership question ("return rather than restitution") represent a hurdle to development? Would it have been possible to counter the loss of eastern European markets more energetically? Would more jobs have been saved if a more moderate wage policy had been pursued? Should economic policy support programs have paid more attention to the preservation of "industrial centers"? Hundreds of such questions could be asked, but they are all now of only historical importance. History does not brook any alternative to what actually took place.

It did not have to happen, but it did: In the first year after monetary union, when production in many sectors of the economy simply collapsed under the tremendous pressure of competition, there was so much new economic activity that the forces of growth soon prevailed. The substantial increase in gross domestic product—with an average growth rate of almost 8 percent in the period from 1991 to 1995—is the clearest proof of the dynamic development of economic activity in eastern Germany. Now, five years after monetary union, the growth process in eastern Germany has a much larger base. Immediately after monetary union, the construction industry became the prime impetus for growth. In this sector, the conditions are just right. There is a great deal of demand due to the significant need for new public infrastructure development, the shortage of business premises, and the desire to bring residential housing up to western German standards. State policy actively assists development in this area through advantageous depreciation allowances, investment incentives, favorable financing terms, and—in the public infrastructure field—the state's own orders. What has really had a positive effect on eastern Germany's production and growth is the fact that the demand for building work is largely satisfied by the eastern German construction industry itself. The service sector also found itself in a similarly favorable position. Eventually, the construction boom will come to an end when demand has been satisfied. But in the meantime, growth has also taken off in the industrial sector, so that it is no longer totally dependent on the construction and service industries.

The initial fall in overall industrial output—by an average of some 40 percent between 1990 and the beginning of 1993 and, as a result, by far more than this in a number of particularly hard-hit industries—was also accompanied by the establishment of new businesses. Moreover, there was the reorientation of privatized enterprises through investment, the development of marketable products, and the penetration of new markets. The process of "deindustrialization" eventually became a process of "reindustrialization." These efforts began to bear fruit in 1994, when industrial production began rising sharply. In 1994, output was 20 percent higher than in the previous year. In the course of the reindustrialization process, a completely different industrial sector has been created from the one that disappeared during the deindustrialization process.

Competitive Handicap

The only industries that will be able to continue and expand are those that benefit from being located in Germany and are successful in maintaining the competitiveness of their production processes. As a result, structural change means a reduction in eastern Germany's existing competitive disadvantages.

The growth process can, however, only really be satisfactory if it is self-sustaining. In other words, growth must be able to continue under its own steam—without special government assistance—based on competitive eastern German enterprises. There are clearly individual exceptions, but the overall economic development is positive; nevertheless, we must not overlook the fact that the overall level of competitiveness remains inadequate. The most important proof of a lack of competitiveness is to be found in companies' unsatisfactory export activity and the enormous disparity between imports and exports.

"Even the 'domestic' markets in eastern Germany are interregional markets..."

The export ratio (the ratio of exports—in this context, not only goods delivered abroad but also goods delivered to western Germany—to gross domestic product) has now risen slightly from a nadir of 18 percent in 1993 to a figure of 22 percent in 1995, but this is still very low. Even the "domestic" markets in eastern Germany are interregional markets (from the perspective of outside traders). Weaknesses in companies' ability to compete can also be found in this area. Compared to the domestic production of goods, the volume of imports (from western Germany and abroad) is unusually high, at 81 percent as of 1995. An inadequate export base not only means that an economy fails to produce goods that could have been sold on external markets, but it leads as well to lost production because foreign suppliers dominate the domestic market.

The Process of Underemployment

The lack of competitiveness is reflected in an extremely high trade deficit (with western Germany and abroad). Overall, low exports are balanced against high imports; in 1995, this left a trade deficit of DM 228 billion in an economy with a gross domestic product of DM 382 billion. There are therefore no grounds to alter the prognosis that eastern German enterprises are still not competitive enough, a diagnosis that is also underlined by macroeconomic observations. The shortage of real investment and human capital is growing ever smaller. There is, however, a lack of "market capital." In other words, it is important not only to produce marketable products but also to be able to sell them. Among other things, this entails experience of sales markets, trust on the part of suppliers and customers, references, and being known in the market. Penetration of supraregional markets is the basis for self-supporting economic growth.

What has been accomplished until now should not allow us to overlook the fact that the economic transformation has given rise to painful adjustment processes, particularly in eastern Germany's labor market. Essentially, this is the reason for the fading of the initial euphoria about eastern Germany's fresh start with a market economy. In fact, the eastern German labor market has been the subject of considerable upheaval, which has been of more than basic significance to the individuals concerned. The negative aspect of the transformation is the rapid loss of jobs since the fall of the Wall. The true extent of underemployment is not fully indicated by the number of registered unemployed (1.1 million people in February 1995); hidden unemployment also exists on a substantial scale (over one million people). For many of the people who have become unemployed—especially for those people who are older—there is no realistic chance of returning to the world of work. It is understandable that a society in which unemployment was never experienced as a direct threat to the individual during the decades of the GDR's existence should now demand the "right to work." But this demand is not usually directed toward obtaining work of any sort; rather, it is directed toward work of a very specific kind (if at all possible, the previous occupation), at a specific location (if at all possible, the previous place of residence), and at a specific rate of pay (if at all possible, the western German rate of pay). Another problem is that the demand for employment is far higher than it is in western Germany. In any event, until now, in eastern Germany a far greater proportion of the population of working age want to work (78 percent in 1995) than in western Germany (70 percent in the same year). Nevertheless, neither of these problems can be blamed on the transformation process as such. They are results of the conditions under which it is taking place.

Initially, wage policy played an ignominious role. It was confronted with the dilemma of fulfilling the workforce's demands for high incomes while not placing insurmountable obstacles in the path of the new market economy through excessive increases in costs. In eastern Germany, pay increases were agreed upon, at least up until 1992, that far exceeded any productivity increases in individual factories or offices, and as a result, unit labor costs increased dramatically.

Most important of all, no regard was paid to the highly differentiated economic situation of individual enterprises. The wage policy did not assist the transformation process in eastern Germany. Eastern Germany will become a "high-wage country" like western Germany, but the right path now has to be found to reach this goal. The economic preconditions for a high-wage country still have to be created. If these preconditions do not exist, the use of nominal wage increases alone would also produce a high-wage country, but only for a minority—an unacceptable number of people would be driven into unemployment.

Growth without Government Subsidies

It will be impossible to cope with the economic transformation process in eastern Germany without considerable government subsidies. An extensive program of support for economic activity played an essential role in the rapid triumph of growth forces in the struggle between degeneration and regeneration. This generally positive view of economic support programs does not ignore the fact that they can lead to individual cases of false development. After German—German monetary union, state economic support was meant to neutralize disadvantage, which was vital. In most economic sectors, investments in eastern Germany entailed significant disadvantages compared with western Germany: poor infrastructure, higher levels of environmental pollution, inexperienced public administrations, the costs of retraining employees in new areas of activity, special difficulties in obtaining financing due to the lack of established banking links, nonexistent connections between companies and established customer/supplier networks, the high cost of compensation payments to implement necessary compulsory redundancies, and the problems arising from nebulous ownership rights. Government support for economic activity was required to stimulate investment and to get the ball rolling despite these disadvantages—a goal that was achieved. The transfer payments that flow from western to eastern Germany are not a waste of resources but a necessary and effective contribution to the "*Aufbau Ost,*" or the reconstruction of the east.

> *"...eastern Germany must face the challenge of creating growth without special measures of economic subsidy and support."*

However, government assistance should not become the rule. In the final analysis, eastern Germany must face the challenge of creating growth without special measures of economic subsidy and support. However, this is not a possibility that can be realized by the end of the millennium. Special economic support measures will continue to be necessary for the foreseeable future, while the economy of eastern Germany still finds itself on shaky ground. If government support were reduced too soon, this could lead to severe economic problems. The economic process in eastern Germany is still far from self-sustaining.

Improving competitiveness is undoubtedly fundamentally the duty of the eastern German entrepreneur—and not the state. Entrepreneurs have to succeed in many areas: the development of innovative products, the optimization of operational processes, the intensification of marketing strategies, and the buildup of a network of contacts in different markets, both at home and abroad. All this depends on the ability and skill of the entrepreneur and not the state, because although the government can do a great deal, it cannot make an individual enterprise competitive.

Government support for businesses, particularly when it comes to promoting investment, continues to be necessary for the time being. In economic terms, however, it would be desirable to establish a selection mechanism to differentiate between good and bad risks. It makes very little sense, for example, to attempt to make up for a chronic lack of finance in a badly managed enterprise. Companies that have financing difficulties should only receive special financial assistance if their situation has been looked at and evaluated closely and assessed positively by a competent specialist body (one could imagine assessment committees within chambers of commerce). This is the Achilles heel of future support for companies. A realistic analysis must thus come to the conclusion that eastern Germany will continue to need special support measures for years to come.

What will the economy of eastern Germany look like in 2010? It will have merged with the economy of western Germany to such an extent that it will no longer be a separately identifiable. The whole German economy will be involved in competition with a Europe that has expanded eastward economically but where it has also opened up substantial new markets. No one can reliably predict which goods will be produced in eastern Germany or how many jobs there will be, because economic development does not follow a simple one-dimensional course just waiting to be discovered. The situation in 2010 will depend on the actions and inactions of the economic players: the entrepreneurs' intensive efforts to open new markets; the willingness of employees to confront technological transformation with further training and to take into account international competition in their demands for working conditions and pay; and the readiness of economic policy makers to devote themselves to structural change rather than to maintaining old structures. Under these conditions, there is no reason not to expect that eastern Germany will be able to come up with a competitive and powerful economy by the year 2010.

Getting Kazak Oil to Market[6]

The desert surrounding the oil field on the northern shores of the Caspian Sea is as barren as the moon. In winter, wolves roam the snow-covered plains; in summer, poisonous sand adders—nicknamed "two-step adders" because their victims can take only a few steps before the venom kicks in—slither across the sand. If the mosquitoes are not biting, it is because a sandstorm has chased them away.

Oil crops up in the most inconvenient spots around the globe—and the Tengiz oil field of western Kazakstan, from which Europe is likely to get as much as 70 million tons of oil a year in the early 21st century, is true to form. Nature has also stored Tengiz oil at considerable depths, under high pressure, and with 20 percent content of hydrogen sulfide, an invisible but lethal gas. The level of the Caspian Sea, furthermore, now only a few hundred yards from the nearest wells, is rising. When the winds are in the wrong direction, the waves lap against the flimsy sand dike built decades ago by Soviet-era oil men to protect the field.

"The powerful Russian oil and gas lobbies kept access to a trickle..."

But now the oil men are employed mainly by Western oil companies, which moved in over the past five years to exploit a resource that the Soviets had neither the money nor the expertise to develop. "I love it here," says Nick Zana, director general of Tengizchevroil (TCO), a joint venture between Chevron, Mobil, and the Kazak government, which has been pumping oil at the Tengiz oil field since 1993. "It's not all roses. But the sunsets are great, and this is a giant oil field. When it's up and running, TCO will be one of the biggest oil companies in the world—by itself!"

This is the attitude that helped Western oil producers survive the difficult years between 1991 and 1995, when they were bogged down by Russian obstructionism and bureaucratic hassles and had to put projects on hold.

The main problem was strategic: The only existing export pipeline from northern Kazakstan runs across southern Russia to the Black Sea port of Novorossiisk. The powerful Russian oil and gas lobbies kept access to a trickle, blaming capacity limitations in the busy pipeline that carries Russian oil from the Urals region and beyond. Without free access to Western markets, TCO has been unable to export more than a few million tons of oil. Last year, daily production dipped as low as 5,000 tons, compared with the peak of 90,000 tons daily planned for the next decade.

Since April, however, prospects have been transformed. The governments of Russia, Kazakstan, and Oman agreed to offer oil producers 50 percent of their stake in the Caspian Pipeline

[6]Article by Sander Thoenes and Anthony Robinson from *Financial Times* Jl 18 '96. Copyright © 1996 Financial Times Syndication. Reprinted with permission.

Consortium, which was formed to build a new pipeline from Tengiz to Novorossiisk. Chevron and Mobil, together with British Gas, Italy's Agip, two small U.S. and Kazak companies, and two big Russian companies, Lukoil and Rosneft, pledged to finance the pipeline in return for guaranteed access.

The agreement was followed by a flurry of related deals. Mobil bought half the Kazak government's remaining stake in TCO for around $1.1 billion, Royal Dutch Shell pledged to finance Rosneft's share, and Vitol, a Dutch oil trader, bought a 90-percent stake in Kazakstan's biggest oil refinery.

Detailed negotiations over the pipeline contracts are now underway. But the crucial element that unblocked the whole deal was the willingness of the Western companies who will foot the bill to concede a 44-percent stake in the project to the Russian government and the two Russian oil companies. By so doing, the oil companies recognized Russia's ability to block the project indefinitely. Meanwhile, TCO has abandoned hopes of selling all its oil on Western markets for a few years and is looking for short-term alternative markets.

Much ingenuity is involved. Crude now goes by pipeline to Lithuania and by train to Finland, and there are plans to send some by barge up the Volga River and down the Don and then to points south. The Kazak government meanwhile plans to ship its share of oil production to northern Iran in exchange for Iranian crude. The U.S. government, which forbids U.S. companies to trade with Iran, has chosen to turn a blind eye, to what its Kazak partners get up to.

Meanwhile, TCO is selling its natural gas to a nearby power plant, flaring off excess liquid gas—and working hard to find a market for the huge quantities of sulfur removed from the oil to make it transportable without corroding the pipeline. Thousands of tons of the bright yellow powder are piled up like a neon pyramid outside of the processing plant. A creative manager recently bartered some for car tires.

War Refugees Trapped by Politics of Oil[7]

It's just 30 minutes down the tracks from Zakir Abassov's abandoned dream home to the hellish place he and his 11 family members live now: a windowless boxcar on an aging Soviet freight train, with no heat, no light, and little ventilation.

But this train is going nowhere; nor are the hundreds of bedraggled Azeri families like the Abassovs who came here four years ago, among the nearly 1 million refugees who fled the fighting between Azerbaijan and Armenia over the disputed enclave of Nagorno-Karabakh.

Their road back home runs through one of the bitter, intractable conflicts that make the Caucasus Mountains politically unstable.

These ancient blood and religious feuds cast a long shadow over the ambitions of Azerbaijan and its post-Soviet neighbors on the Caspian Sea to someday rival the Persian Gulf as a world supplier of energy. The complicated political and territorial disputes that line the possible routes for getting the oil and gas out raise the stakes for the United States and other countries that wish to reduce their dependence on Middle Eastern oil.

For Azerbaijan, which has lost 20 percent of its territory to Armenian forces and where one in seven inhahitants are refugees living in squalor, the ongoing dispute over Nagorno-Karabakh is a source of potential internal strife that could undo dreams of a petroleum-generated boom.

Azerbaijan's president, Heydar Aliyev, recently told foreign dignitaries and oilmen in the bustling capital, Baku, that prosperity was just around the corner. Told of the speech, Zakir Abassov, watching as his wife baked flat "lavash" bread over a rudimentary wood stove on the tracks below his wagon, sensed a bitter irony.

"Really, we had everything we ever wanted back home," Abassov said, nodding down the tracks toward Agdam, where he owned a small café and a house until the Armenian troops overran the town in 1993. Now all he has is this wagon, with nature pictures hung on the rusty steel walls to give the place an air of inhabitability. "I don't see how oil money make this a better place to live."

The mood is no better at a sprawling refugee settlement of grubby mud huts and pathetic-looking plastic tents near Barda, which the 10,000 inhabitants sarcastically call the "Turkish Camp" for the Turkish relief agency that long ago abandoned its

---

[7]Article by David Filipov from *Boston Sunday Globe* N 23 '97. Reprinted Courtesy of The Boston Globe.

aid effort here. No one in this place heard Aliyev's speech: Electricity is one of the many things they do without, along with running water, medical care, a functioning sewer system, and a way to combat rats.

"This is a bad place, and if one person gets sick, they all do," said Elin Suleymanov of the UN High Commissioner for Refugees, which is overseeing a project to build simple limestone settlements for refugees to get people out of places like the Turkish Camp. But the refugee agency is able to target only 140,000 of the refugees from the war. On a tour last week of the regions in Azerbaijan that border Karabakh, Suleymanov pointed out scores of make-shift settlements from the Iranian border in the south to the Caucasus Mountains in the north, the lasting legacy of the conflict.

Both sides committed atrocities, human rights groups say, during the five-year shooting war over the disputed enclave of Nagorno-Karabakh, a mountainous piece of land the size of Delaware, populated by Christian Armenians but located in Muslim Azerbaijan. And although a 1994 cease-fire has held, bitter memories remain from heavy fighting that claimed some 35,000 lives and uprooted hundreds of thousands more.

Like the other dormant-but-unsolved conflicts in the Caucasus, between Georgia and separatist Abkhazia, and between Russia and Chechnya, the roots of the Nagorno-Kairabakh dispute lie in centuries of ethnic hatred that boiled to the surface as the Soviet Union collapsed.

Armenians remember the pogroms in 1990 against their ethnic kin in the Azerbaijan cities of Baku, Sumgait, and Kirovabad. Karabakh Armenians remember the first part of the heaviest fighting over the enclave when their forces were weak and their capital, Stepanakert, helplessly spent days and nights under fierce Azeri bombardment.

But when the tide turned in 1993, Armenian forces struck back with a vengeance, pushing the Azeris out of Karabakh and then occupying six regions that border the disputed enclave. As the suddenly unstoppable Armenian military machine rolled through the Azerbaijan heartland, they reportedly looted and burned villages along the way in what one senior U.S. official described to the Globe at the time as "one of the most disgusting things we've seen."

The people of Boyuk-Bakhmanli remember the day the Armenians seized their village, forcing the entire population to flee across the Arax River into neighboring Iran. The Armenians ultimately withdrew from Boyuk-Bakhmanli, after securing the entire area between Karabakh, Iran, and the Armenian border. When the villagers returned in 1995, there was nothing left of Boyuk-Bakhmanli but the skeletons of houses. Since then, families have lived in the only structures to survive, usually small, unheated stone stables no larger than the train wagons of Barda.

"Most of the wood structures were burned to the ground," said

"...bitter memories remain from heavy fighting that claimed some 35,000 lives..."

Charles Butts of Franklin, Mass., who works for the New York–based International Rescue Committee, which is overseeing the partial rebuilding of villagers' houses in the region. "The idea is to give people their self-respect back."

Now, Aliyev is trying to turn the international demand for Azerbaijan's oil into political leverage to get the rest of the occupied regions back. For the moment, the autocratic former KGB general and Communist Party leader, who has installed a personality cult, appears to have the full support of his people. But the refugees of the Turkish Camp are showing signs of impatience.

"We believe Aliyev when he says we will go home by December," said a former biology teacher from Agdam who gave only his first name, Arif. "If that does not happen, we will see."

The United States, which supported the Armenians during the war, has in the past two years embraced Aliyev and increased efforts to force Armenia to accept a compromise settlement.

These efforts may be bearing fruit. Last month, Armenian President Levon Ter-Petrosian signaled support for a peace plan, advocated by the United States, Russia, and France, under which Armenian forces would have to give up most of the land they captured outside the boundaries of Karabakh to international peacekeepers; the status of Nagorno-Karabakh would be decided later.

But the Nagorno-Karabakh government, led by Arkady Gukasian, opposes any compromise on independence from Azerbaijan. And the 170,000 Armenians in Karabakh and the occupied territories have no plans to leave. Many of them are refugees from Baku and Sumgait, places where no Armenian would dare return to live.

The dilemma in Karabakh highlights a problem of the Clinton administration's strategy in the Caucasus and Central Asia. In focusing on the economic stakes, the White House has frequently glossed over the civil strife and human rights violations that have become defining factors in the lives of most of the region's people.

Hillary Rodham Clinton, during a recent tour of Central Asia, avoided explicit reference to the dismal human rights records of resource-rich Kazakhstan, Kyrgyzstan, and Uzbekistan.

And Energy Secretary Federico Pena, in Baku this month to celebrate the first production of oil from Azerbaijan's offshore wells, praised Aliyev's role in getting the crude moving, but made no public mention of Aliyev's crackdown against opposition politicians and newspapers, or of his government's shoddy treatment of hundreds of thousands of refugees.

This omission was not lost on some Azeris who heard Pena's speech.

"The Americans put oil above everything else in the Middle East, and it got them Iran, a country where everybody hates Americans," said one Azeri official who asked not to be named. "I wonder if they are insensitive enough to do that again here?"

IV. Aid to Russia and Eastern Europe

Editor's Introduction

The four articles in this section discuss the giving of aid to the ex-Communist nations of Eastern Europe and the former Soviet Union as those countries try to become free-market democracies. While none of the writers oppose the idea of aid—all, in fact, support it—most find fault with specific approaches that have been taken.

Articles from both the conservative *Forbes* and the liberal *Nation* are critical of the billionaire George Soros's ostensibly philanthropic activities in Russia and Eastern Europe. Richard C. Morais, writing in *Forbes*, concedes the "considerable good" Soros's money has done in Hungary. Still, he questions Soros's motives for placing his foundation in Hungary in partnership first with that nation's then-Communist government and later with the left-leaning Alliance of Free Democrats. Morais theorizes that Soros has a fear of conservatism, which seems, to Soros, "a stand-in for Nazism." To Morais, such fear—and Soros's power to act upon it—are "pure poison in Eastern and Central Europe, which badly need to develop their free markets." The unsigned editorial in the *Nation* focuses on Soros's 1997 pledge of $500 million in charitable aid to Russia. The writer acknowledges the benefits that such generosity could have while also warning of its potential to "inflame the conflict between Westernizers and nationalists" in Russia. The editorial also suggests that Soros's investment activities in Russia are helping to create the very situation that his philanthropy is supposed to alleviate.

The article "Aboard the Gravy Train" first appeared in *Harper's*. In it, Matt Biven recounts his experiences as a handsomely paid employee of an American firm, Burson-Marsteller, contracted by the United States Agency for International Development (AID) to "sell the notion of free-market capitalism to the people of Kazakhstan," the former Soviet republic. Biven's essay reads like satirical fiction, as he gives a detailed account of blindness on the part of AID; waste on the part of the Burson-Marsteller employees, who were compensated with interest for every expense; and corruption on the part of Kazakhstan bureaucrats—all of which ultimately cheated both American taxpayers and the citizens of Kazakhstan, who never saw the "aid" they were promised.

In a different vein, Charles Weiss Jr., in a piece originally published in *Foreign Policy*, compares the end of the Cold War to the end of World War II. Weiss maintains that there is a need for aid to Russia and Eastern Europe, just as the Marshall Plan was needed to assist—and build good relationships with—enemies vanquished in the Second World War. Weiss points to the way Japan and Germany have emerged as prosperous nations whose ability to compete economically with the United States has benefited all involved. He also weighs the benefits of "a strong Russian government, firmly tied to the world economic and political system" against the danger of "a surly, desperate Russia." Weiss contends that, as in the case of the Marshall Plan, "effective assistance need not be expensive."

Beware of Billionaires
Bearing Gifts[1]

If you've dimly wondered what is happening in Albania, we can, in a brief sentence, explain: George Soros' friends are coming out on top.

Late in February, armed gangs led by gangsters and ex-Communists, many of them veterans of the old secret police state, all but toppled an elected liberal government, and forced the president to appoint a neo-Communist as prime minister. While this was happening, George Soros sat in his London town house and calmly told *Forbes* that his Albanian Foundation is "an excellent group very much on top of the situation."

On top is right: Soros has kept afloat a newspaper, *Koha Jone*, that egged on the coupists with inflammatory antigovernment propaganda. A pyramid scheme had collapsed, costing many people their, savings, and the Soros-supported paper effectively made a call to arms. A top official of the Soros foundation in Tirana boasted to stunned observers: "[President] Berisha's going. We got him."

In an age-old tradition of European political patronage, this multibillionaire speculator routinely taps his billions to fund journals, politicians and educators in Europe and elsewhere. More often than not, these have an exclusively left-wing bias.

Soros, 67, is Hungarian-born but a U.S. citizen. He recently caused a flutter in the February issue of the *Atlantic Monthly* by penning a windy attack on free market capitalism.

Why is George Soros so cozy with people and causes that might be expected to view his kind as parasites?

To understand his charitable works *Forbes* visited the Soros Foundation-Hungary's cream-colored villa in the hills of Budapest. Hungary is not only Soros' native land but where his charities have the longest history. There we met Miklos Vasarhelyi, the 80-year-old president of the Soros-funded foundation. This man, who dispenses millions of dollars a year in a rather poor country, has an interesting past. Vasarhelyi was press officer to Imre Nagy, the Communist Prime Minister executed in 1958 for being too independent. Vasarhelyi stood trial along with Nagy after Soviet tanks crushed the 1956 Hungarian uprising. Nagy and most others were hanged or sentenced to life. Vasarhelyi got just five years, the lightest punishment of the pack.

Thanks to George Soros, this former Communist has risen again. A political party he helped found is a partner in the pre-

---

[1]Article by Richard C. Morais from *Forbes*. Reprinted by permission of Forbes Magazine © 1997.

sent government. That government is a coalition of ex-Communists (now the Hungarian Socialist Party) and a left-liberal group, the Alliance of Free Democrats, a coalition that came to power in 1994 after defeating a rather ineffectual moderate government. Soros blessed the election results.

"These are strong, serious-minded people," he publicly said of the victorious ex-Communists. "I have great expectations in general." Not everyone agreed. One prominent foreign businessman who first considered, then rejected, doing business in Hungary, described the current government as a "bunch of clowns who haven't a clue as to how to run an economy."

Soros has since banged heads with Socialist Prime Minister Gyula Horn, but remains close to his coalition partner, the Alliance of Free Democrats. He provides many AFD leaders with income. Besides Vasarhelyi, for example, Soros' Hungarian lawyer, Alajos Dornbach, is a top-ranked AFD official and a legal adviser to the foundation.

"Soros...gives away more than $300 million through a network of 1,000 employees in 30 countries."

Soros is the great philanthropist of our age—or so his press constantly remind us. Every year, according to his flacks, he gives away more than $300 million through a network of 1,000 employees in 30 countries. When Russian scientists were starving he gave each a year's salary; he brought fresh water to besieged Bosnians; he's providing kindergartens for Gypsies. Good deeds, all.

But there is another side to the giving, a rather nutty political side. The 50 offices maintained by Soros money are spread from Haiti to Mongolia, and all claim that their works are based on philosopher Sir Karl Popper's views of tolerant, open societies. Thus a common name: Open Society Institute.

Behind the nuttiness, there is a consistency. "The people Soros hires," says Mark Almond, a respected Oxford University lecturer, "are noted for their anti-Thatcherite views. You'll be hard-pressed to find a religious dissident or staunch anti-Communist in his foundations."

Johnathan Sunley, the Budapest-based director of The Windsor Group, puts it even more strongly: "Soros is engaged in a one-dimensional ideological laundering of the old Communist/*nomenklatura* at the expense of those who didn't get trips abroad." Sunley means, of course, that real anti-Communists couldn't travel abroad in Communist days; only those in official favor could. Soros has adopted many of these formerly pampered, generally moderate Marxists.

"Soros," says Peter Bod, a former cabinet minister and central bank governor in Hungary, "is the most influential nonelected politician east of the Alps." His power stems not from the ballot box but from his bank account. He wants to see that the old left-wing dictatorships are replaced—not with free market democracies, but with left-wing democracies.

"Yes," the prickly billionaire conceded in an interview with *Forbes*, "clearly there is a political bias in the [Soros] foundation."

Look at the trustees of his U.S. foundation and you will see where the bias lies. One of them is the notorious Lani Guinier, the law professor Bill Clinton tried to nominate as head of the civil rights division of the Justice Department. Once her intemperate brand of politics was examined—such as minority veto power over legislation—even Clinton backed away from her and withdrew his support.

President of the Open Society Institute in the U.S. is Aryeh Neier, a human rights advocate who often embraces extreme liberal positions.

So be careful when you apply the term "philanthropy" to Soros' spending. Not all his causes are political, but he's clearly a would-be social engineer. You wouldn't get far in a U.S. election running on a Soros-style platform, but you might feel quite at home in a lot of U.S. universities.

But back to Hungary. Soros has been working in his native Hungary for the past 13 years. In the early 1980s he was quietly supporting dissidents in Central and Eastern Europe. it was then that the mercurial Vasarhelyi showed up at Columbia University in New York, where he met Soros. The ex-Communist hack seems to have had a considerable influence on the billionaire. With Vasarhelyi's help Soros made a deal in 1984 with the then-government. The first Soros Hungarian foundation had a budget of $3 million and was jointly run by Soros and the Communists. "One of Soros' conditions was that I should be his personal representative," says Vasarhelyi. "He had excellent judgment," says Soros, "and a good understanding of what was possible and what wasn't."

Interesting guy. Vasarhelyi's understanding of what is possible has undergone a number of changes. In 1936 and 1937 he studied political science in Rome because he thought "Italian Fascism showed the way out of an unjust society." He secretly joined the Hungarian Communist Party in 1939 and officially became a member of the Social Democratic Party. "[The Communist Party] instructed [me] to join the Social Democratic Party," he wrote in his 1989 autobiography, "to try and get ahold of key positions, but to continue following the leadership of the Communist Party.

By the late 1940s the Communists ruled Hungary and Vasarhelyi became a top-ranked "journalist" spouting pure Communist propaganda. Then he turned his coat again. By the mid-1950s, he had joined the ranks of "goulash" Communists disenchanted by Stalinism, but still in love with Karl Marx. After serving his relatively mild prison term, Vasarhelyi eventually got a job at a literature academy, was given a passport and allowed to travel. The dissidents we talked to said dissidents normally didn't get such perks. Says OSI's Neier: "We always regarded him as strongly committed to the Open Society principles, and he is held in high regard."

Everyone likes Vasarhelyi. References to him are to be found in recently released internal records of Communist Party meetings about a 1989 political demonstration. Vasarhelyi and others negotiated with the government on behalf of the dissidents. According to the records: "it is worth talking to...Vasarhelyi on whom we have influence" and "if the [speeches] get into Vasarhelyi's hands we would be able to get ahold of them." Vasarhelyi strenuously denies collaborating with the Communists.

Maybe that was wishful thinking, but it's a revealing comment nonetheless. Vasarhelyi of course no longer calls himself a Communist but neither is he a big believer in free markets. "I was and always am very critical of capitalism," Vasarhelyi tells *Forbes*.

Give Soros credit. His money does do considerable good. Between 1984 and 1989 he and Vasarhelyi helped undermine the Communist Party's control of information by trading photocopying machines to cultural and educational institutes for Hungarian currency; the currency was then used to give grants to dissidents and to writers of all political stripes.

But along the way Soros seems to have developed delusions of grandeur. He wasn't satisfied with helping end Communist totalitarianism. He wanted to decide what kind of government would replace it. In 1990 a new center-right coalition government was voted into power in Hungary which killed the Soros-government agreement. That's when the foundation began its partisan support.

Vasarhelyi denies that there is any political bias in his foundation. The Soros Foundation, for example, gives to the youth clubs and pays for Gypsy dance troupes (the Gypsies are a repressed minority in Europe).

Gabor Ivanyi is a former AFD member of parliament, and a Methodist minister who runs homeless shelters in Budapest. Last year Soros Foundation Hungary gave Ivanyi $38,000 for mattresses, an ambulance to pick up homeless who were freezing on the streets and for TB treatments. Ivanyi is a genuine man of goodwill.

But study the foundation's 1980s modus operandi and you'll see it always mixed applauded works with politically motivated projects. With Vasdrhelyi's AFD pals in power again, we found the relationship with certain sectors of government very cozy. The AFD-controlled culture ministry and the Soros foundation, for example, both subsidize periodicals. We matched the most recently published lists of subsidies and found 77% of the periodicals that got major government handouts also received subsidies from the Soros foundation. It seems to us a foundation dedicated to an Open Society would go out of its way to assist periodicals not supported by the government of the day.

How reformed are Soros' ex-Communists? Not very. A few years back, Gyorgy Litvan, a Soros friend of longstanding, a former adviser to the foundation's board and director of an institute given Soros' grants, attacked historian Maria Schmidt. She had uncovered secret police files indirectly confirming that Alger Hiss had been a Soviet spy. Her work was widely published in the U.S. and led to a Reader's Digest article in Hungary. Then she bumped into Litvan. Schmidt says Litvan lambasted her for her "mentality," and said he would do everything he could to stop her working as an academic in Hungary.

Litvan tells *Forbes* he never said such a thing, but admits he used his power to block her from making a documentary on the secret police. "I dislike her," he says. "She is on the far right." This Soros friend has an interesting idea of what constitutes "far right." It seems to be anyone to the right of Alger Hiss.

Interviewing him in London, *Forbes* asked Soros why he supports turncoats like Litvan and Vasarhelyi. His reply was—shall we say—a bit confusing. "They [as ex-Communists] know better what democracy is than perhaps those who were always opposed to [the regime]." What an insult to those true democrats who paid, sometimes with their lives, for their beliefs.

That's outrageous, typical Soros gobbledygook. Exactly what does he believe in? A utopian vision of a sort of borderless, multicultural world, where people respect one another and the well-to-do take care of the less-well-off. But Soros' friend Byron Wien, managing director of Morgan Stanley International, comes closer to the truth when he says: "Soros is terrified of right-wing nationalism."

"Soros annually pumps some $60 million into outfits in Hungary..."

Understandable perhaps in a man who spent his boyhood watching Nazis and their Hungarian supporters at work. In testimony to the U.S. Congress in 1994, Soros insisted that Eastern Europe's ex-Communists "want to get away from Communism as far as possible. Their reemergence constitutes a welcome extension of the democratic spectrum." Soros went on: "The real danger is the emergence of would-be nationalist dictatorships. They are playing in a field definitely tilted in their favor."

Thus, for Soros, a rosy glow seems to surround the left, while conservatism seems, to him, a stand-in for Nazism. That may seem relatively benign when expounded in American universities. It is pure poison in Eastern and Central Europe, which badly need to develop their free markets.

Soros annually pumps some $60 million into outfits in Hungary, among them his Central European University, whose goal is to educate an "administrative elite." Here students can not only bone up on macroeconomics but also on such American imports as feminist literary theory and how the media "constructs gender and sexuality, whether heterosexual or homosexual."

We found Soros' "cultural elite" unbelievably arrogant. A chirpy Open Society Institute press officer told us over a five-star Kempinski Hotel breakfast that she wanted *Forbes* to see what Soros "means to the little people."

Vaclav Klaus, the Czech Republic's prime minister and a tireless advocate of free markets, has a good notion of what Soros' ideas mean to "the little people." Klaus, in effect, kicked Central European University out of Prague. The no-nonsense Klaus wasn't afraid of Soros' ideas. He just didn't want Soros money buying up Czech intellectuals.

Soros returned the insult: "Klaus embodies the worst of the Western democracies." Maybe, but the Czech Republic is easily the most prosperous, modern economy in Central or Eastern Europe.

Say this for Soros: He knows his way around the law. His country foundations are usually local legal entities but often receive funds, says his New York press officer, from the New York-domiciled foundations. That's very interesting.

According to the IRS tax code, to enjoy tax-exempt status a private foundation cannot "intervene, directly or indirectly, in any political campaign on behalf of (or in opposition to) any candidate for public office...."

You can dismiss George Soros as a kooky rich man who uses his money to collect politicians and intellectuals the way some rich people collect castles and old masters. And in a way he is ridiculous, flying about the world, holding press conferences and writing books and articles that nobody can understand.

On the other hand, money can do a lot of harm in politics, especially in poor, small countries.

In Budapest in 1944 George Soros lived a double life. His father, a lawyer and editor of a journal in Esperanto (a now almost forgotten effort to develop a common language for the world), forged official papers to disguise the family's Jewish heritage. The papers saved the family, and during the Nazi occupation, when German and Hungarian fascist allies rounded up 300,000 Jews, young Soros posed as the Christian godson of a Hungarian government official. The 14-year-old George Soros sometimes found himself accompanying his supposed godfather as he seized the property of Jewish families bound for slaughter.

Heroic? No, but how many heroes are there when survival is the issue and resistance futile? It's typical of Soros that he purports to remember that time not as a terrifying ordeal but as an adventure. "The happiest year of my life," he calls it.

Read George Soros' frank personal statements and meet the billionaire in his elegant but slightly tatty London home—light switches falling out of the wall, piles of laundry on the bathroom floor—and you can't help but rather like the man. Yet sometimes the openness seems a bit phony.

Example: After George Soros challenged Europe's Exchange Rate Mechanism in 1992, becoming the "man who broke the Bank of England" and probably the first person to make $1 billion in a month, he lectured: "It behooves the authorities to design a system that does not reward speculators." Yeah, I did it, but you shouldn't have let me. It's the system. So he's a capitalist but hedges his bets by supporting socialist causes.

The key to understanding George Soros is that he skirts, by his own admission, a kind of lunacy. It's both his strong point and his weak point. "Next to my fantasies about being God," Soros told British television, "I also have very strong fantasies of being mad. In fact, my grandfather was actually paranoid. I have a lot of madness in my family. So far I have escaped it."

Just.

One bout of instability came in the early 1980s. His fund was doing extremely well when he walked away from his partner, first wife and family. It was a "very intense emotional process to correct errors [in the financial markets]," he explains. "The psychic cost of running the fund was very high. The more successful I was, the more I was punished by having more money to run."

During this turmoil Soros walked through the City of London and was convinced—wrongly—that he was having a heart attack. "It made me realize that maybe it wasn't worth it. To have a heart attack and be knocked out is really losing the game."

He spent a few years devoting himself to his intellectual and charitable interests, remarried and eventually pulled off his greatest financial coup by betting against the British pound.

Unable to resist pondering his navel, eager to dazzle with his erudition, Soros has produced several books, all impenetrable to the point where some people think he is pulling their leg. His recently published *Atlantic Monthly* article, "The Capitalist Threat," is a collection of pretentious and incomprehensible musings about capitalism, the implication being that, though he didn't mention them by name, Reagan and Thatcher were bad guys. "The article was misunderstood," he says. "I was not attacking the capitalist system. I was attacking the excesses of the capitalist system."

Oh.

When he went through his personal crisis in the early 1980s, he says he felt he was acting out the conflict between his parents. We couldn't resist asking: Are you projecting onto capitalism and the financial markets your own personal anxieties?

"Maybe so," he answered. "The insecurity I feel actually corresponds to the conditions in the market better than the equilibrium that the professors of economics deal with."

Looking into himself, Soros sees the world. Looking at the world, he sees—George Soros. Madness is close to genius.

St. George & the Kremlin[2]

Billionaire foreign policy redux: Hard on the heels of Ted Turner's September pledge to donate $1 billion to the United Nations over ten years comes financier George Soros' announcement of $500 million in charitable aid to Russia through his Open Society Institute over the next three years, dwarfing U.S. aid programs there. Soros is a complicated figure, at once patron of civil liberties East and West and speculator in Third World currencies. He leaked news of his gift to *The New York Times*, which ran a hagiographic front-page story complete with a color photo of the financier next to an infant in an incubator. The Russian reporters at Soros' Moscow press conference were less reverent, pelting him with questions about the relationship between his gift and the more than $2.5 billion he has invested in Russia's privatized state enterprises.

Those questions need to be asked. Soros' gift will not solve any national problems but could alleviate some of the fallout from Russia's collapsed infrastructure—by fighting tuberculosis, retraining career soldiers for civilian life, strengthening education. Yet it's an unprecedented intervention by a foreigner into Russian affairs. It's not hard to imagine how such intervention, no matter how well meaning, will inflame the conflict between Westernizers and nationalists, generating a ferocious political backlash.

This is all the more likely because of Soros' looming presence on Russia's political and financial scene, from his potential gain as a currency trader in the shift from old to new ruble next year to his sponsorship of Internet expansion in the former Soviet Union. Soros told reporters he hopes Moscow's banking oligarchy will start acting like "legitimate capitalists" instead of "robber capitalists," but his own Russian investment partners are some of the most rapacious "robber capitalists." This year Soros purchased 25 percent of the vast state-run Syazinvest telecommunications company in tandem with a former finance minister. Some analysts claim the company was worth considerably more than Soros and his partners paid; the deal is under criminal investigation. At his press conference, Soros made no bones about seeking even more foreign investment for Syazinvest (and admitted he had already invested in a number of Russian oil and gas companies), despite government rules restricting the next round of bidding to Russians.

In the meantime, capital flight from Russia is now estimated to be at least $2 billion a month, exceeding all foreign investments, credits and loans. If Soros' Russian partners were not stripping

---

[2]Article from *The Nation* 265:3-4 N 10 '97. Copyright © 1997 *The Nation*. Reprinted with permission.

the country of former state assets at fire-sale prices—while the Yeltsin government promotes the belt-tightening demanded by international financial institutions in thrall to advisers like Jeffrey Sachs—the country might not be in such dire straits and Soros' philanthropy might not be so badly needed.

Soros' donation, like Turner's proposed gift to the U.N., is also connected to a larger, worldwide issue: the replacement of industrial nations' foreign aid programs with reliance on transnational investment and charitable giving. In 1996 private capital flows to developing countries totaled $234 billion—four times the size of the industrial world's foreign aid programs combined. These capital flows, reported the London-based group Earthscan a few days before Soros' announcement, are "not at all focused on poverty and social needs" and in fact have exacerbated inequities within nations and internationally. And it's getting worse: the World Trade Organization's Multilateral Agreement on Investment, currently being negotiated, is expected to require government to open all enterprises to foreign investors, just as Soros is now demanding in the telecommunications deal.

Even *The New York Times* seems worried about Soros' "dual role" and philanthropist in Russia. Nevertheless, it praised him in an editorial for reflecting "American values" But when has doing business with semi-criminal oligarchs been consistent with America's values? "I have not become a player in Russian politics," Soros insisted to the press. "I have become a player in the Russian market." But in Russia, the two are inextricable—certainly in the eyes of tens of millions of Russians who will ultimately pay the price.

Aboard the Gravy Train: In Kazakhstan, the Farce that Is U.S. Foreign Aid[3]

Nina Timofeyeva, the sour-faced Russian woman who ran the St. Petersburg real-estate agency Poisk ("Search"), sat behind her desk, ignoring my accusations and cutting her fingernails. As each clipping fell, she blew on it, sending it skittering across the desktop. Some fell onto the dirty linoleum floor, others into my lap.

"I'm not going to talk to you anymore about the money," she said finally. "From now on, you talk to the Boys."

The money referred to was the apparently irretrievable $7,500 that my wife, Svetlana, and I had given Nina as a down payment on an apartment. The Boys were the unpleasant crew-cut thugs who worked for her. Or maybe she worked for them; such things are hard to determine. My wife and I had long wanted to buy a modest St. Petersburg apartment, and in the late summer of 1994 we had borrowed money and signed an agreement with Poisk. A few days later, Svetlana was summoned to Poisk for what she thought was a routine meeting—something to do with the documentation of our apartment purchase—and instead found herself alone in a tiny room with six large men—the Boys—who reminded her that they knew where we lived and where her parents lived, then demanded that she hand over *another* $7,500 or lose both the apartment and the original $7,500.

Svetlana went into hiding at her parents' summer cottage while I sought the U.S. consulate's advice on how to deal with the situation. That advice boiled down to two possible scenarios:

(a) I forget about the $7,500; or

(b) I buy a gun, hire a bodyguard, check into a hotel, and then—and *only* then—call the police.

Scenario (b) would probably unfold as follows: The cops would kick in the door at Poisk, club the Boys into submission, and demand back my $7,500. Then the cops would summon me to the precinct, where they would return, oh, say, $2,000 of our money. Then the Boys would pay me a visit.

Neither scenario appealed, so the advice I took in the end was Nina's: I talked to the Boys. Which is to say, I performed for them. I played—convincingly, I thought—the dumb foreigner, so naive that he just might pose some heretofore unthought-of threat to their operation. I waved around a government press card, sponsored by the *Los Angeles Times*. I dropped the names of big-shot cops and KGB officers. I boasted that the U.S. con-

---

[3]Article by Matt Bivens, editor of the *St. Petersburg Times*, in Russia, from *Harper's* 295:69-76 Ag '97. Copyright © 1997 Matt Bivens. Reprinted with permission.

sulate was already aware of their activities and would "take steps" if my wife or I were hurt.

Soon they had warily agreed to return our money; their reasoning seemed to be that for $7,500, it was not worth the trouble either to kill me or to ignore me. But as the days went by, they came up with excuse after excuse, and Svetlana and I began to accept the idea that we would never see the money again. We sensed that we had come to the end of that happy period during which a couple can live comfortably on the modest income of a freelance journalist. Now we needed money.

So I turned to the Dark Side of the Force. I applied for a job in public relations.

I had heard of an opening in Almaty, Kazakhstan, with the New York–based Burson-Marsteller, the world's largest public relations agency, and although I once would have scoffed at the idea of working in P.R., I quickly convinced myself that this posting would be different: Burson-Marsteller was working under a contract from AID—the U.S. Agency for International Development—and this meant that I would be helping the Kazakhstanis, not shilling for some corporation.

In Kazakhstan, as throughout the Soviet Union on the day in 1991 that it collapsed, the government owned everything—not only the telephone system and the factories but every barbershop, every gas station, every bakery. As if to underscore this fact, businesses did not even have names, just numbers—Bakery No. 1, Bakery No. 2, and so on. The government of newly independent Kazakhstan vowed to put these concerns back into private hands, and the United States Congress sent help: AID contracted corporations such as Ernst & Young and Deloitte & Touche to offer economic and legal advice on how, exactly, one goes about privatizing an entire nation, and it brought in Burson-Marsteller as well. As described in an outline of U.S. assistance programs in Kazakhstan, published by AID in 1994, Burson-Marsteller's task was to ensure that "the Kazakhstanis understand the privatization process and participate actively in it." In other words, Burson-Marsteller was to sell the notion of free-market capitalism to the people of Kazakhstan. That meant pro-privatization TV commercials, newspaper ads, and press conferences; it meant developing a logo—a galloping Pegasus wrapped in the word "privatization!"—and plastering it on billboards and city buses; it meant courting the local press; it meant keeping people informed about how to buy shares in corporations and when the auctions would be held for barbershops and bakeries.

I knew nothing of P.R. and little of privatization. But I was an American, I spoke good Russian, and I was willing to leave St. Petersburg on short notice. A single phone call to Burson-Marsteller's Washington, D.C., office landed me the job.

The next day Nina and the Boys paid me back, minus $250 for their "services."

With the money returned, the pressure to leave journalism was off, and I thought briefly about turning down the P.R. job. But there was really no turning back now; Burson-Marsteller had made me an offer I couldn't refuse: $53,518 a year after taxes, insurance benefits, free housing, a driver, a maid, a $2,000 moving allowance, and an additional $25 per diem ($9,000 a year) in spending money. All told, a $70,000-a-year package; after only a few months, it would grow to $90,000. I was twenty-six.

The main event of every day was lunch. Lunch was always at a fancy restaurant, with your driver waiting out front. More than thirty-five U.S. companies or organizations were on the AID payroll in Kazakhstan, offering advice on everything from drafting laws to wearing condoms, and every single one of them seemed to be as high on lunch as Burson-Marsteller was. The hours before and after lunch were generally a blur of meetings between consultants, consulting companies, consortia of consulting companies, and groups of consortia of consulting companies. Fridays I would retrieve a crumpled ball of business cards from my suit-coat pocket and incorporate them into a memo summarizing my work week: Monday met with so-and-so, discussed such-and-such. Tuesday met with such-and-such of the this-and-that group. Mostly I was describing lunch.

My co-workers turned out to be young Americans like myself with humanities degrees. In the States, we would have struggled to distinguish ourselves from thousands of applicants for entry-level jobs. Here, we were expert consultants to a foreign government, with hefty salaries and lofty titles. I was the National Media Coordinator. My main duty was to run the Kazakhstan Press Club. I also administered a TV show, a couple of radio shows, and a smaller Burson-Marsteller office that bought newspaper and radio ads, but I was told to concentrate on the press club.

A good part of my training consisted in looking through the files left by my predecessors, and from those files I learned, for example, that Burson-Marsteller had a "cost-plus" contract with AID, which was a fairly standard deal: AID would reimburse all of the costs we incurred, "plus" pay about 7 percent on top of that—our profit margin. In other words, the more we spent the more we earned. Here was a receipt for thousands of blue shopping bags emblazoned with the yellow Pegasus logo. (The bags themselves choked the closets and corners of our office. Unaware of their significance—they were, after all, a gift from the American people to the people of Kazakhstan—I had taken hundreds home for use as trash-can liners.) And here were other receipts, for billboards, key chains, and even watches, all sporting the privatization Pegasus. Meaning that all of it was foreign aid, earnestly referred to by Burson-Marsteller as "educational material."

Many of the files concerned the press club itself, which had opened days before my arrival to positive coverage in the

Kazakhstani press. Burson-Marsteller had come up with the idea, then convinced AID to fund it. I came across a pair of unusually candid internal Burson memos discussing how to sell AID on "the Cadillac of all press clubs." One was titled "What Makes Ed Happy," Ed being a man at AID with clout. "I think...we can grow this to a rather pretty little business," mused a predecessor.

AID does fund programs to help former Soviet journalists, but Burson-Marsteller had no such contract. What it did have was a broad mandate to build support in Kazakhstan for free markets, and so the pitch for the press club blurred ideas such as capitalism, democracy, and free speech into a single blotch of "good American things that good people ought to support." It worked. Soon Burson-Marsteller was raking in the cost-plus on a press club decked out with a computer and laser printer, monster TV, video recorder, satellite dish, and subscriptions to CNN, MTV, the *Wall Street Journal-Europe*, and the *International Herald Tribune*. In addition to being a rather pretty little way to spend U.S. tax dollars, the club provided Burson-Marsteller with ready access to local journalists, who were taught, through the club's events and publications, that all of the *best* journalists supported privatization. The company's connection to the club was never concealed, but neither was it volunteered or explained. If Kazakhstan's journalists asked about the club's origins and mission, we would answer that it was aid from America, a gift from the same friendly people who had brought them Radio Liberty and the Voice of America.

For me, the club presented a plausible excuse to escape the main Burson office and relax before (or after) lunch. The club's wooden chairs were somewhat uncomfortable, though, so I sent my staff out shopping for stuffed armchairs, which I assumed were being billed to the U.S. government, along with everything else. I was part of the team.

Kazakhstan is an ecological disaster, with oil reserves, wedged between Siberia and China. It is the home of the Semipalatinsk nuclear testing range—the Soviet answer to the Nevada flats— and the Virgin Lands agricultural campaign launched by Nikita Khrushchev, in which millions of acres of pastureland were over-plowed into dusty worthlessness.

National Geographic has suggested that Ust Kamenogorsk, a small city in northern Kazakhstan, may be the most frightening-ly polluted city in the former Soviet Union. Ust, as the locals call it, is just a two-hour drive from the Semipalatinsk nuclear test site. It is also the home of industrial giants such as the Ublinsky Metallurgical Works, where, according to Greenpeace, an explosion of some sort in the late 1980s coated the city with a fine film of zinc dust. Citywide nosebleed epidemics that stop as sudden-ly and inexplicably as they start are common.

Newspapers in Ust were overcharging us for ads about privatization. This was actually to our profit, but the naive young

American stationed there, not accustomed to Cost-Plus Think, felt it ought to change. A seminar, we reasoned, could wow locals into a new respect for Burson-Marsteller and the U.S. government, after which we would get drunk together, become friends for life, and ad rates would go down.

Seminars are the bread and butter of the foreign-aid community. They can be billed as "training," and training the locals is very fashionable at AID. More important, seminars produce "deliverables"—a deliverable being any physical proof of our work. Examples of deliverables from a seminar include written agendas and programs, local media coverage, and carefully composed photographs: serious Kazakhstanis at desks in a classroom; wise Americans leaning on overhead projectors; racially mixed groups of happy Russians and ethnic Kazakhs engaged in solving happy imaginary problems; post-seminar Americans, Russians, and Kazakhs drinking to international friendship. All of it—photographs, agendas, news clippings—goes into a box delivered to AID in Washington, D.C. Deliverables are the sole benchmark by which AID evaluates success or failure.

"Deliverables are the sole benchmark by which AID evaluates success or failure."

Burson-Marsteller was always rich in deliverables, but we still loved seminars. Battling the logistics energized the whole office, and seminars provided valuable evidence of our expertise—for how better to prove that someone is an expert than to feature him as a speaker?

As National Media Coordinator, I was slated to speak. This would not be the first time. Some weeks back, my boss, George Nikolaieff, had decided to hold a seminar at the press club for our workers in the regions outside Almaty. I suggested a talk on journalistic ethics, which George thought was a fine idea. Then I learned that I would be addressing, among others, journalists paid a Burson-Marsteller salary to orchestrate positive news coverage of privatization. When the day arrived, Almaty's real journalists were shooed away from the press club and the doors were locked. Introduced in glowing terms as a journalist published by the *Los Angeles Times* and the *Associated Press*, I stood up, gave a vague, noncommittal speech, and sat back down. I wondered briefly how I would answer if anyone asked about the ethics of a journalist taking money from a foreign P.R. company to praise the government, but it never came up.

Nikolai Ushkov, the hard-drinking editor of his own newspaper in Semipalatinsk, made the two-hour drive along snowy, decrepit roads to witness my next attempt to hold forth on "ethics" and "integrity." He did not think much of it. As he said at the seminar, and elaborated on after a few shots of vodka at the evening banquet, my insistence that journalists not take money from businessmen in return for favorable news coverage was incorrect. "I don't like taking money for hidden advertisements," he said. "But I need to."

The local authorities in Semipalatinsk had already crushed Ushkov's first newspaper, *Slovo* ("The Word"), with an oppressive tax on advertising. Backed by a local businessman, Ushkov launched a second paper, *Novoe Slovo* ("The New Word"), but a few mornings after Ushkov reported that modestly paid local officials were somehow able to afford palatial homes in the suburbs, that same businessman turned up crying: he'd been visited by the tax inspector. Ushkov had come to our seminar with hopes of hearing how he could get financial backing; instead, he heard me.

The morning after the banquet, as we treated our hangovers Semipalatinsk-style—alternating glasses of cheap red wine with glasses of cheap instant coffee at a rate of about a glass every three minutes—Ushkov told me frankly what he needed: money. I gave him the phone number for the Eurasia Foundation. The Eurasia Foundation does what most people probably think of as foreign aid: it gives small grants (usually less than $50,000) for concrete projects. But when I called some days later to catch up, Ushkov told me that *Novoe Slovo* had been shut down. "The [oblast governor] doesn't let me run my newspaper. He says, 'Yes, you tell the truth, and I like that to an extent. But to another extent...'"

"Did you call the Eurasia Foundation?" I asked.

"I got some very polite documents from them; they even sent me a brochure. But they said that since I am a commercial newspaper, I couldn't receive a kopeck," he said. Noting that the Eurasia Foundation didn't seem to believe that his paper wasn't turning a profit, Ushkov apologetically hastened to blame himself: "I probably didn't fill out the forms correctly."

After my encounter with Ushkov, I began to look more critically at what I was doing. I realized that for a negligible sum— far less than half of my yearly salary—Ushkov could be the kind of journalist he deserved to be and Semipalatinsk Oblast could have a real newspaper. Instead, we wasted his time, and then bragged about it to the U.S. government, which paid us to do it all over again.

And yet...I was making more money, and working less, than I ever had before. I had plenty of time to spend with Svetlana, and we had decided, in the first flush of financial security, to have a child. And so I resigned myself to being one of those useless yet well-paid people—wedding coordinators, dog psychologists, and the like—who clutter the earth doing, well, doing nothing. I told myself I could live with that, for now.

George asked me along to a meeting with Sarybay Kalmurzayev, the chairman of the State Property Committee. Kalmurzayev was the government's top privatization official, a tyrant who held the veto over everything we did. That day we needed Kalmurzayev's approval on some television ads.

I had hoped to see a hard sell: a team of executives oozing American self-confidence, an exchange of business wit. Instead, Kalmurzayev shouted and we groveled. We sat meekly through a vague tirade about our incompetence. Then, when Kalmurzayev began ticking off demands, we perked up and scribbled furiously on legal pads.

Demand: *An end to all polling and sociological research.*

Kalmurzayev had seen a newspaper poll indicating that Kazakhstanis mistrusted privatization, so all of sociology had to go. He may have had something there. We had spent thousands of AID dollars on polls of our own but let no one see the results—not even AID. Too often the findings suggested that our propaganda campaign was failing.

Demand: *A seminar for Kalmurzayev and his workers on the principles of advertising and P.R.*

"You're always holding seminars to help journalists, but what about us?" he yelled. "We need training, too!"

Demand: *Lots—no, millions—of pocket calendars.*

"Local officials were naturally disconcerted by the arrival of all these well-intentioned foreigners..."

When he had finished scribbling, George announced that we would be happy to spend U.S. taxes to print pocket calendars and to teach Kalmurzayev's Soviet-trained bureaucrats all of Madison Avenue's tricks. When co-workers later asked in shocked if hushed tones why we were spending $69,000 on five million pocket calendars for a country whose total population was just seventeen million, George played what he considered a trump card: "Kalmurzayev personally requested it."

As I considered this logic, I remembered a story about the earliest days of the American humanitarian aid mission to Almaty. Like many of the new post-Soviet states, Kazakhstan had gladly accepted offers of U.S. aid. But instead of money, America sent hundreds of consultants like me. Local officials were naturally disconcerted by the arrival of all these well-intentioned foreigners with their fancy clothes, loud voices, and bad Russian. So to smooth things over, a party was planned: the Americans and Kazakhstanis would whoop it up at a water theme park.

George wore a pair of red swimming trunks that day. Those trunks caught the eye of a local bureaucrat, who suggested a trade: his ratty Soviet shorts for George's snazzy red trunks. George declined. The bureaucrat got angry: he wanted those trunks. George began to realize that having an enemy in the local bureaucracy could jeopardize Burson-Marsteller's lucrative U.S. government contract. There was nothing left to do, he recounted to me sheepishly, but take off his pants and hand them over.

Back at the press club, I popped the pilot of our soap opera, *Iskateli Schastya* ("Seekers of Happiness"), into the VCR and settled into one of my armchairs. I had once naively asked George how a soap opera could be considered foreign aid. His answer: "It's not a soap opera, it's social engineering."

The six-part miniseries, set and filmed in Almaty by a production company called Ulkiza, follows two fictional families—one Russian, one Kazakh—who are thrown together by circumstance, become partners, and together achieve a certain level of economic security. Along the way, privatization is shown in a glowing light. In the violent opening scene, two thieves (part of an action subplot) sneak into a museum and spray some sort of aerosol in a guard's face. When Kalmurzayev saw this he hated it. "Why are you scaring people with your soap opera?" he yelled.

I myself preferred earlier drafts of Ulkiza's script, as described to me by an American colleague who had vetoed them. They featured nuclear submarines surfacing in the ocean and fire-breathing dragons swooping down from the skies, and were much too ambitious ever to be filmed. One episode merits a fuller description: The Kazakh and Russian families decide to build a simple house but can't figure out how. Suddenly a hot-air balloon soars into view. The balloon has "Soros Foundation" emblazoned on it. It lands. Americans leap out of the basket, build the house, and sail away. The Kazakhstanis wave and cheer.

Anyone working for AID in Kazakhstan, directly or indirectly, was entitled to a $94 per diem on top of his or her salary. The Latin term is pure Duckspeak: only through euphemism can one argue that generously paid people deserve an additional $94 every day, including weekends (or $34,310 a year)—just for the hell of it. We at Burson, however, were not getting the full AID-mandated $94; our per diem was a mere $25. AID had allocated the money, but Burson-Marsteller had refused to claim it for us. The reasoning here was that all per diems dropped to around $25 on days spent outside of Almaty, and Burson merely wanted to protect us from the stress of an income that fluctuated with travel. In other words, the company assumed that we would prefer to make about a fourth of what we could in return for knowing exactly how little that amount would be.

My fellow young Americans and I held a secret meeting. We wanted the $94 per diem. We discussed the possibility of a strike but opted instead for a quieter barrage of memos and faxes. It succeeded, and it felt strangely good: we had set a specific goal, worked toward it, and achieved it in an empirically measurable way. For the first time since my arrival, I felt like a real doer.

Then things turned ugly.

With George away on vacation, and me left in charge, a $75,000 wire transfer from the States got lost between banks. Ad agencies came to be paid; we asked for their patience. Newspaper ads were scheduled to go out; we asked editors to carry the ads on credit. Then Mirhat Nigmatulin came by. A short, dark man with a mustache, always in a black overcoat and a black fedora, Nigmatulin was the very picture of the sleazy Soviet bureaucrat: Boris from "Rocky and Bullwinkle." He was Kalmurzayev's press secretary. We had dubbed him "Pig-matulin," and one of my predecessors had placed a doll of a pig in a dress above the office door to represent him.

Nigmatulin was furious. He stood beneath the pig in the dress and screamed. What was this about us having no money? Did we know that we owed the Butya ad agency—an agency Nigmatulin had *personally* recommended—about $3,000? (How did he know this?) Or that we owed Atamura—the privatization-committee press—$69,000 for the five million pocket calendars they had printed? We owed him $69,000! Where was it?

The Atamura contract was in the files. In addition to the printing and paper costs, Atamura had included an author's fee, presumably for the five-sentence text exhorting citizens to support privatization; office rent; storage; transport; banking services; a "labor fund"; medical insurance; "social" insurance; and a road-building fund. An additional 5 percent of this running total was added for an "investment fund." Then an additional 10 percent of the new total was added for "rush printing." Then 10 percent of *that* was added as Atamura's profit margin. Grand total: $69,000. Where was it?

Olga Kim, Burson's locally hired accountant, had been complaining for weeks about Atamura's bizarre charges. Since when, she asked, did printing a calendar also involve building a road, or insuring the printer's employees, or paying their office rent? George had told her to drop it. But, as she was quick to point out, this week George was gone, and I was the boss.

I was still gaping at the contract when Olga laid the phone bill out in front of me and solved a small mystery: Although we paid the bill religiously, the phone company had briefly cut off our service in September, October, November, and December. Why? Because we paid our phone bills through Kalmurzayev's office, and *he* hadn't paid the bill. An exasperated Olga had gone directly to the phone company with our November bill of $6,662.40—only to learn that Kalmurzayev's office had padded in $4,309.75 of fictitious charges. When Olga challenged Kalmurzayev's accountant about this, he had sneered, "What, are you with us or with them?"

After learning this, and in the wake of Nigmatulin's visit, the last person I wanted to see was Kalmurzayev, but I had some more TV commercials that needed his approval. These ads, filmed by an agency called Charm, were silent shorts in the style of Charlie Chaplin (Stalin's favorite), spoofing government-run businesses and then showing those same businesses under new and idealized private ownership. In one, a sullen woman at a Soviet dry cleaner accepts a suit coat, ditches the cigarette dangling from her lips, dons a gas mask, and disappears for hours. She returns with the wrong coat, and again with the wrong coat, and again, until finally the customer gets his coat, shrugs it on, and storms out, an iron mark burned into the back.

It was the iron mark that Kalmurzayev cited in vetoing the ad. "They never left iron marks on your back at the Soviet dry cleaner," he said, and then came out from behind his desk to take my arm. Examining the sleeve of my tweed suit coat, he found a thread and began to tease it. "No, the strings would be all loose and frayed, and they'd start coming out, like this."

We began to argue. I noted that the ad was a farce—no one wore gas masks at the dry cleaner, right?—and suddenly Kalmurzayev was screaming that we owed Atamura $69,000 for the pocket calendars. "You owe us $69,000!" We owed Butya, an agency he had *personally* recommended, $3,000! What business did we have using an incompetent ad agency like Charm when we hadn't even paid Butya? We should have hired Butya instead! We were paying tens of thousands for a soap opera, but we had hired an incompetent director! Where did we find that awful Ulkiza company? "All of Kazakhstan is laughing at you! Why didn't you ask me?" he said. Naming a prominent figure in Kazakhstan's film industry, Kalmurzayev demanded that we reshoot the soap opera under that man's direction. Moreover, Kalmurzayev stated, from now on he himself would decide whom Burson hired to produce ads and shows. I started to reply, but Kalmurzayev turned and left. End of interview.

Back at the office, Olga handed me Burson-Marsteller's contract with Ulkiza. We were paying a whopping $110,000 for the soap opera, or $18,333 per episode—an outrageous amount. (By contrast, the economic news program I was in charge of cost us only about $1,200 per episode.) But Ulkiza's director was probably splitting the loot with friends in the office of Nursultan Nazarbayev, the president of Kazakhstan. It was thus best to let Ulkiza overcharge us, not merely for the cost-plus but because it was worth courting the goodwill of anyone with such powerful friends. It was a red-swimming-trunks situation.

Let us suppose that Burson's AID contract is up for extension (as it soon would be). AID sends a man to check things out. He visits, say, Kalmurzayev. What do they talk about? Probably the AID man asks Kalmurzayev for an "honest assessment": Who among the Americans is doing good work? Kalmurzayev cries, Burson-Marsteller! They are doing crucial work, saving our economy! Give them more money!

And that is exactly what AID does.

Weeks later, when asked to document his expenses with receipts, the soap opera director took deep offense. He would do no such thing, he said. Fear of the tax inspector would keep his employees from admitting that they had received such high salaries. When Olga pressed him, he grudgingly suggested that his employees might own up to having received a *tenth* of their stated salaries. It was an awkward moment: the man had effectively admitted to stealing not only from us but from his own employees. This was later confirmed when Olga interviewed the actors, some of whom broke into sobs when they learned how much they were supposedly being paid.

Yes, almost everyone was winning: young Americans with fat paychecks, corporations with fat contracts, bureaucrats fattened by theft. Only those involved abstractly were losing: the American taxpayer, whose altruism had been twisted; and the

"Fear of the tax inspector would keep his employees from admitting that they had received such high salaries."

Kazakhstanis, who were seeing Soviet corruption thrive on American aid. Congress sets aside billions; AID gives it to Americans. Proud U.S. government spokesmen inform the Kazakhstanis that they will soon benefit from millions of dollars in aid. Instead, they are saddled with hundreds of American "experts," and to the humiliating injury of publicly receiving humanitarian aid is added the insult of not even getting it. Feeling cheated, the bureaucrats scheme, and soon they are steering what's left of the foreign aid toward friends or relatives or themselves.

I recall a grim breakfast at the home of William Courtney, the U.S. ambassador to Kazakhstan. The Republicans had swept Congress, and Jesse Helms was grousing about the bottomless "foreign financial ratholes" (e.g., my Maryland checking account) into which AID was shoveling money. Courtney, troubled by privatization's plodding pace and low reputation, called for radical suggestions from the sixty-odd "experts" gathered there. We discussed, among other options, covertly lobbying the program's opponents in Kazakhstan's parliament. At one point, Courtney asked, "Should we shut privatization down? Or shut it down in half of the country, as a demonstration?"

I wondered how the American ambassador would do that—shut down another government's number-one domestic policy.

The United States Information Service official then made an announcement: "There's someone from ABC News in town, so please be careful who you talk to!"

This anxious plea could be AID's motto. When senior AID staff in Washington discussed how to fend off congressional hostility, they concluded that dishonesty was the best policy. Notes from the meeting describe their strategy as "delay, postpone, obfuscate, derail." Months after that memo was made public, AID spokesman Jay Byrne still refused to criticize it or to back away from the tactics it called for. "We have a very clear strategy with regard to the [hostile] legislation, and that is to defeat it," he explained to the *Washington Post*.

Titillating tales of foreign-aid idiocy have been trickling into Washington for years. Lawrence Pope, the U.S. ambassador to Chad, once intervened to keep AID from funding a study on "Viability of the Chadian State." In a State Department cable, he wondered, "What exactly would we have done if they concluded that it wasn't [viable]?" The *Moscow Times* has reported that AID spent $200,000 in 1994 to renovate an apartment for the organization's director for Russia. It has spent money promoting Haiti as a relocation destination for companies tired of shelling out the U.S. minimum wage. It has used American tax dollars to build pay toilets in Indonesia and to advertise golf courses in Ireland. Given the ludicrous nature of such projects, it is little wonder that the organization respects its own privacy; and Burson-Marsteller, which has downplayed everything from the *Exxon Valdez* spill to the Bhopal disaster to Argentina's Dirty War, is well equipped to serve in this regard.

Friday was dress-down day at the office, but some of us started earlier in the week. So on the day the AID auditor arrived in a three-piece pinstriped suit, looking serious and white and mid-fifties and patrician, I was in jeans, and my female twenty-something colleagues were dressed for after-work aerobics and jogging. He must have been surprised at our youth, assuming, of course, he'd seen our salaries.

He first interviewed our business manager, Naya Kenman, a woman in her twenties wearing a gray sweatshirt and black shorts over tights. They had barely begun when a co-worker strolled in, picked up the telephone, dialed fourteen digits, and said, "Mommy? Hi, it's me!" The auditor's eyebrows rose. Naya spoke more loudly and tried to draw his attention to the hardships we had imposed on ourselves in the name of cost-efficiency. She explained how Burson-Marsteller had arranged with DHL to send a twice-monthly package from Washington, because consolidating all mail was much cheaper than sending documents piecemeal.

On cue, the DHL man arrived, a huge package in his arms. In his wake was another co-worker, clapping excitedly. "It's my L.L. Bean clothes, they're here!" she cried, tearing into the package to pull out a sweater and a parka. Other colleagues, unaware of the auditor, rushed to see if their orders had come in, too. I hoped our man from Ust Kamenogorsk wouldn't start talking about the Soloflex he was planning to order from the States, though he at least intended to pay for shipment.

George then joined the audit interview. The auditor asked about a letter given AID contractors that allowed us to fly for reduced rates on the government airlines. How much, he asked, was this saving taxpayers? Very much, answered Naya, and then she put forth an illustration: "For example, I'm taking a vacation, flying part of the distance inside Kazakhstan on a cheap ticket, and I'm saving hundreds!" To the auditor's queer expression, George added, "She probably shouldn't be doing that, should she?"

No, the auditor said, she shouldn't.

Despite all this, the interview lasted only about an hour. There was no painstaking examination of documents, no double-checking the math or the bids. Nothing came of it, nor of the memos that I and others (including Naya) eventually wrote to our superiors. According to a 1996 report by JNA Associates, a consulting firm studying AID's work in the former Soviet Union, no omnibus AID contract has ever had a full financial audit.

Shortly thereafter, I quit. The *Los Angeles Times* had offered me a job covering the war in Chechnya, for a salary that was about one-third what I was making in Kazakhstan. Svetlana and I discussed it for all of ten minutes before we decided. Burson-Marsteller wished me well and offered, should I change my mind, to take me back. They have since made overtures to hire me on three separate occasions, to work in either Almaty or Moscow.

Those offers have not been entirely unattractive: I liked many of the people I worked with at Burson, and the company always treated me fairly. We made some wonderful new friends in Kazakhstan, took French lessons and tennis lessons and drawing lessons, traveled around the world, ate out every night, and still banked about $4,000 every month. That's not bad.

But then there are the red swimming trunks. When I think of them I see the American foreign-aid mission for the farce that it is, and I know I've made the right decision. All three of the principal actors are here, cast in truth's cruel light: the grasping bureaucrat, who can be fun to pal around with but is usually after something; the American consultant, whose first loyalty is to his corporation and who sees keeping the locals fat and happy as the best measure of success. And hovering over both is AID, ready to award its multimillions once the swimming trunks are handed over. Foreign adviser and local bureaucrat, American and Kazakhstani zip past each other on the water slides, laughing and waving and pledging eternal friendship, playing nice for befuddled old Uncle Sam, who smiles and waves back and keeps on sending the money.

Eurasia Letter: A Marshall Plan We Can Afford[4]

The June 1997 commencement at Harvard University will mark exactly 50 years since the address by Secretary of State George Marshall that launched the Marshall Plan. That plan laid the cornerstone for both the economic and political recovery of Western Europe after World War II and the ensuing decades of peace and prosperity. This anniversary coincides with the shaping of a new postwar world, one that may well determine the course of the next 50 years.

Looking back 50 years to today, what will our children and grandchildren say about our response to the fall of the Soviet empire? Why, they will ask, did we rush to return to "normalcy" after the Cold War when we knew that a similar pattern after World War I had led to catastrophe? Why did we not follow the pattern set after World War II of helping defeated enemies back to their feet and integrating them into the international political and economic structure?

Why, in short, did the world not help Russia and the other nations of the former Soviet empire to provide a decent life for their citizens and to rejoin the family of nations?

Altogether, the United States and Europe spent some $107 billion on aid to former communist countries from 1990 to 1994, an amount that is actually greater than the inflation-adjusted value of Marshall Plan assistance. But much of this aid was either in the form of tied trade credits or shackled with other conditions that rendered it minimally effective. In any event, the history of the Marshall Plan shows that more important than money is a clearly articulated, high-profile commitment from government, business, and labor, backed by the broad involvement of the general public. This commitment shows concern, inspires confidence, and focuses assistance on the needs of the recipients rather than on the self-interest of the donors.

One small part of the Marshall Plan—the productivity assistance program—offers a remarkable, inexpensive, and little known precedent that even today can send a clear message to the people of Russia, Eastern and Central Europe, and Central Asia of the West's commitment to their recovery. It can show the people of these nations that democracy and free markets can give them a better life and are worth the sacrifice. A program of productivity-oriented study tours—modeled on the productivity assistance program—would have the added benefit of letting large numbers of ordinary Americans come into contact with

---

[4]Article by Charles Weiss, Jr., lecturer at the Paul H. Nitze School of Advanced International Studies at Johns Hopkins University, and president of Global Technology Management, Inc. from *Foreign Policy* 106:94-109 Spr '97. Copyright © 1997 by Carnegie Endowment for International Peace. Reprinted with permission.

people from former communist countries who are working against great odds to create honest businesses and democratic institutions. Such tours would tap into America's latent idealism and help to counter the indifference voters now feel toward foreign affairs.

A Disaster Waiting to Happen

The disastrous situation in Russia and most of its former empire is too obvious to ignore. An unfettered free market, unsupported by institutional infrastructure, has left the new "transitional" countries with widespread poverty and despair; large numbers of unpaid workers and military personnel; mafia control of key sectors of the economy; a small, disreputable class of newly rich whose wealth is based mostly on theft and asset stripping; and an impoverished and disgruntled military that is unable to perform elementary security functions. The initial wave of enthusiasm for the West has been replaced by pervasive distrust.

"Nor is it in America's interest that Russia remain internally weak."

No great power, however humbled, is likely to permit such a situation to continue. The United States should expect that Russia will reconsolidate and regain at least some of its former strength and should prefer that it do so under a government that is reasonably friendly to the West. Nor is it in America's interest that Russia remain internally weak. Surely there are few greater threats to the world's geopolitical security than a prolonging of the current political weakness and economic disorder in a country that has thousands of nuclear weapons and that stores under primitive conditions tons of weapons-grade plutonium derived from decommissioned weapons. Surely there are few threats to environmental security more important than the absence of effective government in a country that covers a ninth of the Earth's land surface and is home to a still larger fraction of its most serious environmental trouble spots.

Russia and the countries of Eastern and Central Europe and Central Asia face political, economic, and social transformations that will be much more far-reaching than were changes in Western Europe following World War II. But the risks of failure at the end of the Cold War are as serious as they were at the end of each of the two world wars. Despite the reelection of Boris Yeltsin, Russia may yet sink back into its historic sullen hostility, prompting higher Western defense budgets and an increased potential for geopolitical and environmental mischief.

Current strategy is based on the self-fulfilling proposition that Russia is beyond the West's influence and is likely to remain hostile to the West and to its own neighbors. The West plans to extend NATO to the Polish-Russian border, to build up reform-minded states, Ukraine, and the Baltics as best it can, and to leave Russia and the rest of Eastern Europe and Central Asia to their own devices.

In short, the United States plans to stand back while one of several readily foreseeable disasters unfolds in Russia: the rise of a weak, adventurist government under Vladimir Zhirinovsky or some more sophisticated nationalist; the recovery of Russian political unity under a militaristic, hostile government bent on revenge and the reestablishment of a Russian empire; or the continuation of a feeble government unable to prevent the removal of fissile material from poorly protected sites in an increasingly impoverished military-industrial complex.

Does the United States really want Russia to succeed? Would it prefer that Russia remain a weak, unstable power, unable to defend its economic and political interests or to provide the basic necessities for its citizens? I would argue that America has less to fear from the missiles of a strong Russian government, firmly tied to the world economic and political system, than from the possibility of self-destructive behavior from a surly, desperate Russia, from an accidental missile attack due to a lack of command and control, or from the diversion of nuclear weapons to a rogue nation or terrorist group. The world has less to fear from a "second China" than from a "Weimar Russia with nukes."

Or does America perhaps fear creating a new Japan? Would we be better off today if the Marshall Plan had not succeeded and the U.S. economy dominated those of Western Europe and Japan the way it does those of Latin America? After all, Japan and Western Europe may be America's most important competitors, but those countries are also America's most important markets. America sells more agricultural exports to well-off people than to poor ones and more computers to sophisticated industries than to backward ones.

And true to the tenets of trade theory, our foreign competitors are blessings in disguise. They provide us with cheap clothes, good cars, and VCRs, and they help to keep our own industries sharp. For example, Japanese manufacturing technology, absorbed by the United States in response to competitive pressures, has greatly contributed to the growth in American manufacturing productivity. As for employment, the export of low-productivity jobs to Mexico or the Far East makes it possible to keep high-paying managerial and technical jobs here. America's problems of under- and unemployment are rooted in its schools, not its foreign trade.

Can We Afford to Make a Difference?

The Marshall Plan productivity assistance program, now largely forgotten, showed that effective assistance need not be expensive. This program brought 24,000 West Europeans and later several thousand Japanese, Koreans, Taiwan Chinese, and others to America for four- to six-week study tours. These guests saw for themselves how American businesses were run and how production was organized. These productivity tours brought about immediate increases in the productivity of West European firms, enabling them to show European consumers that a market economy can improve their lives. The cost was low: about 1.5 per cent of the cost of Marshall Plan capital assistance, spread over a period of 12 years.

The study tours of the productivity assistance program were aimed at achieving quick improvements in productivity and in the supply and variety of affordable consumer goods. They were organized to cover a particular branch of industry (steel foundries, machine tools, electric power production, etc.) or a particular function (materials handling, time-and-motion studies, standardization, or research management).

Topics, participants, and itineraries were carefully selected with the help of local industrial leaders by productivity offices located in Western Europe and staffed by local people. Participants were required to write detailed technical reports and to disseminate their findings to their colleagues through months of lectures and seminars after their return home. Even the many firms that seemed hopelessly old-fashioned and inefficient were helped to restructure themselves, without basic changes in national economic policy. Many recovered and reached international levels of quality and productivity. To cite a few examples from France, the French wool, foundry, and mechanical and electrical construction industries all were able to double hourly wages between 1949 and 1956 by virtue of labor productivity increases largely due to the Marshall Plan. Similarly, the introduction of hybrid corn by the Marshall Plan productivity assistance program gave rise to a quick 25 to 50 per cent increase in production. At the firm level, a major French shoe manufacturer reported a rapid 50 per cent increase in production and a 20 per cent increase in wages, based on such reforms as better lighting, heating, and ventilation systems. "A shivering workman doesn't produce very much," the owner was quoted as saying.

"...introducing Americans to entrepreneurs from former communist countries...may also rekindle an interest in foreign affairs among the American public..."

Such a program, adapted to today's conditions, could raise productivity and incomes in Russia and the former Soviet Union and help to restore the pride of ordinary Russians and other former Soviets in their own accomplishments. Study tours today could also introduce participants to the workings of the institutional infrastructure of democracy and free markets: stock markets, insurance companies, real estate agencies, election commissions, social security systems, and so forth. As a byproduct, introducing Americans to entrepreneurs from former communist countries who struggle to build their countries under trying circumstances may also rekindle an interest in foreign affairs among the American public, much as the establishment of the Peace Corps did almost 35 years ago.

In contrast with the Marshall Plan, current efforts by the West to help Russia and the countries of Eastern and Central Europe and Central Asia have been inadequate, halting, and fragmented. Despite the commitment of large sums of money, these efforts have been conducted with no clear statement of purpose, minimal public involvement, and little effort to build political consensus.

Even the technical assistance programs have been designed to spend money in the United States and Western Europe rather than in the countries needing assistance. Expensive consultants have been dispatched to the former communist countries to offer advice that is roundly criticized as being patronizing and ignorant of local conditions. Few of the exchange programs that bring people to the West have sought to increase industrial productivity.

In fairness, the Bush and Clinton administrations and their European counterparts have gone as far as they could without taking significant political risk. But their efforts fall far short of what is needed to convince the leaders and the ordinary citizens of former communist countries that they too have a stake in the world system. In any case, American aid efforts are apparently about to end, on the grounds that Americans have done all they can do and that the taxpayer will contribute no more.

The Marshall Plan was much more than the gift of some $13 billion. True, the capital assistance was a donation of unparalleled generosity, one that Winston Churchill called "the most unsordid act in history." In 1994 dollars, the value of Marshall Plan assistance was $86 billion—or 1.26 per cent of U.S. gross national product—disbursed over four years. Even this extraordinary gift was not nearly enough to cover the cost of the reconstruction of Europe. The main capital for the reconstruction of Western Europe came from *domestic* sources, not from the United States. Nor did the money for reconstruction come from direct foreign investment; there was in fact little such investment until the 1960s.

In retrospect, the greatest immediate importance of the Marshall Plan was as a symbol of American commitment and leadership. It produced an immediate psychological lift and restored European confidence at a time of widespread despair, so that Europeans would invest their own money, time, and effort in their reconstruction. It also provided a political and economic cushion against the consequences of what today would be called "structural adjustment."

Through the Marshall Plan, the United States sent a clear message to Western Europe, which could be summarized this way: "Your success is important to us. Our goal is your recovery, not just increased exports for ourselves. We will not abandon you and are determined to see the job through. All we ask from you is a commitment to democracy, to general market principles, and to the objective of improving the life of ordinary citizens in your countries. We will respect your wishes and will share with you the things that you need. But we do insist that you face your problems, that you tell us what you need, that you justify your requests to us and to each other, and that you present a unified proposal for help."

Laying the Postwar Foundation

The enduring legacy of the Marshall Plan and of the spirit of cooperation it encouraged is the set of institutions that to this day binds the nations of Western Europe to each other, to the United States, and to the rest of the world: the Organization for Economic Cooperation and Development (OECD), the European Union (EU), and NATO. Less well known, but of critical importance in the 1940s and 1950s, were the European Payments Union and the European Productivity Agency.

Reduced to essentials, the strategic underpinnings of the Marshall Plan were four. First was economic security. A growing economy was seen as the bedrock of political stability. Second was the decision that Germany must be encouraged to recover politically and economically and to rejoin the world community as a constructive member. Third was the realization that only a political and economic system that included all of Western Europe and the United States was big enough to balance and integrate Germany. And finally was the use of money to create, in historian Theodore White's words, "a field of force, as invisible yet as energizing as electricity."

"...only a political and economic system that included all of Western Europe and the United States was big enough to balance and integrate Germany."

These strategic principles remain valid. They can be adapted to the situation in Russia and the newly independent states of Eastern and Central Europe and Central Asia.

The success of the Marshall Plan depended on its architects' careful attention to the politics of leadership. First, the Marshall Plan was a comprehensive, integrated response to a critical situation. Marshall himself was in the habit of telling his staff, "Don't fight the problem; solve it." Solving the problem of the reconstruction of Western Europe required a sustained commitment, from both the United States and the West European countries themselves. U.S. security was defined not only in military but in economic terms.

Second, the Marshall Plan was adopted with the backing of the American people and the Congress after a sustained six-month lobbying and public education campaign that was launched with the unstinting support of President Harry Truman. Top American foreign policy officials who are now legend took part: Marshall himself, Dean Acheson, Averell Harriman, and George Kennan. The president enlisted the high-level involvement of business and labor, both of which provided essential political support. The business community was also a source of key management personnel and a door-opener for technical assistance missions, while labor was an essential ally in overcoming the opposition of communist-dominated European unions.

Truman's presidential leadership took place in a political situation not so different from that of the past two years: widespread public indifference to foreign affairs, eagerness to get back to normal living after a long and costly war, and a feisty new Republican majority in Congress, jousting with a beleaguered president. On the Hill, critical leadership came from Republican senator Arthur Vandenberg, chairman of the Senate Foreign Relations Committee.

Third, political, business, and labor leaders in the United States and Western Europe made a commitment to achieving practical results from Marshall Plan assistance, even when this involved short-term political costs. A top Republican business executive, Paul Hoffman of Studebaker—then a leading car manufacturer—was recruited to head the program and was allowed a free hand in managing it.

Hoffman insisted that Marshall Plan assistance emphasize solving the problem in Western Europe rather than gaining domestic political advantage in America. For example, he insisted that European nations not be required to import U.S. goods if the same goods were available in Europe. For his part, Truman made sure that the executing agency of the Marshall Plan was independent of cabinet departments and reported directly to the president.

Fourth, the Marshall Plan was based on regional cooperation. European countries were forced to justify their requests for assistance to each other before they presented them to the United States. In this way, they got to know each other and got into the habit of seriously discussing their problems and their policies. This process created immediate pressure for the lowering of trade barriers and for economic policies that would stand up to outside examination. It laid the foundation for later European cooperation, which replaced the centuries of hostility that had preceded World War II. It also created a framework for the distribution of Marshall Plan money that, in turn, laid the institutional groundwork for postwar prosperity and relative peace: The EU, the OECD, and the world trading system (first the General Agreement on Tariffs and Trade and now the World Trade Organization), along with NATO exist today as a result.

Last, Truman and Marshall recognized that European recovery would take time. They took a long view of political developments in Europe, which at the time were typified by the "revolving door" governments in Italy and France and the substantial communist vote in democratic elections in these and other countries.

Marshall and Truman also recognized that different European countries would follow different models of the market economy, from the relatively free market policies in Germany and strong government intervention in Great Britain to *dirigisme* in France. The plan was open to all countries willing and able to abide by its principles: the free market; the expansion of trade; democratic procedures; and the social compact among workers, owners, and consumers. In Marshall's words, it was "directed not against any country or doctrine but against hunger, poverty, desperation and chaos." Eastern Europe and even Josef Stalin's USSR were invited to join—though probably in the hope that they would refuse, given the obvious difficulties of getting congressional approval for their participation.

New World, Similar Problem

There are many differences between today's situation and that faced by Western Europe in the aftermath of World War II. But are those differences sufficient to justify the world's timid response to the Russian situation?

To be sure, today's problem is much more challenging. Russia is bigger, more populous, and politically more complicated than postwar Germany. It is also much more difficult to integrate into a global political structure. Its historical burden is greater, its economic structure more unsound, and its legal, financial, and institutional foundations for markets, democracy, and civil society more tenuous. Unlike Germany, which was occupied by Allied forces and governed by leaders committed to economic and political reform, Russia suffers from rampant corruption and an ambivalent attitude toward reform. On the Western side, the American public has much less confidence in its own government today than it did at the end of a victorious and just war. Nor is there a Stalin or a threat of communist invasion against which to mobilize public support.

"...Russia suffers from rampant corruption and an ambivalent attitude toward reform."

Propitious circumstances led to regional cooperation at the end of World War II. Western Europe was willing to respond to proposals from its own leadership and to American prodding in the direction of regional cooperation. Europe was concerned about the spread of communism and feared that the United States would withdraw from Europe and lose interest, as it had after World War I, especially after the 1946 congressional elections, which gave control of Congress to isolationist-minded Republicans. While the countries of postwar Western Europe remained suspicious of one another's motives—as a result of their long-time mutual hostility—national leaders and the public were anxious not to repeat the history of the interwar period. Whatever the misgivings of France toward a possibly resurgent Germany or of Great Britain toward continental Europe, there was a consensus that Western Europe must cooperate to avoid further war. Many of the postwar leaders had formed the habit of cooperation during the common wartime effort. In contrast, the legacy of the communist system, both economic and emotional, now makes it difficult to reestablish regional political and economic relationships in Eastern and Central Europe and Central Asia.

Not all of the differences between then and now favor postwar Western Europe, however. Today's problems are greater, but so are the resources available to assist economies in transition. The world economy is many times larger than it was in 1947. Many countries (not just the United States) are helping, private industry and global financial markets are vastly bigger, and bilateral and multilateral aid agencies and a wide variety of nongovernmental organizations can serve as models and vehicles for assistance. Advances in information technology and telecommunications allow new ideas to spread quickly. They have made it possible to relieve the isolation of previously remote areas and have made it more difficult for governments or private interests to inhibit communication or to conceal information. Most importantly, today we have the history of the Marshall Plan itself to show that recovery and reintegration really can work.

The differences between then and now are important, but so are the similarities. By 1947, the American assistance program for Western Europe had put $11 billion into uncoordinated, bilateral, humanitarian and infrastructure assistance programs that actually cost almost as much as the Marshall Plan itself and were subject to many of the same criticisms as current American and West European aid programs for Russia. Until Marshall's Harvard speech, the United States had been only weakly committed to modest transitional assistance to European relief and reconstruction. Indeed, Marshall insisted that the period of assistance be held to four years, on the grounds that Congress and the public would not support a longer-term program.

Like the Soviet empire after the fall of the Berlin Wall, postwar Europe faced widespread poverty, the disruption of trade patterns, political instability, and, in several countries, hyperinflation. Few goods were of export quality, raw materials were in short supply, and shortages of foreign currencies at fixed exchange rates (the so-called "dollar gap") left Europe without the dollars needed to buy U.S. commodities and capital equipment. Foreign investment was scant. Defense conversion was an acute problem. Hopelessness and the fear of social unrest predominated. All these problems have echoes in Russia, Eastern and Central Europe, and Central Asia today.

On the economic front, Western Europe inherited from prewar times a system of inward-oriented economies protected from competition and cut off for decades from mass consumer markets and from advances in the technologies of mass production. Cartels shielded inefficient firms from bankruptcy by guaranteeing them a share of controlled and protected markets. Manufacturing plants were small and obsolete, wages and productivity low, low-cost consumer goods limited in quantity and variety, and costs and prices high. Even plants in the same industry operated in isolation from one another and from world trends in markets and technology. Industrial management emphasized short production runs aimed at the high end of small, protected economies. Technology, marketing, and management outlooks were all 20 to 30 years out of date. Many government and business officials had vested interests in retaining obsolete practices.

In short, postwar European industry needed a new mentality, not just a restoration of infrastructure. This is where the productivity study tours had relevance.

Marshall Plan Productivity Assistance

The Marshall Plan consisted of four principal elements: a framework for the presentation of multistate, regionally agreed upon proposals for assistance; a system for the settlement of intra-European trade; grant and loan aid; and productivity tours and other forms of technical assistance. Of these, the program of productivity study tours could make an especially dramatic contribution to improving the current situation of countries in Eastern and Central Europe, the Russian Federation, and Central Asia.

Such a program could enable tens of thousands of Russians, East and Central Europeans, and Central Asians to visit Western Europe, the Pacific Rim, and those parts of Central Europe that are making progress in their transition to democracy and free markets. These visitors would see for themselves how to raise productivity and produce affordable consumer goods, how government and private service industries operate, and, more generally, how an open society functions.

"...CCI...in 1996 brought 200 Russian and Ukrainian entrepreneurs...to the United States to study... industries..."

This idea has already been tested on a small scale with 12 productivity tours, involving visits by some 180 participants from Kazakhstan to countries in Western Europe. The visits were funded by a loan from the World Bank and carried out by a German organization descended from the original Marshall Plan program. A somewhat similar program, funded by the United States Information Agency and carried out by the Center for Citizen Initiatives (CCI)—a nongovernmental organization based in San Francisco—in 1996 brought 200 Russian and Ukrainian entrepreneurs from small- and medium-sized businesses to the United States to study such industries as food processing and construction. In both cases, participants were carefully selected for their management track records and, in the case of the World Bank program, for their performance in seminars on Western economics and management methods. A strenuous work program discouraged boondoggling and shopping sprees.

The first evaluations of these tours were strongly favorable. Participants returned home enthusiastic and confident that they could apply American management and production techniques to the very different circumstances of the former communist economies. Many of the visitors started by designing marketing strategies, often for the first time, talking with their customers, studying demand, reexamining the design of their product, and surveying competitors' prices.

Returning Kazakh entrepreneurs, like their European counterparts 40 to 50 years ago, instituted inexpensive changes that enabled them to greatly expand production, enter new markets, and improve quality and productivity. To cite two examples from a garment tour, a coat manufacturer in Almaty, the capital of Kazakhstan, increased the labor productivity of his firm by 13 per cent within a month of his return without additional investment. The owner of a garment enterprise in the town of

Taldyqorghan, some 140 miles northeast of Almaty, had been on the brink of closing out of fear that her business was too small to compete with government-owned behemoths. Instead, she used what she had learned in Taiwan to win a government contract. She is now hiring personnel and redesigning her workshop. A Volgograd contractor inspired by his participation in the CCI program has begun to develop modular building techniques, while a St. Petersburg farmer has tripled the size of his 10-acre truck farm and plans to mechanize—and then double it again.

The most heartening aspect of the productivity tours launched to date has been the enthusiasm of the American and European hosts. Small towns across America have volunteered housing, transportation, and meals in support of the CCI tours. European and American companies have opened their doors to reveal management and production techniques that, while not the most advanced, are within the reach of the participants. Local newspaper coverage has been favorable. These tours should be followed up with supplementary information and assistance, using the Internet and other tools of the information age.

The cost of these programs is modest. Experience to date suggests that at least 800,000 former Soviets could be brought to the United States or to other Western countries for $1.5 billion—a fraction of current U.S. spending on aid programs that are far less effective. These costs could be spread over 10 years and shared with allies. The World Bank and the U.S. Agency for International Development are discussing expanding these programs but at a scale that would meet only a tiny fraction of the overall need.

The Marshall Plan–type tours would differ from existing programs in several aspects:

• The **objective** of the tours would be the quick delivery of consumer goods to the local market through either rapidly increased productivity and broadened product mix—using existing plant capacity—or increases in the productivity of government or service industries.

• The **teams** would consist of 15 to 20 key people—one to three senior managers plus supervisors and trainers from each selected firm along with government officials—in short, whoever can understand, implement, and spread the new ideas.

• The **tour design** would feature a series of intensive, tailor-made, one- to two-day visits to plants or organizations that had been picked for their similarity to those in the home country.

• A local plan **staff** member with detailed knowledge of an entire branch of industry would design and lead the respective tours. This special feature is beyond the capabilities of most universities or training institutions.

• Team members would publish a detailed **technical report** after each tour and would then give seminars to colleagues in other plants—creating an amplification process that would reach into all corners of even a vast country like Russia.

• **Follow-up technical services** would help tour participants to put their new ideas into practice by providing advice on product and process design, standardization, manufacturing practices, labor relations, and markets.

These tours and technical assistance programs should be extended to the dozens of closed military cities, three of which still specialize in the production of weapons-grade plutonium for want of an alternative. Helping firms in these cities to diversify into civilian manufacturing should be a priority of U.S. assistance policy, even if doing so entails extra difficulty and expense.

In addition to this technical assistance, it would be useful to establish a joint economic council, perhaps within the framework of the Organization for Security and Cooperation in Europe, to facilitate discussions among East and Central European leaders about shared economic, political, and environmental problems of the transition to free market democracy. One aim would be to identify areas of commonality, which would lead to the establishment of voluntary and economically rational intraregional trade patterns to replace the artificial patterns that prevailed under communism. Currently, the former communist countries are pitted against one another in efforts to win bilateral concessions and membership in trading blocs like the EU. Thus, they have played down opportunities to reestablish old trading relationships with other ex-communist countries.

"...the strategic lessons of the Marshall Plan have been largely ignored."

From Enemies to Partners

Russia, Central and Eastern Europe, and Central Asia are not America's to lose. Their fate is in their own hands. Only they can decide how much sacrifice they are willing to make to effect the reforms they need. The West can influence their internal processes only at the margins.

At the same time, the United States must do what it can to ensure that its erstwhile Cold War antagonists become strong, constructive partners. As the postwar recovery of Western Europe demonstrates, the transformations of Russia and the countries of Eastern and Central Europe and Central Asia—and their integration into the world political and economic system—will benefit both the donors of assistance and its recipients. If these countries fail to make the transition, the likely scenarios are awful: political instability, nuclear anarchy, depression, social unrest, environmental devastation, and, worst of all, a return to authoritarian rule and militant nationalism.

So far, the strategic lessons of the Marshall Plan have been largely ignored. The people of Central and Eastern Europe, Russia, and Central Asia sense that the West does not really care whether they either take their places in the world economic and political order as market-oriented democracies or slip back into stagnant authoritarianism and repression. This belief has fostered a great disappointment among voters in the struggling new democracies and among those leaders who staked their political futures on the hope of tangible results from friendship with the West—and with the United States in particular.

A full-scale Marshall Plan today would be politically infeasible and probably unwise given the many institutional weaknesses in the countries of the former Soviet Union. Fortunately, the dramatic expansion of private capital and technology markets makes it possible for at least some of the impact of the original Marshall Plan to be achieved through a major program of technical assistance.

An effort of this magnitude requires articulate and prominent leadership by the president of the United States and the senior members of Congress. Top leaders of American business and labor should also be enlisted to work with their overseas counterparts to determine what assistance is needed and who should deliver it. The National Planning Association, a 60-year-old policy and research institute in Washington, D.C., has proposed forming an economic assistance council, under the direct supervision of the White House, to enlist the help of business and labor leaders in organizing such exchanges.

The original Marshall Plan showed that strategic thinking followed by action can shape the course of history. Summarizing the accomplishments of his generation, Truman once told Henry Kissinger, "We completely defeated our enemies and made them surrender. And then we helped them to recover, to become democratic, and to rejoin the community of nations."

If then, why not now?

Bibliography

An asterisk (*) preceding a reference indicates that an excerpt from the work has been reprinted in this compilation or that the work has been cited.

Books and Pamphlets

Baranovskii, Vladimir, ed. Russia and Europe: The Emerging Security Agenda. Oxford University Press '97.

Borneman, John. Settling Accounts: Violence, Justice, and Accountability in Post-Socialist Europe. Princeton University Press '97.

Bowker, Mike. Russian Foreign Policy and the End of the Cold War. Dartmouth '97.

Buckley, Mary, ed. Post-Soviet Women. Cambridge University Press '97.

Carlton, David and Ingram, Paul, eds. The Search for Stability in Russia and the Former Soviet Bloc. Dartmouth '97.

Crawford, Keith. East Central European Politics Today: From Chaos to Stability? Manchester University Press '96.

Crowley, Stephen. Hot Coal, Cold Steel: Russian and Ukrainian Workers from the End of the Soviet Union to the Post-Communist Transformations. University of Michigan Press '97.

Daianu, Daniel. Economic Vitality and Viability: A Dual Challenge for European Security. Lang '96.

Davies, R. W. Soviet History in the Yeltsin Era. St. Martin's Press '97.

Davis, Junior Red. The Transition to the Market Economy: Critical Perspectives on the World Economy. Routledge '97.

Dawidowicz, Lucy S. The Golden Tradition: Jewish Life and Thought in Eastern Europe. Syracuse University Press '96.

Drabek, Zdenek. Conference on Regional Economic Integration and Global Economic Cooperation: The Case of Central and Eastern Europe: Forum on Debt and Development '97.

Drakulic, Slavenka. Cafe Europa: Life After Communism. Norton '97.

Furmanek, Rick. Stranded in Moscow: an American's Story of Life in the New Russia. Square Peg Press '97.

Garnett, Sherman W. Keystone in the Arch: Ukraine in the Emerging Security Environment of Central and Eastern Europe. Carnegie Endowment for International Peace '97.

Holmes, Leslie. Post-Communism: An Introduction. Duke University Press '97.

Ioffe, Gregory and Nefedova, Tatyana. Continuity and Change in Rural Russia. Westview Press '97.

Karatnycky, Adrian, Motyl, Alexander, and Shor, Boris, eds. Nations in Transit: Civil Society, Democracy, and Markets in East Central Europe and the Newly Independent States. Transaction Publications '97.

Kurti, Laszlo and Langman, Juliet, eds. Beyond Borders: Remaking Cultural Identities in the New East and Central Europe. Westview Press '97.

Levesque, Jacques. The Enigma of 1989: The USSR and the Liberation of Eastern Europe. University of California Press '97.

Lewis, Alfred, ed. Privatization and Entrepreneurship: The Managerial Challenge in Central and Eastern Europe. International Business Press '97.

Longworth, Philip. The Making of Eastern Europe: From Prehistory to Post-Communism. St. Martin's Press '97.

O'Neil, Patrick, ed. Post-Communism and the Media in Eastern Europe. Cass & Co. '97.

*Pipes, Richard. A Concise History of the Russian Revolution. Vintage '96.

*——, The Unknown Lenin. Yale University Press '96.

Ramet, Sabrina P. Religion, Politics, and Social Change in East-Central Europe and Russia. Duke University Press '98.

Rein, Martin, ed. Enterprise and Social Benefits After Communism. Cambridge University Press '97.

Roskin, Michael. The Rebirth of East Europe. Prentice-Hall '97.

Royal Institute of International Affairs. Ukraine and European Security. Pinter '97.

Sergeyev, Victor. The Wild East: Crime and Lawlessness in Post-Communist Russia. Sharpe, M.E. '98.

Sinyavsky, Andrei.The Russian Intelligentsia. Columbia University Press '97.

Skak, Mette. From Empire to Anarchy: Postcommunist Foreign Policy and International Relations. St. Martin's Press '96.

Slobin, Mark, ed. Retuning Culture: Musical Changes in Central and Eastern Europe. Duke University Press '96.

Tracey, Patrick Austin. Political Reform Leaders in Eastern Europe and the Former Soviet Union. Facts on File '97.

Turnock, David. The Eastern European Economy in Context: Communism and the Transition. Routledge '97.

Urban, Michael E., Igrunov Vyacheslav, and Mitrokhin, Sergei. The Rebirth of Politics in Russia. Cambridge University Press '97.

Who's Who in Russia Since 1900. Routledge '97.

Williams, Phil, ed. Russian Organized Crime: The New Threat? Cass & Co. '97.

Witter, Sophie, ed. An Introduction to Health Economics for Eastern Europe and the Former Soviet Union. Wiley '97.

Zacek, Jane Shapiro, ed. The Legacy of the Soviet Bloc. University Press of Florida '97.

Additional Periodical Articles with Abstracts

For those who wish to read more widely on the subject of Russia and Eastern Europe, this section contain abstracts of additional articles that bear on the topic. Readers who require a comprehensive list of materials are advised to consult *Reader's Guide Abstracts* and other Wilson indexes.

NATO keeps door open as it expands eastward. John D. Morrocco. *Aviation Week & Space Technology* 147:37 Jl 14 '97

In a decision that represents a watershed in NATO's history as it extends eastward, the alliance voted at a recent summit in Madrid to invite Poland, Hungary, and the Czech Republic into the allied fold. Talks with the three new member nations are expected to last about six months, with formal entry for the three scheduled for 1999. In addition, NATO has signed a special partnership pact with Ukraine and has inaugurated a new consultative council that comprises neutral countries such as Switzerland and Russia as well as other Eastern European countries, such as Romania and Slovenia, whose quest for full membership in the alliance was deferred for at least a year.

Westward (and eastward) ho for airlines in Eastern Europe. Michael A. Taverna. *Aviation Week & Space Technology* 147:79-81 N 17 '97

After concentrating for several years on establishing links with Western European air-lines, Eastern European carriers are turning to strategic alliances with U.S.-based air-lines and other cooperative stratagems to encourage growth and development. The change in direction is partly intended to compensate for the limitations and shortcom-ings of a number of partnership agreements with Western European airlines, which were established in the years after the fall of the Berlin Wall.

Joining the march of folly. Ronald E. Powaski. *The Bulletin of the Atomic Scientists* 54:18-22 Ja/F '98

Part of a special section on the debate over NATO expansion. The Clinton administra-tion's campaign to expand NATO into eastern Europe runs counter to U.S. interests. In July 1997, at a NATO summit in Madrid, Spain, three countries that had been Soviet allies in the defunct Warsaw Pact—Poland, Hungary, and the Czech Republic—were invited to join NATO. Despite the administration's repeated assertions that NATO expansion is not aimed at any country, it is well known that the expansion is intend-ed to constrain Russia. The maintenance of peace in Europe should involve all the European states, including Russia, because, as 20th-century history shows, outcast states tend to become enemies of America. Moreover, including Russia as a full partic-ipant in the European international structure would help insure that democracy will endure there.

NATO. *The Bulletin of the Atomic Scientists* 54:18-39 Ja/F '98

A special section on the debate over NATO expansion. Articles discuss the Clinton administration's campaign to expand NATO into Eastern Europe, the benefits to European stability of expanding NATO, Bulgaria's desire to join NATO, the chances of the U.S. Senate approving NATO expansion, the European Union's acceptance of NATO's pronuclear posture, and the problems presented by the absence of a real U.S. policy toward Russia.

Credit where credit is long overdue. Karen Lowry Miller. *Business Week* 120+ S 15 '97

Debt financing has become big business in the former Soviet bloc countries, and the market is still growing. Russian and Eastern European borrowers have issued $3.32 billion in new debt in the past 18 months alone, according to IFR Securities Data: London. Credit Suisse First Boston (Europe) reports that total debt from the region, including private placements, could reach $20 billion by the end of 1997, compared with $5 billion in 1996. Claude Chaubet-Bride, associate director of business development in Eastern Europe for Standard & Poor's Corp., notes that those who invest in the former Soviet bloc countries can earn far higher yields for the same level of risk found in other emerging markets.

How Russia can avoid the Asian abyss. Patricia Kranz. *Business Week* 46 Ja 19 '98

Russians are engaged in a great discussion over how to develop a new Russian-style capitalism. The choice is between American-style open markets or a more closed, directed form of economic management that has thrived, until recently, in Asia. Given Asia's difficulties, the choice should be a simple one, but the establishment in Russia is resisting change. President Boris N. Yeltsin could build a lasting legacy by consolidating and accelerating initiatives to make Russia's market fairer and more open, but if he concedes to the oligarchs, Russia will stay a country of the very wealthy and the very poor, and a collapse in the Asian style could well lie ahead.

NATO expansion: the view from Central Europe. Jakub Trojan. *The Christian Century* 114:567-8 Je 4-11 '97

Part of a special section on NATO expansion. Every discussion on the expansion of NATO inevitably draws attention to the vital concerns of eastern European countries. Only an internationally guaranteed stability will make the democratic development of central European countries irreversible. In addition, only a flourishing democratic system in these countries is likely to have a positive effect on the more distant areas of eastern Europe, which appear to be less stable, partly as a result of the absence of democratic traditions. In consequence, the expansion of the security zone eastward, rather than representing a threat, in fact constitutes an illustration of what would make the democratic transformation of eastern European societies ultimately feasible. The writer of an accompanying article on the subject responds.

WCC's cold-war record upheld. *The Christian Century* 114:117-18 D 3 '97

The general secretary of the World Council of Churches (WCC) has strongly supported and defended the part played by the ecumenical organization in Eastern Europe during the cold war. Konrad Raiser, a renowned Lutheran theologian from Germany, was responding in an interview to recent contentions that the WCC had done too little to back dissident groups within the churches of Eastern Europe under communism and that the organization needed to embark on a self-critical analysis of its activities during the cold war. During the cold war, the activities of the WCC's member churches in Eastern Europe were often rigorously controlled by the authorities. At times, this caused criticism from outside by those unwilling to tolerate any state interference, who suggested that some church officials actively collaborated with communist regimes, thus compromising their principles for the sake of the survival of their churches.

Why die for Danzig? Joshua Muravchik. *Commentary* 104:40-5 O '97

The debate over the expansion of NATO into Eastern Europe has begun in earnest. Different points are emphasized by different critics, but for some of them a major theme, after the issue of the budgetary costs of expansion and of equitable burden-sharing among the allies, is that Americans should not be forced to "die for Danzig," that is, to go to war for the sake of a European ally. Another argument against enlargement, one that also amounts to an argument against NATO's continuance even in its current form, is that the best organization for preserving peace in post-cold war Europe is no longer NATO but some larger international body. The argument that occupies foreign-policy specialists the most, however, is that NATO expansion will arouse sensitivities or fears among Russians that will undermine the standing of pro-Western democrats in Russia, which in turn will benefit the nation's Communists and nationalists. The writer responds to these arguments against NATO enlargement.

Europe lost & found. Manuela Hoelterhoff. *Conde Nast Traveler* 32:238-52 + My '97

Part of a tenth anniversary special issue. Conde Nast Traveler selected six uniquely Eastern European sites to celebrate the new freedom of Eastern Europe for both its inhabitants and its visitors. The following are photographed and described: Sanssouci Palace, Potsdam; Kutna Hora, Czech Republic; Monastery Succevita, Romania; Leonardo's Lady with an Ermine, in Krakow; Chersonesos, Ukraine; and Kizhi Pogost, Russia. Tourist information is provided for each site.

The oil rush in the Caucasus. Robert E. Ebel. *Current History* 96:344-5 O '97

Part of an issue on Russia and Eurasia. Attracted by oil, foreign investors are returning to the Caucasus. Toward the start of the century, the region's oil was considered an international prize, and foreign investors, led by Great Britain, flocked to the area. The region's present oil potential is immense and cannot be realized in an acceptable time frame without foreign capital. One reason for the oil's significance is that, following the construction of pipelines, the Transcaucasus is expected to become an important corridor for the movement of oil to markets outside the former Soviet Union. Although Transcaucasian and Caspian oil will not be critical, these new supplies will be important at the margin, restraining OPEC's market share and giving importers security through diversity of supply.

"The politicians treat ordinary people as garbage." Paul Klebnikov. *Forbes* 161:56 + Ja 12 '98

General Alexander Lebed's dire prognosis for Russia cannot be ignored. Lebed, who led troops in Afghanistan and in a number of ethnic conflicts, is hugely popular among ordinary Russians. He supported Boris Yeltsin in the second round of the 1996 presidential elections and was given the powerful position of secretary of the security council, from where he halted the war in Chechnya. Lebed was later dismissed by Yeltsin in a power struggle. Even allowing for his bitterness and his well-known political ambitions, Lebed's criticism of the Yeltsin government is fairly frightening, and he hints at the possibility of a military coup. In an interview, Lebed discusses his view of the situation in Russia.

How big is too big? Andrew Phillips. *Maclean's* 110:26-7 Jl 14 '97

The leaders of NATO will discuss the expansion of the alliance at a meeting to be held shortly in Madrid. The controversial expansion plan raises a number of issues, including that of which countries should be invited to join. America, which provides the largest share of NATO's budget and its nuclear umbrella, favors the admittance of the three former East Bloc countries with the longest record of democratic government, market reform, and good relations with their neighbors: Poland, Hungary, and the Czech Republic. America's refusal to admit Slovenia and Romania at the moment has angered Italy and France, who accused the Americans of dictating to their European partners. Canada has indicated that it will support the Americans, although it favors a broader approach in principle. In early 1997, Russian leaders strongly opposed any expansion, but, in late May, Russia accepted NATO expansion as part of a new arrangement in which Russia is a partner with NATO in European security. The implications of the expansion for Canada are discussed.

The case against NATO enlargement: Clinton's fateful gamble. Sherle R. Schwenninger. *The Nation* 265:21-2 + O 20 '97

Having gained Moscow's acceptance of NATO enlargement with the signing of the NATO-Russia founding act in May, the Clinton administration must now win Senate approval of its plan to expand the organization. The White House promotes enlargement as a strategic decision that would produce a peaceful and cohesive Europe, help strengthen democracy in Central and Eastern Europe, and safeguard America's ongoing involvement in Europe's affairs. Opponents of NATO expansion fear that it would create new dividing lines in Europe and have a negative effect on the effectiveness of the Western alliance.

NATO's stealth costs. William D. Hartung. *The Nation* 265:21-3 N 24 '97

A spending free-for-all to finance NATO expansion is taking place via special Pentagon loan programs. The largest potential lies in a taxpayer-supported, $15 billion arms export loan guarantee fund set up by Congress at the prompting of Lockheed-Martin and other big weapons exporters in 1995. To date, eight eastern and central European nations are among the 37 countries eligible for loans under the fund, and the first commitment—for $23 million worth of pilotless drones for Romania—was concluded this summer. If anything is to wake the public up and prompt questions about the largest expansion of U.S. military commitment since the cold war was at its peak, it should be the fact that NATO expansion will see billions of dollars of taxpayers' money flow into the coffers of such well-heeled military conglomerates as Lockheed-Martin and Boeing.

Portrait of a village. Lida Suchy. *National Geographic* 192:78-93 N '97

The Hutsuls of Kryvorivnya village, an isolated part of Ukraine's Carpathian Mountains, have managed to preserve their distinct culture and identity despite centuries of domination by foreign lands. The writer, whose father's family fled to the United States from the area 50 years ago to escape Soviet occupation, describes a trip to the village. Photographs of the Hutsuls and the area they live in accompany the text.

The battle of Madrid. *National Review* 49:15 Jl 28 '97

On June 26, 50 former U.S. officials, senators, diplomats, and experts asserted that expanding NATO into eastern Europe is an enormous error. The group foresees NATO enlargement destroying the alliance, antagonizing Russia, and bankrupting central and eastern Europe—and possibly the United States. Opposition to NATO expansion is the result of a dubious partnership between liberal, moderate, and extreme grassroots isolationists, however.

Growing pains. Charles Gati. *National Review* 49:27-9 Je 16 '97

As the expansion of NATO moves closer, many questions, particularly concerning Russia, remain unanswered. Unless America hesitates or Western public opinion turns far more skeptical than it currently is, the parliaments of Western Europe and Canada will ratify NATO's decision to expand further without much debate. It is too soon to tell which way members of the U.S. Senate will vote on the issue, but two basic questions will shape the outcome of their vote. The first is whether the White House can succeed in keeping together the diverse coalition currently in favor of enlargement. The second is whether the candidate countries can succeed in strengthening the impression that they can become reliable members who will be able to contribute to the alliance. After the details of enlargement and Russia's new relationship with the alliance are made clear, the second phase of enlargement will reach a successful conclusion in 1999.

NATO weal. Adrian Karatnycky. *National Review* 49:43-4 N 10 '97

The North Atlantic Treaty Organization's decision to expand is a key event in European history. The very expectation that the alliance would move eastward has added to striking improvements in the security of Central and Eastern Europe. For the last year, there has been a wave of diplomatic activity among the nations of East-Central Europe, spurred by their wish to join the alliance and other Western institutions. This diplomacy has led to treaties that have settled long-standing border disputes that were the source of instability, tension, and potential armed conflict. There has also been a flurry of agreements designed to increase trade and economic cooperation in the area. Moreover, as Russia realizes that its reduced economic and military power means it will have a more limited role in the region, it has tried to better relations with states it once intimidated.

The danger of NATO expansion. Robert Vincent Daniels. *The New Leader* 80:11-13 Jl 14-28 '97

The Clinton administration's resolve to enlarge NATO by including Poland, Hungary, and the Czech Republic may be a serious foreign policy miscalculation. Doubts over the expansion of NATO revolve primarily around the implications of the move for the U.S. commitment to Europe, but the implications for Russia have not drawn serious attention. In Russia, the reaction of political leaders to NATO expansion has been universally negative, and the contention that enlargement will end the division of Europe is viewed as highly disingenuous. From the Russian perspective, NATO expansion moves the dividing line further east and implies that Russia does not belong in the picture, which heightens Russian security concerns and exacerbates nationalistic resentments. The writer posits that the expansion of NATO could result in a second cold war with Russia.

The false pretense of NATO expansion. Paul M. Kennedy. *New Perspectives Quarterly* 14:62-3 Sum '97

If NATO expansion is to be accepted by the U.S. Senate and the American people, the opinions of military planners should be known. It is likely that members of the military will not feel comfortable in asserting that the armed forces could give adequate protection to the borders of new member states, following a period in which those forces are being significantly reduced. If the economic pressures on the army continue, for example, there may be as few as eight effective divisions spread around the world. Even if relatively small U.S. ground forces were still based in Western Europe should a crisis with Russia occur in the future, there may be some doubt about the ability of the military to get to the eastern battlefields. The writer discusses historical precedents in which peacetime commitments were not accompanied by corresponding military preparations.

Bosnia, the skunk at the NATO party. *New York Times* 14 O 5 '97

NATO's plan for eastward expansion could well depend on developments in Bosnia over the next nine months. Bosnia is likely to be a divisive issue in the United States Senate next spring, as June 1998 is the date set by President Clinton for the withdrawal of American troops, just when the NATO expansion plan moves into the most critical period of consideration. Nevertheless, Bosnia and NATO expansion are linked, and the White House and the Senate should not be afraid to put them on the table at the same time.

Prosperity's traffic jams Eastern Europe's roads. Jane Perlez. *New York Times* 4 N 2 '97

All across Eastern Europe, and particularly in richer Poland, people are purchasing cars in an explosion of ownership that has come with better economic conditions and the growing acceptance of credit, but unlighted, narrow, rutted roads are jammed with the new autos, as well as old cars, transport trailers, horsecarts, and pedestrians. In Poland, the number and severity of accidents have become a national concern, although the authorities concede that little is being done about it.

NATO's salesman finds the U.S. tough territory. Elaine Sciolino. *New York Times* 3 N 9 '97

The Clinton administration wants NATO secretary-general Javier Solana of Spain to sell the idea of NATO expansion to Congress and the American people, but he seems an odd candidate for that task. He once fiercely opposed Spain's entry into the alliance, but even more telling is the almost total lack of recognition he has in the U.S. However, Charles A. Kupchan, professor of international relations at Georgetown University, says that Solana is appropriate for the expansion debate "because he makes everyone feel included." Solana is profiled.

A promised land of frozen milk and honey. Michael Specter. *New York Times* 5 F 8 '98

The image of Siberia is one of coldness, remoteness, and undesirability, but the actual Siberia, while cold and huge, has a vast trove of natural resources. Those, like Japan, who invest in Siberia's oil, gas, coal, timber, and other resources, face the not insignificant and costly task of getting and moving the raw materials, as most are refined far from where they are found.

Armenia's turmoil. *New York Times* 18 F 9 '98

Armenian president Levon Ter-Petrossian's resignation earlier this month was a disturbing development for peace and ethnic harmony in the Caucasus. The resignation of Ter-Petrossian increases chances that a cease-fire that has been in place since 1994 will end, and it also formalizes the growing hold on power of an unsavory band of military and security officials.

The most tainted place on earth. Michael Specter. *New York Times Magazine* 48-52 F 8 '98

Once a main site of chemical-weapons production in Russia, Dzerzhinsk, with a population of 300,000, may be the least habitable city on Earth. Located 250 miles east of Moscow, Dzerzhinsk has for decades produced tons of deadly gases: DDT, blister gas, mustard gas, and rocket fuel. When these chemical weapons were no longer required, they were buried in rusting barrels that have expanded and burst with age. That contributed to the formation of a festering reservoir of toxic waste known as the White Sea, which like the city itself was a secret until 1991. According to biologists who have taken samples, the sea may contain the world's highest concentration of dioxin, which can cause cancer even in minute doses. Photographs of the region accompany the text.

Eastward expansion. Melinda Liu. *Newsweek* 129:43 My 26 '97

Moscow had little leverage from the start in its negotiations over its future relations with NATO, which is offering membership to a number of former Warsaw Pact states. That pact is gone, and NATO is about to grow eastward whether Moscow agrees or not. Boris Yeltsin is now set to meet with Bill Clinton and other NATO leaders to sign the new accord that will allow NATO to welcome new members for the first time in 15 years. This expansion has been described by State Department spokesman Nicholas Burns as the most significant foreign-policy initiative since Clinton's presidency began. The Czechs, Poles, and Hungarians are certain to be invited to join NATO later this summer, while the Romanians and Slovenians are lobbying to join them.

A diplomatic triumph for Bill Clinton. Christopher Ogden. *Time* 149:51 My 26 '97

Thanks to the recent signing of a new European security pact with Russia, NATO enlargement—Bill Clinton's top foreign-policy objective for his second term—has moved a step closer to reality. The accord between NATO and Russian, called the Founding Act on Mutual Relations, clears the path for former Moscow satellites to join the Western alliance. The act is the most significant foreign-policy development since the demise of the USSR, and it has strategic implications that will remain for decades. In addition, it will take the sting out of Russian anger that NATO growth was going to occur whether or not Moscow liked it. Implemented correctly, the pact will soothe, but, diplomatic denials notwithstanding, it is still a crushing surrender for Russia and a diplomatic victory for Bill Clinton and the Western nations.

Red phoenix rising? Communist resurgence in Eastern Europe. Roger W. Fontaine. *USA Today* 125:48-53 N '96

An article based on a Cato Institute Policy Analysis. Communist parties are gathering momentum throughout the former Soviet bloc. The collapse of communism in Eastern and Central Europe gave rise to a belief that the struggling new democracies' path to prosperity appeared clear with the aid of Western governments and international financial institutions. In the immediate post-cold war period, however, the transition to democratic capitalist societies has been more erratic and difficult than most Western experts anticipated. Various communist, reformed communist, and neocommunist parties have exploited the transition to obtain power or mount serious challenges to non-communist reform factions. The rise of such parties in Estonia, Latvia, Lithuania, Poland, Hungary, the Czech Republic, Slovakia, Romania, and Bulgaria is discussed.

Nazi victims receive first Swiss payments. Richard Z. Chesnoff. *U.S. News & World Report* 123:6 D 1 '97

The Swiss Fund for Needy Victims of the Holocaust has paid out its first $10 million to tens of thousands of needy Holocaust survivors in Eastern Europe. The $200 million voluntary fund was set up by Swiss bankers and businessmen as a way of atoning for their country's wartime profiteering from the Nazis after the publication of lists of some 5,559 dormant bank accounts, many of which belong to Holocaust victims.

Taking aim at Europe's ghosts. Richard J. Newman. *U.S. News & World Report* 123:34-7 Jl 14 '97

With the demise of the Soviet Union, the most historic thing about the upcoming expansion of NATO may be that the organization has accelerated its own demise. Poland, Hungary, and the Czech Republic will be formally invited to join the body, but if this expansion makes NATO too unwieldy, it could ultimately develop into a European statesman's nightmare, a mini-United Nations. Moreover, military force may not be the correct tool for shaping the future of Europe. As a military alliance, NATO does not dare to expand to protect the countries most in need of protection—the tiny Baltic states, who arguably have most reason to fear Russia—and as an economic alliance, its role would logically be superseded by the European Union and other trade blocs.

The lessons of the Marshall Plan. Bill Clinton. *Vital Speeches of the Day* 63:546-8 Jl 1 '97

In a speech made at the Commemorative Event for the 50th Anniversary of the Marshall Plan in the Hall of Knights in Binnenhof in The Hague, the Netherlands, the U.S. president discusses NATO expansion. For the first time, a new NATO and a new Russia have agreed to work as partners in order to tackle challenges to their common security in a new and united Europe. In addition, NATO will remain open to all those capable of sharing the responsibilities of membership. Via NATO, the United States has the potential to defend freedom, reinforce democracy, lessen old rivalries, expedite integration, and provide a stable climate in which prosperity can increase in eastern Europe. The legacy of the Marshall Plan is also discussed.

The Warsaw Pact. John J. Hamre. *Vital Speeches of the Day* 64:166-8 Ja 1 '98

In an address delivered to the World Peace Luncheon in Birmingham, Alabama, John Hamre, deputy to the secretary of defense, discusses how the United States is going to preserve peace in Europe. The code to preventing war in Europe in the 21st century is to extend the democracy, stability, and affluence of Western Europe into Eastern and Central Europe, all the way to Russia. The key to that is inviting new members into NATO. As the Senate prepares to consider the enlargement of NATO, it is essential that all Americans join in this debate, particularly veterans in support of enlargement. Through the cold war, Americans stood with the free people of Europe, and now, having emerged triumphant, there is a historic opportunity and a very serious challenge. George Marshall's vision of a Europe healed, complete, and free must be brought about to guarantee that Americans never again have to engage in combat and die on European battlefields.

Eastern Europe opens the files. Natalie Nougayrede. *World Press Review* 45:10-11 Ja '98

An article excerpted from the October 22, 1997, issue of Le Monde of Paris, France. The debate on how to confront the past in former Communist countries still rages on. The Romanian, Bulgarian, Czech, and Hungarian governments have passed or proposed laws to allow citizens to consult secret police files, and the Right in Poland is calling for a purge of former agents of the secret police. The opening of the files in East Germany in 1992 resulted in a stampede of Germans consulting their files, but this also led to vast purges in the civil services, provoking criticism by human rights organizations. The Czech lustrations have been subject to the same reproaches, and the process is at a standstill in Poland, with citizens having no access to police archives.

Russia's smoldering anger over NATO. *World Press Review* 44:9-10 Je '97

Part of a cover story on worldwide concern about a new cold war. An article excerpted from the April 4, 1997, issue of *Asiaweek* of Hong Kong. By pushing military expansion through NATO's Eastern European enlargement, the West touches Russia's rawest nerve and risks igniting a new cold war. Russia is well aware that NATO enlargement is the West's reward for winning the cold war and comes largely at its expense. The move, imposed on a weakened and unstable Russia, will probably be a source of unease and potential instability for many years. A confidant of President Yeltsin has warned that the move will prompt Moscow to reassess its foreign policy and possibly boost its ties with China, Iran, and India. NATO enlargement should be made more agreeable to the Russians and less disruptive to global stability.

Index